Water-Mill Inns of France

Water-Mill Inns of France

A Gastronomic Guide to Romantic Country Inns

BY

Marvin Luther

RECIPES TRANSLATED FROM THE FRENCH
AND ADAPTED BY

Winona Luther

Illustrations by Nixon Galloway

Corinthian Publications, Redondo Beach, California

Library of Congress Catalog Card No. 95–071951

Publisher's Cataloging in Publication Data:

Luther, Marvin and Nona
    Water-mill inns of France/ by Marvin and Nona Luther. Illustrations
    by Nixon Galloway.
        p. cm.
    Includes bibliography and index.
    ISBN: 0-9649085-4-9
    1. Hotels, taverns, etc.—France—Guidebooks. 2. France—Description
and travel—Guide-books. 3.Cookery, French. I. Title.
TX910.F8.L88 1996
647\.944401—dc20

Printed in the United States of America

Frontispiece: Ar Milin', Châteaubourg, Ille-et-Vilaine, Brittany.

Cover design by Robert Howard.

Published by Corinthian Publications: SAN 298-8615.
P.O. Box 3028, Redondo Beach, CA 90277-3028, U.S.A.

TABLE OF CONTENTS

ACKNOWLEDGEMENTS

Our thanks to the many mill owners for their time, patience, and enthusiasm for the project, and to the scores of chefs for their recipes and the opportunity to share their talents with our readers. (Owners and chefs are too numerous to list here, but their names appear near the end of each chapter. And we received so many recipes that we couldn't include them all—the others will find a place in a planned cookbook.)

Thanks to author/mentor Kit Snedaker for her patient guidance, and to author Judith Pacht for her encouragement and example. And thanks to Susan Clifford for her professional editorial suggestions.

FOREWORD

As we near the end of this century, which has provided us with atomic energy, supersonics, electronics, and the "information super-highway," we find an increasing need to escape the pressures of modern industrial society, and seek the tranquil beauty of the countryside—we unconsciously search for the simpler past, with less traffic and noise, with more friendliness and relaxation. An abundance of diversions, near to nature, are healthy for the body and mind, and essential for modern man to maintain his equilibrium.

Visitors to provincial France long to see the "real France." Sated with traditional sights and cities, they wish to sample the provinces' diverse terrains, folkways, and culinary delights. They want to escape *le stress* in a quiet place, where life proceeds at a different pace. They seek to understand the French, and their heritage.

What better place to center such activities than in a verdant river valley, near a small village, in an ancient mill, carefully restored and converted to a comfortable inn—with a gifted chef preparing tantalizing regional fare.

At a time of proliferation of electronic and information technology—which all of us depend on, and few of us understand—the mills, these ancestral machines, have a reassuring simplicity. To understand them, it is sufficient to see them. Mills were the quintessence of user-friendly machines. And mill-inns provide the quintessence of friendly innkeepers. As the Luthers note in this book, mill owners often make you feel like a guest in the home of a friend.

Marv and Nona Luther are the ideal couple to write a guide to mill-inns. They lived in France, and love regional France and the French. They also love French food and wine (Nona has a certificate from Paris' *Cordon Bleu*, and for 13 years they owned a firm importing fine French wines to the U.S.A.). And they love mill-inns, having visited more than a hundred over the past several years.

Vive la France des provinces, vive la cuisine française, vive le vin français, et vive French Water-Mill Inns!

Annie Candoré

Author of *Guide des Moulins en France* (Horay, Paris)
Founder and Past-President of *Moulin Étape*

ABOUT THE AUTHORS

Marv and Nona Luther lived for six years in Europe: two years in France, and two each in Holland and Germany with frequent visits to France. In California, they formed Bay-Vintners Imports for the import of fine French and German wines. They sold the wine firm, but continue frequent visits, often staying at water-mill inns.

When not traveling or writing, they share time among their family, sailboat, and kitchen. Nona earned a diploma at the Cordon Bleu in Paris, and taught classes in French cooking. She translated and adapted the recipes for the book.

ABOUT THE ILLUSTRATOR

Nixon Galloway is past-president of the Society of Illustrators of Los Angeles, and recipient of their Life Achievement Award. His work has been exhibited in the White House, the Pentagon, the Air and Space Museum, and the Kennedy Space Center. He has won awards in London, Dallas, New York, Chicago, Washington D.C., Pomona and Los Angeles.

THE SECRET INNS OF FRANCE

Here's one of the best-kept secrets in France: the most-congenial, most-memorable, most-romantic country inns are converted water mills. Along with fine food and lodging, they offer tranquil seclusion, ample activities, and an atmosphere that is friendly, casual, and flavored with nostalgia. And the mills bewitch. There is magic in the sylvan setting, the murmuring water, the elegant rusticity, and in the arcane machinery and archaic wheels.

For centuries, mills were the heart of rural France, numbering in the tens of thousands and adapted to an astounding variety of tasks: not only to grind grain, make paper, and saw wood, but also to press oil from nut meats, weave ribbon, make cloth, even forge metal. The mill wheels and gears formed the mills' signatures, and most mill-inns have preserved these parts. They add an extra dimension to a visit—taking us back to a simpler time.

Yet even before World War I, the mills of France began to grind to a halt. Steam, diesel, and electric power had won the day. A few still struggle along, but most stopped operating by the sixties. The conversion to inns started slowly, accelerated after 1975, and by 1996 more than 200 restored water mills operated as inns or as restaurants.

A typical mill sits along a stream in a forest of oaks, beeches, and elms. The vine-covered buildings of heavy timbers and stone are three or four centuries old. At one end of the main building a large, wooden wheel dips into the millrace. A stone terrace, sprinkled with bright umbrella tables, overlooks the pond. Flowers flourish from spring through fall. The mill is cool in the summer, and cozy and comfortable all year.

The inns are like a choice B&B with fine restaurant added. The typical mill is small—three to 20 bedrooms. Its dining room, also small, is decorated with old copper utensils and bric-a-brac, and old faience sits on the open beams. Furnishings are antique. The owners

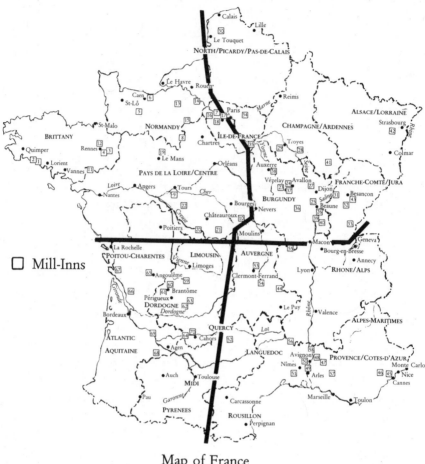

☐ Mill-Inns

Map of France

are husband and wife, often descendants of the original millers. One serves as chef, the other as host or hostess. The warmth of their welcome makes you feel like a guest in someone's home.

Although the emphasis is on tranquility and gastronomy, guests find much to do besides eating. Mills offer quiet walks along the stream, and colorful gardens in which to sit and read, or muse. A small village dozes nearby, and the modern world seems far removed. They often have tennis courts and heated swimming pools. If fishing is your love, the trout and perch in the streams and ponds are eager, and the chef may prepare the catch. Boating? Some mills have boats. In any event, golf, boating and riding are nearby.

Mills make a relaxing base for local touring. The Moulin Fleuri, for example, is within 30 minutes of 18 of the great châteaux of the

Loire. From the terrace of the Vieux Moulin at Pont-du-Gard, the ancient Roman aqueduct seems close enough to touch. Four exquisite mill-inns are less than an hour from the prehistoric caves of Les Eyzies-de-Tayac and the Vézère, and from the Dordogne River with several villages rated among "the most-picturesque in France[34]." Colorful markets take place weekly at towns and villages near the mills.

After a bit of sight-seeing, guests return to the mill's garden to have an apéritif and think about dinner. The demanding world is far removed. "It doesn't get any better than this," is a frequent comment. And when you've seen one, you haven't seen them all—each mill has its own character, its own personality.

As discussed in Chapter 25, we discovered French water mills while on a wine-buying trip to Burgundy. A friend took us to dinner at the then recently-converted Hostellerie du Vieux Moulin, "Inn of the Old Mill," in the hillside hamlet of Bouilland—so tiny that at the time, before the French modernized their communications system, the inn's telephone number was 15.

We'll never forget that first dinner, served *al fresco* on a patio overlooking a green wood and a gentle stream: foie gras followed by large, luscious trout from the mill's own pond, the trout served with a superb cream sauce, accompanied by a fine Meursault. Époisses, chaource, and other cheeses were served with a Mazis-Chambertin. Dessert was a pleasant, peasanty pudding. The owner joined us for Coffee and we felt at home, with friends.

The inn and the village bewitched us. We have traveled to France many times since, frequently seeking-out mills, and still have a special fondness for our first. We watched it grow in elegance to where, in 1990, it received its second Michelin star, and watched Bouilland grow in size to a population of 145. And we have found many other mills, and small villages, with the same friendly charm.

This guide features 40 of the authors' favorites: their facilities, personalities, activities, food and wine—including some recipes to help you recall and recreate favorite delights of the regional cuisine—and suggests things to see and do in the vicinity. Additional recommended mills, covered briefly, bring the total to 70. All but three of the inns were water mills. The three were animal-powered but were too fine to resist inclusion. We have visited all mills listed, and many more.

To ease the task of trip planning, the book divides France into regional quadrants. The preceding map shows this division, and indicates mill locations. The quadrants are the subjects of the next four parts of the book. Parts contain a map, a regional summary, and nine to eleven chapters describing mills that offer something special.

These chapters begin with a sketch, and a description of the mill and its amenities. They introduce the owners and chef, recommend specific rooms when appropriate, and list any caveats. The FOOD & WINE section reviews the restaurant food, cellar, and service, and comments on special dishes. Most chapters include recipes for dishes described—the chefs providing the recipes, and Nona translating and adapting them to American kitchens.

The SIGHTS & SUCH section describes recreational facilities and local sights. Sidebars summarize key data for ready reference, with prices computed at 5.00 francs per dollar: room prices for a double room, and meal and pension prices per person. At the end of each Part, two to 12 additional recommended inns are briefly described (most of these are "restaurant only," i.e., no rooms).

We hope and expect that you will delight in your own visits to the Secret Inns of France. Please write us your impressions and comments—you may see them acknowledged in the next edition. (Write c/o Corinthian Publications, P.O. Box 3028, Redondo Beach, California 90277.)

INDEPENDENT TRAVEL IN FRANCE

In our view, the way to enjoy the delights of provincial France is *not* as part of a group tour, but independently, whether by road, air, or rail, or some combination. You can go where you want, when you want, for as long as you want, see just what you want, and stay and eat where you want. And it's not that big a deal. Everyone is friendly and helpful, and while it is useful to know a few words of French, it's not essential.

TRAVELING BY CAR: This provides the greatest flexibility. Europe by Car or Renault or Citroën can make all arrangements, as can Hertz, Avis, Budget, Kemwell, and others. If your stay is three weeks or longer, lease the car (a purchase–repurchase plan) in lieu of simple rental. This will save the 28-percent rental-car tax.

U.S. citizens may drive legally in France, for up to six months, with a driver's license from one of the States. Some say that an international license may be useful—perhaps if you encounter a suspicious gendarme—but in seven years of driving in Europe, we have never needed one.

The French Government Tourist Office issues "Motoring in

France," which delineates the rules of the road. The most important rule to note is that of *Priorité à Droite*, priority to the right. Unless otherwise indicated, vehicles must yield to those approaching from their right. On major roads a yellow diamond road sign tells drivers they have priority over all. A crossed-out yellow diamond, or *Stop, Cédez le Passage*, or *Vous n'avez pas la Priorité* mean the drivers no longer have priority, and must give way to the right.

The major roads vary from fast, modern *Autoroutes*—labeled with an "A," such as "A6"—to *routes Nationale*, labelled with an "N" (e.g. N20), to *routes Departmental*, with a "D" designation. Speed limits are specified by type of road, e.g. 135, 110, and 90 kilometers per hour (kph), for A, N, or D roads. In town, the limit is 50 kph, unless otherwise posted. If stopped for speeding, you may have to pay a hefty fine on the spot.

The rules for parking: You may park by a blue sign with white "P." The words *Parking Payant* mean that you need to buy a ticket from a nearby vending machine, and display it on your dash. *Zone Bleue* parking requires display of a *Zone Bleue* disk, which you buy from a tobacconist or newspaper shop.

One of the delights of driving in France is picnicking—look for the roadside sign with the profile of a picnic table. Shop for your picnic before noon (the shops close for lunch). You'll need a *charcuterie*, to buy patés or terrines or ham or quiche, a *boulangerie* for bread or rolls or cakes, and an *épicerie* for fruit, pickles, bottled water. You can find all of this and much more at a *supermarché* or *hypermarché* (supermarket), but the individual shops are more charming.

TRAVELING BY AIR: Half a dozen regional airlines have flights to major—and many not so major—cities. Car rental is available at the airports. However, the flights may be infrequent—ask your travel agent for schedule information.

TRAVELING BY RAIL: The TGV *(Treins à Grande Vitesse*—high-speed or bullet trains) are a fast, fun way to get from one major city to another (at 300 kph or so). TGV stations are few, but car rental is available. You need advance reservations for the TGV, and the French Government Tourist Office can tell you where to make reservations and buy tickets in the U.S.—also where to find schedules for the local trains. The smaller local trains are slower, and may require train changes and waits for connections.

HOTEL AND RESTAURANT GUIDES: We like the Michelin red guide *France*[32], and the GaultMillau guides: *The Best of France*[28] (in English), and *France*[27] (in French). The French version is more up-to-date, and covers more establishments. Michelin rates restaurants using rosettes in place of stars, but most people call them stars anyway (a three-star Michelin restaurant is the best France has to offer). Gault-Millau rates restaurants with zero to four toques (chefs' hats). *Le Guide,* for which Michael Bond's fictional Monsieur Pamplemousse is an inspector, uses zero to three stock pots.[5] All of this has nothing to do with the Government's flawed system of zero to four stars for luxuriousness, which we show in the sidebar following each mill-inn's description.

USING THE TELEPHONE: France is divided into two zones: (1) Paris and the Île de France, and (2) the rest of the country (the provinces). All numbers have eight digits, which include the city codes for all of France except Paris and vicinity, for which you must precede the eight-digit number with a "1" city code.

To call from the U.S.: dial 011 (the international access code) + 33 (the code for France) + the eight-digit number. If calling to the Paris area, precede the eight-digit number with 1.

To call the U.S. from France: dial 19 (wait for dial tone) + 1 (the U.S. access code) + area code + the local number.

To call within France: Between two numbers within a zone (the Paris area, or the provinces): dial the eight-digit number. From the Paris area to the provinces: dial 16 (dial tone) + the number. From the provinces to the Paris area: dial 16 (dial tone) + 1 + the number.

Most public telephones accept only plastic cards *(télécartes),* available from a post office, tobacco shop, or newsstand. This may be preferable to calling from a hotel, since hotels routinely add surcharges. Telephones that accept credit cards are becoming common.

Emergency numbers: 15 for an ambulance; 17 for police.

APPENDICES: Appendix A: alphabetical listing of the mill-inns.

Appendix B: Bibliography and references; comments on maps, tourist guides, and other useful reference books. Superscripts in the text refer to items in this appendix.

Appendix C: A few basic recipes for sauces *et al,* which are used in two or more other recipes.

I. NORTHWEST FRANCE

Brittany, Normandy, and the Loire/Center have little in common historically, culturally, or gastronomically. But then, it is the same in many of the other French regions. Even after centuries of life under a strong, sometimes repressive central government—which tried to force uniformity—tremendous diversity remains.

The map on the next page shows Northwest France. It indicates mill-inn locations, with references to chapter numbers.

BRITTANY: The old name of Brittany is *Ars Mors* or *Armorica*, "country of the sea," a land almost surrounded by 1,500 kilometers of jagged coastline (roughly 1,000 miles). Some of the coast has gentle sandy beaches, some violent rocky spurs. The seas—the English Channel, the Bay of Biscay, and the Atlantic Ocean—have a tremendous impact on the lives and food of the Bretons.

This is an exotic land of mystery, legend, and superstition, where the people are Breton first, and French second. They jealously preserve their own language and customs, which are a fascinating blend of the Christian Celts who came here from Britain in the 5th to 7th centuries, and the original natives (those responsible for the mysterious menhirs and dolmens). As counterpoints to their many spirits, fairies, and demons, the Bretons have literally hundreds of saints (fewer than a dozen of which were canonized by the Vatican). Each founder of a Christian village was worshipped as a saint. And there are saints for every trade and every ailment, including baldness. For centuries, saints replaced doctors. The most vital event in the life of many villages is the annual *Pardon*, when the whole village dons ancient costumes and marches to the parish close, to beg the saint to cleanse them of their sins, and cure their illnesses.

The best time to visit is mid-May to early October. If you go in July or August, when most of the French (and millions of British, Germans, and Japanese) take their annual holiday, be sure to reserve long in advance.

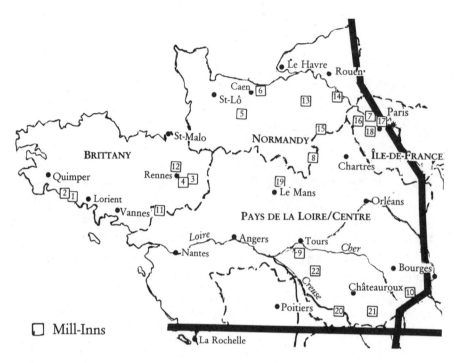

Mill-Inns

Northwest France

There are several daily flights and many trains from Paris to Brittany. From Paris by car, expect almost five hours to Rennes, two hours more to Quimper.

Breton cooking tends to use the finest materials, in the simplest preparations. Most important is the seafood from the rugged coasts and offshore waters. The spiny lobster *(langouste)* is outstanding, as are the Belon and Cancale oysters, and the clams, shrimp, scallops, and fish. The lobster is served grilled or with cream, or in a rich hot sauce which makes a dish called "Armoricaine" (sometimes mis-called "à l'Américaine," which originated due to a mistake on a Paris restaurant menu). Also try *cotriade*, made and served in the same manner as *Marseille bouillabaise*, with local fish and omitting the saffron and lobster—it is also called *bouillabaisse bretonne*.

The coastal salt-pastures *(pré-salés)* produce lamb and mutton which are famous. Leg of pré-salé mutton with beans is an ancient, delicious dish. Game, Nantais ducks, Rennais chickens, and pork products are also tasty.

A regional specialty is the pancake (*crêpe*, found at *crêperies*), and the *galette*, or scone. Crêperies often offer a meal composed of three courses of crêpes. They typically stuff the first crêpe with seafood (salmon and shellfish), and the second with ham, cheese, and mushrooms. The third: a flaming dessert.

The principal drink is cider (generally inferior to the cider of Normandy). The only Breton wine is Muscadet, grown near Nantes, and perfect with seafood. A Muscadet vineyard tour takes in the best districts (see Michelin's green guides *Côte de l'Atlantique*—for vineyard data—and *Brittany*).

NORMANDY: The name Normandy comes from "northmen," the pillaging pirates from the north (Vikings from Denmark and Norway) They settled here in the 10th century, adopted Christianity, made reasonable laws, and built many castles, churches and cathedrals. They weren't too busy, however, to have time to conquer Britain, and William the Conqueror became King of England as well as Duke of Normandy. William and his conquest are the subject of the famous 70-meter (233-foot) tapestry at Bayeux. After the Hundred-Year War, in 1469, Normandy became a French province.

Despite many wars and battles, Normandy wasn't badly scarred until it's greatest disaster came in World War II. In 1940, the cities of Upper Normandy were ravaged by fire, and in 1944 the destruction was completed as the Calvados and Contentin beaches became the beachheads for the Allied invasion. However, the rural and agricultural communities were relatively unscathed, and remain much as they have been for centuries.

One of France's great gastronomic provinces, Normandy is the dairyland of France, and also famous for its apples, and its numerous seaports and fishing villages. So the cuisine—you guessed it—is based upon cream, seafood, cream, apples, cream, and cheese. The cream goes well with fish, chicken, veal, sweetbreads, vegetables—even game. The thick, slightly sour *crème fraîche* is great on fruit and berries, as well as in cooking.

Meats include beef, pork, lamb, poultry, and game, plus pré-salé lamb and mutton from the fields near Mont-Saint-Michel. Nona and I have a prejudice against tripe, so will only remark that it's a big thing in Caen and elsewhere, in soups, and in sausages such as *andouille*.

Normandy cheeses are world-renowned. From the Auge region come the *Pont-l'Éveque* and *Livarot* (they've reigned for 700 years) and the newer *Camembert* (they've only been making it 190 years).

From the Bray region come the fresh *suisses, demi-sel* double cream, *bondon* and other *Neufchâtel* farm-house cheeses, and *Brillat-Savarin*.

The most popular drink is apple cider, for which Normandy has been known since the middle ages. A pear drink is made in the same manner. But it is the distilled cider, Calvados, which permits Normandy to lead the rest of France in alcohol consumption.

A Norman tradition is that in the middle of a meal, before the main course, you toss down a glass of Calvados, to refresh the palate and ready you for the delights to come. This is a *trou normand*, or "hole" in the meal (restaurants often substitute a Calvados sorbet for the fiery apple brandy).

LOIRE/CENTER: The longest river in France, the Loire flows from the Massif Central northward to skirt the southwest edge of Burgundy, then curve westerly to the Atlantic. The region is best known for La Vallée des Rois, "Valley of the Kings." Between Orleans and Angers, along the Loire and its many lovely tributaries— the Indre, Cher, Loir, Vienne, and Sarthe—you find dozens of old castles, Renaissance châteaux, picturesque villages, and vineyards.

Caves abound: mushroom caves, wine caves, and cave-houses built into the cliffs. Nona and I once visited Montrichard to see the late J.M. Monmousseau, a well-known wine grower. He invited us to his home that evening, to hear some music. His house was on the top of a cliff, and the entrance was at the base: a door built into the rock. This led to an elevator, which carried us up to the house.

(Tourists also abound, but the sights are worth the wait in line. See the Michelin green guide *Châteaux of the Loire*.)

The Loire is the land of "good food, merry drink, and calm digestion." This river and its tributaries furnish pike, salmon, perch, and shad. Forests provide game and game birds, and the farms produce pork, veal, chicken and duck. Vegetables are important— especially asparagus, lettuce, and cabbage. A variety of mushrooms come from caves and forests. In contrast to most of northern France, recipes call for more oil (walnut, hazelnut, and olive) than butter.

According to legend, the famous *Tarte Tatin*—an upside-down, caramelized apple pie—was invented by the Tatin sisters at their hotel in Lamotte-Beuvron some time in the late 19th century. The hotel is still in business, and still making their tart (33 kilometers south of Orleans).

1. LES MOULINS DU DUC

Moëlan-sur-Mer, Finistère, Brittany

"Oh yes, the Queen Mother stayed here," M. Quisterbert said proudly. Which, I must admit, impressed me. It implied elegance, opulence, and gentility. If it's good enough for the mother of Queen Elizabeth . . . But the reference was not needed—Les Moulins du Duc speaks for itself. Its two old, stone mills formerly belonged to the regal Duke of Brittany, which gives it a certain royal cachet. And the story-book setting evokes images of feudal days and chivalrous knights.

A small hidden valley, wooded and green, forms the backdrop. The two mills and six or seven cottages, all with stone walls and slate roofs, date from the 16th century. Other granite buildings, since added, make up a small hamlet, brightened by profuse beds of geraniums, hydrangeas, and asters. A small lake, or large pond—filled with trout, salmon, and ducks—reflects the ancient buildings and a wide terrace. The Belon river wanders through the park and feeds the lake, on its way to the famous oyster beds, and to the Atlantic eight kilometers away.

The Quistrebert family bought one mill in 1968, later bought a second, and gradually restored and added other buildings. The main mill, on the lake, contains the public rooms and a museum's-worth of mill mechanisms. Other buildings share the 22 bedrooms and five suites. A narrow road winds among them to an enclosed, heated swimming pool.

Our favorite suite is "Tymylin," a small, two-story cottage. Nona, barely five-foot six, had to stoop to pass through an entrance sized for a 16th-century miller. The narrow sitting room, roughly eight by 20 feet, has the entry at one end, opposite a window over-looking a wood. On one side a door opens to a modern bathroom, on the other a stairway leads to a loft with king-size bed. Old mill parts flank the stairs.

A little private terrace—with a table and chairs—spreads in front of Tymylin, by a lawn and the river bank. A delightful place for dozing or reading. Or playing dominoes. Or sipping apéritifs. For an apéritif, though, we prefer the friendly terrace by the lake.

FOOD & WINE

In the main mill, a door in the entry opens to a large room with a well-stocked bar, a lounge to the left, and a view of the huge mill wheel on the right. At the rear, stairs lead down past massive cog wheels to the restaurant: two stone-flagged rooms at the river level, with views of the wheels and the stream.

For years, through 1986, the Moulins du Duc had a Michelin star, GaultMillau toques and membership in the prestigious Relais & Châteaux chain. Then chef Shigeo Torigaï left, to be followed by a revolving door of less-gifted chefs. The present chef, Thierry Quilfen appears to have both talent (he worked under Barrier in Tours), and a desire to stay. He has already earned a toque. If he provides stability, we may soon see the other honors restored.

Quilfen's specialties feature local ingredients, which means many products of the sea. He graciously shared some recipes with us, one of which we present below: *Escalope de bar à l'oseille* (filet of bass in a sorrel sauce). The wine list is small, good, and costly.

Oyster lovers must visit Port Belon, on the Belon River six kilometers west of Moëlan. Experts consider Belon oysters to be the best in France. They grade them by size, the larger costing more, and the smaller tasting better. Get oysters at La Cabane, a small bar-restaurant. (You might count your dozen—once we found only 11, and they cheerfully corrected the shortage.)

SIGHTS & SUCH

At the secluded Moulins du Duc you can fish or row in the lake, fish in the river, walk in the woods, swim in the pool. You can stew in the sauna, and workout in the exercise room. Or you can eat, drink, and relax.

It is tempting to remain at the inn, but there's too much else to see and do in Finistère. Tennis, golf, riding, and beaches are nearby. The towns of Moëlan-sur-Mer and Quimperlé are worth a visit, but we find most exciting the coastal ports and villages.

On the coast 5.5 kilometers south of Moëlan, the small fishing port Doëlan overlooks the entrance to a deep, sheltered estuary. Eight kilometers farther, the small port Le Pouldu lies at the mouth of the Laïta River. It has a monument to Gauguin, who lived and painted here for a time.

Between Le Pouldu and Lorient are several beach resorts and a zoo. At Lorient you can get a boat to Monet's fabulous Belle Île, a few miles off the coast. Continue southeast to Auray, and find a pretty harbor on the Loch (or Auray) River, and an imposing array of 15th-century stone houses. And then, drive down the Quiberon peninsula, visiting Carnac, with many megaliths dating to 6000 B.C. Also, in Carnac, Quiberon, and Belle-Île are spas called by such names as Institute de Thalassothérapie. *Thalassa* means "sea." These spas offer the "restorative powers of brisk sea air, salt water, and the nourishing Breton climate."

For sights west of the Aven estuary, see Chapter 2. For all of the Finistère coast, see the green Michelin guide *Brittany.*

After sightseeing, return to the terrace on the lake for an apértif and a chat with other guests, and with the ducks.

SEA BASS FILETS WITH SORREL
Escalope de bar à l'oseille

2 lbs. (1 kg.) sea bass filets   salt
1½ lbs. (700 g.) sorrel*   4 Tablespoons (50 g.) butter
1 pint (45 cl.) thick cream

Make 2½ cups (60 cl.) fish stock from the bones and head of the fish. Reduce by two-thirds.

Wash the sorrel and cut into very thin slices *(chiffonnade)*. Cook the sorrel with the water that clings to it in 2 tablespoons (30 g.) of butter until it is dry. Add the cream and the fish stock to make a thick sauce.

Place sea bass in the sorrel sauce. Cover and cook 10 minutes over a low fire, without boiling. Remove the fish and keep warm. Rectify the seasoning of the sauce and add the rest of the butter.

To serve, place some sauce on a plate and top with the sea bass. Noodles are a good accompaniment.   Serves 6.

* *If sorrel is unavailable, try chard or a similar green, with lemon juice.*

★ ★ ★ ★ LES MOULINS DU DUC, 29116 Moëlan-sur-Mer. Tel: 98 39 60 73. Fax: 98 39 75 56.

PROPRIETORS: The Quistrebert family.

ROOMS: 22, plus 5 suites, all with bath or shower and WC, direct telephone, TV, mini-bar.

PRICES: Rooms: 440 to 805 F; ($88–161). Suites: 1010–1300 F ($202–260); ½-pension: 525–910 F. ($105–182). Breakfast: 55 F. ($11). Menus: 90 (Lunch), 135–320 F ($18 (L), $27–64), children 60 F. ($12). Credit cards: AE, DC, EC, MC, Visa.

AMENITIES: Bar, lounge, terrace, 150-acre park, Belon River, ponds, woods. Free trout and salmon fishing. Indoor, heated swimming pool. Sauna and gym. Parking. Tennis 1 km., riding 15 km. Golf: 4 courses nearby. Beach and water sports 5 km. Dining inside, or on the terrace.

ASSOCIATIONS: Moulin Étape; Relais du Silence.

MARKET DAYS: Pont-Aven: Tue; Riec-sur-Belon: Thu; Concarneau Mon, Fri; Pont-l'Abbé: Wed–Sat; Quimperlé: Fri.

DIRECTIONS: From Moëlan-sur-Mer, N 2 km on D116, then follow signs to the mill. Moëlan-sur-Mer is on the South Brittany coast, 23 km. W of Lorient, 20 km. E of Concarneau.

OPEN: Mar 1–Jan 19.

2. LE MOULIN DE ROSMADEC
Pont-Aven, Finistère, Brittany

"This is an exquisite resting place, a countryside almost too pretty, with boats from the sea, and mills on the water, lost in a confusion of foliage . . . an operatic decor."

More than a century ago, François Coppée thus described Pont-Aven, the village made famous by Paul Gauguin and the artists he diverted from impressionism. In 1886-1896, Pont-Aven was a placid mill town, set in Southwest Brittany six kilometers from the sea, where the Aven River broadens into an estuary—a small village about to become a cosmopolitan art colony. The Moulin de Rosmadec and 14 others still ground grain, as they had for 400 years.

The mills have all stopped working, and while most were abandoned, the Moulin de Rosmadec survived as an inn. The main building has two stories of gray stone walls, steep slate roofs, and mullioned windows. Red and pink hydrangeas hug the walls, red and pink roses climb around doorways and windows, and pots of red and pink geraniums crowd sills and lintels. In this busy tourist town, Rosmadec's riverside setting is an oasis of calm and grace.

You reach it from the Place Paul Gauguin, through a 40-foot passage barely wide enough for a car. The drive then broadens, with room for five cars to park along the river. At the end, a portal leads to the inn's front terrace and entrance.

Gabrielle Sébilleau greets you warmly, and shows you around the inn. From the tiny reception and bar area, a door leads to the courtyard and a secluded rear terrace, on a spit of land pointing downstream in the Aven River. A ship's bell sits on a stone column near an antique well. Modern white tables and chairs with bright red cushions make a pleasing contrast to the old stone walls and well. A place to sit and read, shaded by beech trees, or to enjoy an apéritif or lunch. Or, to watch the families of ducks.

The ducks face upstream in the river, paddling just enough to remain stationary. They dunk their heads to gobble some tidbit, then boast about it to the others. Periodically they swim closer to the terrace to discuss the matter with guests.

Double doors open from the bar to the larger of two dining rooms. This room has oak floors, and dark, massive ceiling beams covered with heavy planking. Windows along two sides keep the room from being somber. Antique faience, lamps, and Breton bric-a-brac crowd the walls—a mini-museum of Breton culture. Pink linen covers the 12 well-spaced tables, all with fresh flowers and sparkling silver and crystal. At one end of the room sits a large, stone fireplace. The head of a boar glares down from above the mantel.

To the left of the fireplace, a door leads to the lower dining room: small, airy, cheerful, and brightened by windows looking out on the rear terrace and river—ideal for lunch. Most prefer the main dining room for dinner. Be sure to make reservations (resident guests have their choice of tables).

In a separate, new building are the four large and comfortable guest rooms, each with modern decor and furnishings. All of the rooms have well-furnished baths, telephone, television, and air conditioning. Mme Sébilleau named the rooms for flowers. Our favorite, the "Cyclamen," overlooks the river, the front terrace, and the passage. One evening as we looked out the window, a sixth and seventh car pulled into in the narrow driveway, blocking the first five. When someone wanted to leave, the hotel staff had to find the invaders, and ask them to back out. No one seemed to mind. However, you can park in the zone bleue area, 100 yards away in the Place de l'Hôtel de Ville, next to the Place Paul Gauguin.

FOOD & WINE

Some come to Brittany for the unspoiled coastal scenes and picturesque villages, and to Pont-Aven for the serenity Gauguin found. Nona and I come for the lobster, and the best place for the lobster is the Moulin de Rosmadec. The mill rates a Michelin star and a GaultMillau toque—some think it the finest restaurant in Brittany. This is arguable, but I've no doubt that Frédéric Sébilleau's grilled lobster, *Homard grillé Rosmadec*, and his *Homard Breton flambés au whiskey* (lobster with a cream sauce, flamed with scotch) *are* the finest (see recipe). The dishes were invented by Sébilleau's father Pierre, who had the secret of grilling lobster without losing its moist succulence. (Pierre is still around to help his young son.)

Other specialties include starters such as *Fonds d'artichauts aux morilles* (artichoke hearts with morel mushrooms) and *Huîtres chaudes farcies aux amandes* (warm oysters stuffed with almonds). An outstanding dish is the *Magret de canard rosé au cassis* (duck breast with black currants—see recipe). For beef, we like the *Coeur de filet de boeuf grillé à la moëlle*. A nice dessert is *Sabayon de fruits frais*, a zabaglione with several fresh fruits.

The short wine list has a few token Burgundies and Bordeaux, and well-selected Loires. With seafood, try the dry, refreshing Muscadet, and with duck or steak, the red Saint Nicolas de Bourgueil.

This is a rich area for discovering Breton cuisine. Oyster lovers must visit the Belon River, six kilometers to the east, for the best oysters in France (see Chapter 1). In Riec-sur-Belon is the charming Mélanie restaurant, with an old-Breton decor and atmosphere. Here the late Curnonsky—"Prince-elect of the Gastronomes," prolific food author, and founder of the monthly *Cuisine et Vins de France*—lived out the war years. Too old to fight, he could still eat, drink, and flirt with the legendary Mélanie. The restaurant displays photographs of them enjoying a respite from the war.

In Concarneau, 15 kilometers west, the best-known restaurant—and perhaps the best—is Le Galion. An old Breton inn, Le Galion specializes in classic seafood. In the walled city (La Ville-Close) on the islet in Concarneau's bay, several *crêperies*—such as the Crêperie Éole and the Crêperie l'Écume—offer the delightful all-crêpe meal mentioned earlier: the first crêpe stuffed with seafood, the second with ham, cheese, and mushrooms, and the third a flaming dessert.

Another fine seafood source is Chez Jacky, a fisherman's bistro in the Port-du-Belon, seven kilometers south of Pont-Aven. She serves a superb seafood platter, and of course the Belon oysters. For a snack, get excellent Breton pancakes at the Crêperie des Chaumières, a thatched-roof cottage in Kerascoët (on the west side of the Aven estuary, almost to the sea). Or, shop on Place Paul Gauguin, in Pont-Aven, for a Breton picnic.

SIGHTS & SUCH

With as many mills as houses, in Gaughin's day someone wrote:

> *"Pont-Aven, ville de renom,*
> *15 moulins, 14 maisons."*

(Fifteen mills, 14 houses.) Pont-Aven changed. The population grew to 3000, as sophisticated Parisians replaced most of the peasants. Shops and galleries now line the thoroughfares and squares.

The tourist office, on the main square, will give you a walking map. For example, the Xavier-Grall walk, accessible by foot bridges, leads along a flowered islet, between two arms of the river—a lovely place for the picnic. Just east of the tourist office, a museum displays a fine collection of post-impressionist paintings.

The walks along the river must give as much pleasure today as a century ago. Northeast of town, on the right bank, lies the Bois d'Amour, a large wood of oak and beech, named for the romantic trysts it invited through the years. Painters still come here for the pervasive calm, the large old trees, the ever-changing river—its reflections perturbed by the current as it washes the large granite rocks—and the wispy clouds that transform the light. Little signs along the paths identify painters associated with specific views.

Near the Bois d'Amour, the Chapelle de Trémalo, an early Breton country chapel, contains the 16th-century wooden crucifix that inspired Gauguin's *Yellow Christ*. Several other old stone churches are within six kilometers.

Between Pont-Aven and the sea, picturesque hamlets are sprinkled along both sides of the estuary. After extensive restoration, some look the way they did centuries ago. Of particular interest: Kerascoët, mentioned earlier, and the port of Kerdruc.

Concarneau, France's third largest fishing port, holds a colorful fish auction Mondays through Thursdays, between 7 and 10 a.m. This auction, like the village market, appeals to all the senses, and you'll probably see some creatures you've never seen before. While there, visit La Ville-Close, even if not interested in crêpes. Walk around the granite ramparts, which date from the 14th to 17th centuries, and enjoy the views from the towers. Visit the Shellwork Display Center, and the large Fishing Museum. Return to Pont-Aven along the coast (45 kilometers, two hours). This trip includes dramatic views of the sea, and the towns of Kerascoët, Port Manech, Kerdruc, and Névez.

From Concarneau—or from Beg-Meil or Port-la-Forêt—you can take a boat up the Odet River, the "Prettiest river in France," to Quimper, for 400 years the faience capital of Brittany. One can see the colorful pottery in the museum, or in the pottery workshops.

Pont Aven makes a good base for visiting the jagged coast of Cornouaille (named after England's Cornwall), and other sights of western Brittany. See the Michelin green guide *Brittany*.

When finished with the day's sight-seeing, return to the Moulin de Rosmadec for a quiet apéritif, a chat with the ducks, and a memorable dinner.

LOBSTER FLAMED WITH WHISKEY
Homards Breton flambés au whisky

This is a beautiful dish! It would be great for a Valentine's Day dinner for two. So simple but elegant, and quite rich.

2 1.5-lb (800 g.) lobsters*   cayenne pepper
3 cups (70 cl.) cream   3.5 oz. (100 g.) butter
5 oz. (15 cl.) oil   salt, pepper
4 oz. (12 cl.) Scotch whiskey

Cut the lobsters in two lengthwise. Pour the oil in a pan and brown the flesh sides. When golden brown, turn them, place in an oven-proof casserole, and flame with ¾ of the whiskey. Salt and pepper lightly.

Add the cream and the cayenne, and cook for 10 minutes in an oven preheated to 375°F (190°C).

Put the lobster on a serving plate, and keep warm. Reduce the cream on a low fire. Correct the seasoning. Add the rest of the whisky, and reduce several minutes.

Pour the sauce over the lobster, and serve hot.

Serves 4.

* *You can two substitute lobster tails – a half pound each.*

DUCK BREAST WITH BLACK CURRANTS
Magret de canard rosé au cassis

3 cups (75 cl.) crème de cassis   1 cup (25 cl.) veal stock*
1 cup (25 cl.) vinegar   salt and pepper
Fresh currants*   4 6-oz. (180-g.) duck breasts

In a sauce pan, reduce the crème de cassis and vinegar by half.
Add the veal stock and reduce again by half. Season with salt and
pepper and add the currants.

Season the duck breasts and sauté on both sides until done (they
should be pink inside). Cut the breasts in thin slices.

Place cassis sauce on the plates and fan the slices of deck breast
on the sauce.

Serves 4.

* If fresh currants are not available, try dried cranberries.
Chicken or beef stock may be substituted for veal.

★★★ LE MOULIN DE ROSMADEC, 29123 Pont-Aven, Tel: 98 06 00 22.
    Fax: 98 06 18 00.
PROPRIETORS: Pierre & Gabrielle Sébillau. CHEF: Frédéric Sébillau.
ROOMS: 4, with bath or shower and WC, direct telephone, TV, air conditioning.
PRICES: Rooms: 400–470 F ($80–94); Breakfast: 40 F ($8). Menus: 160–400 F
    ($32–80). Credit cards: AE, MC, Visa.
AMENITIES: Bar, two river-front terraces. Parking. Dining in two dining rooms or
    on terraces. Tennis, riding, golf nearby.
ASSOCIATIONS: Les Cuisiniers et Hôteliers de Métier.
MARKET DAYS: Concarneau: Mon, Fri (fish auction Mon–Thu); Fouesnant: Fri;
    Pont-l'Abbé: Wed–Sat; Pont-Aven: Tue; Riec-sur-Belon: Thu; Névez: Fri, Sat.
DIRECTIONS: In center of Pont-Aven, So. Brittany coast: 14 km. E of Concarneau,
    31 km. W of Lorient.
OPEN: Mar 1–Oct 15, Nov 4–Jan 31; Restaurant closed: Wed; Sun dinner
    Sep 3–Jun 18.

3. AR MILIN'

Châeaubourg, Île-et-Vilaine, Brittany

Ar Milin'—Breton for "old mill"—was originally a large flour mill, though better known as a hydroelectric plant. For the first half of the 20th century, besides grinding grain, it furnished electricity for the town of Châteaubourg, leading to the town's nickname: "the city of light" (with more-obvious justification than Paris').

The inn is in the middle of the Vilaine River and in the middle of town, but after you turn into its 12-acre park, you are completely unaware of the village. This park boasts a lake (too big to call a pond), complete with swans, woods, lawns, the curving river, pleasant paths, and a majestic old mill—an imposing building of stone and wood, with a millrace running underneath.

Guest rooms in the mill are small but pretty, with modern baths and antique furniture. Balconies overlook the park—a pleasant place to sit and listen to the songs of river and birds. Be sure to reserve a room in the mill, *not* in the annex. The latter, at the back of the park near the not-so-silent railway, was added for use by attendees of seminars and weddings, which represent the bulk of the inn's business. Modern motel in style, it is comfortable, but lacking in charm.

The inn's public rooms are a delight. The semicircular, well-supplied bar, and the lounge—with black leather-covered armchairs—give the cozy feeling of a private club. At mealtime, choose between the two dining rooms. One is bright and airy, with three walls of windows overlooking the park. The other is elegant rustic: heavy hand-hewn beams, huge fireplace, mullioned windows, and antique chandeliers. We like the first at luncheon, the second at dinner.

FOOD & WINE

Chef Bertrand Poulnais' specialties are "the cuisine of the market, in the rhythm of the seasons." Most are traditional, but some are downright unusual. He shared the recipes for two of these dishes: *Rillettes de maquereau à la ciboulette* (minced mackerel spread, with chives); and *Crème brulée aux pruneaux* (crème brulée with prunes— a refreshing variation).

In case the unusual turns you off, we found these more-traditional dishes exceptional: *Canard sauvageon de domagné au beurre d'herbes* (wild duck with herb butter); *Croustillant de caille aux ris de veau* (crisp quail with veal sweetbreads); and for dessert: *Meringue Rennais aux pommes* (meringue with apples—an ancient recipe from the Rennes region). On another visit, we enjoyed *Farci de canard au foie gras parfumé au Layon* (duck with foie gras, prepared and served with semi-sweet, white Coteaux-du-Layon wine, from the Loire).

For other local wines, try the Muscadet-sur-lies Château de la Galisonière and the red Bourgueil. Burel has a good list of Bordeaux graves, and a fine Pouilly Fumé.

No matter the season, you can't go wrong dining here.

SIGHTS & SUCH

The activities available within the park are numerous (see sidebar). If you are a bird watcher, bring your handbook: more than 20 species of bird live in the park, from tiny sparrows to swans.

The walks within the park may satisfy you, but a 1.5-hour trek in the surrounding woods starts just 200 yards from the inn. This walk lets you discover a second mill, another pond, the Château du Val, and a peacock farm. The hotel staff will direct you.

Châteaubourg is just east of Rennes, the capital of Brittany. With over 200,000 inhabitants, Rennes has problems typical of a big city—too much traffic, too little parking—but is well worth a visit. In particular, the Museum of Brittany and the Museum of Fine Arts (on the first and second floors of the same building). Nearby are several other museums and châteaux.

Châteaubourg is only one hour from the Emerald Coast and the cities of Saint-Malo, Mont-Saint-Michel, Cancale, and Dinard. (See the Michelin green guide *Brittany*.)

With all there is to see and do, you might make Ar' Milin your home for several days.

MINCED SPREAD OF MACKEREL WITH CHIVES
Rillettes de maquereau à la ciboulette

This is a pleasant variation on pork or rabbit rillette. The mackerel flavor is strong enough to make it work.

2 lbs. (1 kg.) mackerel   ½ bunch of chives
2 cups (50 cl.) cream   juice of 1 lemon
¼ cup (12 cl.) white wine

Bring cream and wine to a boil, and reduce 5 minutes.

Filet and bone fish, place in a large frying pan, and cover with the reduced cream and wine. Add lemon juice and a little salt. Poach 4 minutes, let the fish cool, then drain, reserving the liquid.

Flake the filets, removing skin and dark portions of flesh. Add chives, and mix well. Add enough of the poaching liquid to obtain the consistency of a thick paste.

Serve on toast, or on lettuce leaves as a salad.

Serves 6 to 8.

CRÈME BRULEE WITH PRUNES
Crème brulée aux pruneaux

4 oz. (120 g.) pitted prunes   1 cup (25 cl.) cream
4 egg yolks   ¾ cup (20 cl.) milk
4 tablespoons sugar   4 tablespoons Armagnac
                                 or other brandy

Cut prunes into quarters and marinate in the Armagnac for an hour. Drain and reserve the liquid.

Beat egg yolks and sugar together. Add the milk and cream.

Divide prunes into four custard cups. Add the egg cream mixture and the Armagnac marinade. Place cups in a baking pan and add boiling water around them. Bake 45 to 50 minutes at 325°F (165°C).

Remove from oven. Sprinkle the custards with granulated sugar and place under the broiler to caramelize the sugar. Watch carefully so they don't burn.

Serve warm or cold.

Serves 4.

★ ★ ★ AR MILIN', 30, rue de Paris, 35220 Châteaubourg. Tel: 99 00 30 91.
Fax: 99 00 37 56.
OWNER/HOST: M. Michel Burel.
ROOMS: 30, plus 1 suite, all with bath or shower and WC, direct telephone, TV.
PRICES: Rooms: 325–593 F ($65–119). Suite: 640–715 F ($128–143). ½–pension:
396–572 F ($79–114). Breakfast: 49 F ($10). Menus: 99–196 F ($20–39).
Children: 66 F ($13). Credit cards: AE, DC, EC MC, Visa.
AMENITIES: Bar, lounge, terrace. 12-acre park crossed by the river, with 3
waterfalls, lake, pond, many different kinds of trees, 20 kinds of local birds.
2 dining rooms, tennis court, volley ball, ping-pong, boules, pedalo boats,
kayaks, fishing. Interesting walks. Riding 1 km. Golf 15 km. (4 courses within
20 km.) Parking.
ASSOCIATIONS: Moulin Étape; Châteaux et Hôtels Indépendants.
MARKET DAYS: Rennes: Sat, Place des Lices—one of the nicest markets in France;
Hédé: Tue.
DIRECTIONS: In Châteaubourg: 23 km. E of Rennes, 320 km. W of Paris (2 hours
by T.G.V., 3 by auto on A11/A81). 25 km. from Rennes airport.
OPEN: Jan 3–Dec 21; Restaurant closed: Sun dinner (Oct–Mar).

4. HÔTEL GERMINAL
Cesson–Sévigné, Ille-et-Vilaine, Brittany

Imagine a romantic mill-inn isolated on its own private island in the middle of the Vilaine River. The Hôtel Germinal, a four-story flour mill, dates from 1883. It is located only five kilometers from the center of Rennes, the capital of Brittany. At the edge of the peaceful, green village of Cesson, it sits near an old Roman bridge that is still in use (one car at a time).

Louis Goualin purchased the mill in 1930, and his children modernized it. His grandson, also Louis, was born in what is today the dining room of the inn. He worked in the mill for a few years, and in 1974 converted it to an inn. He is now your host and chef.

Mme Goualin will welcome you, and give you a room with a river view. The 20 guest rooms are well-furnished, with well-appointed bathrooms, direct telephone, TV, and furniture of warm, wild-cherry wood. Some have canopied beds. All provide a quiet, comfortable night.

FOOD & WINE

Mme Goualin loves the elegant dining room, whose large bay windows open to views of the river and trees. You can dine on the sheltered terrace looking out on the river. And you can dine well.

Chef Goualin specializes in fish, lobster, and other products of the sea, and has an astonishingly large selection. Fixed-price menus give a choice among six to eight items for each course. Here's a sample meal we enjoyed, for 88 francs: *La terrine de saumon* (salmon terrine—see recipe), *Les noisettes de porc à la moutarde* (pork filet with a mustard sauce), and a choice among cheeses, pastries, or sorbets. Excellent dishes, at a favorable price. The limited wine selection offers good value.

It would take a while to exhaust Goualin's offerings, but you may wish an occasional change. Of the restaurants in Rennes, the finest and best value is Le Palais—rating three GaultMillau toques and a Michelin star, with menus from 98 to 220 F. There are 10 other toques in the city, and another at Ar Milin' in Châteaubourg, 15 kilometers east of Cesson (see Chapter 3).

SIGHTS & SUCH

The site offers pleasant walks along the river and through the village (13,000 inhabitants), tennis in village courts, and punting and fishing. Also in town—across the bridge, almost immediately on the right—is the Manoir de Bourgchevreuil, with large, well-kept herb and rose gardens worth a visit.

Bird lovers flock to Bruz, 12 kilometers south of Rennes, for *Le Parc Ornithologique*, with 210 species. For golf, you need drive only eight kilometers.

Since Cesson is near the center of Rennes, the Rennais attractions are almost within walking distance. And the Emerald Coast, with Saint-Malo and the Mont-Saint-Michel, is less than an hour away (see Chapter 3, and the Michelin green guide *Brittany*).

SALMON TERRINE
La Terrine de saumon

1 lb. (500 g.) salmon filet	1½ cups (375 g.) *crème fraîche*
½ lb. (250 g.) whiting or	or heavy whipping cream
other white-fleshed fish	2 egg whites
salt, pepper	2 oz. (60 g.) spinach

Line a terrine mold with a wide strip of aluminum foil.

Cut a bar of salmon two inches (5 cm.) wide, and the length of the terrine mold. Salt, pepper, and set aside.

Put remaining salmon, cut in small pieces, in a blender. Add salt and pepper and blend until puréed. Add 1 egg white and blend. Add ¾ cup cream and blend until all is a smooth purée. Set aside.

Follow the same procedure for a purée of the white fish. When the purée is finished, add the spinach and purée until smooth again. Set aside.

Fill the terrine mold by placing half the salmon purée in the bottom. Top with half the white fish purée. Place the filet of salmon in the center of this layer and cover with the other half of the white fish purée. Top with the rest of the salmon purée.

Place the terrine in a flat pan and add about 2 inches boiling water to the pan. Bake for 40 minutes at 325°F (190°C).

Slice and serve either hot or cold.

Serves 6.

★★★ . HÔTEL GERMINAL, 9, cours de la Vilaine, 35510 Cessons-Sévigné. Tel: 99 83 11 01. Fax: 99 83 45 16.
PROPRIETORS: M. & Mme Louis Goualin. CHEF: Louis Goualin.
ROOMS: 19, all with bath or shower and WC, direct telephone, TV.
PRICES: Rooms: 325–420 F ($65–84). Breakfast: 45 F ($9). Menus: 88–250 F ($18–50), children 50 F ($10). Credit cards: CB, EC, MC, Visa.
AMENITIES: Bar, lounge, terrace, river, private island, parking. Fishing, swimming, tennis, riding, punting: 1–6 km. Golf 8 km.
ASSOCIATIONS: Moulin Étape; Logis de France.
MARKET DAYS: Rennes: Saturday, Place des Lice—one of the nicest markets.
DIRECTIONS: In the town of Cesson-Sévigné, 6 km. E of Rennes on N157 (341 km. W of Paris). N on rue des Vieux Ponts.
OPEN: Jan 5–Jul 31, Aug 22–Dec 19. Restaurant closed: Sun.

5. HOSTELLERIE DU MOULIN DU VEY
Clécy, Calvados, Normandy

A lovely vine-and-rose-covered water mill in a scenic valley cut through the hills by the Orne River, the Moulin du Vey is a welcome stop for a day or a week. The majestic valley, surrounded by green, rolling hills, provides a restful haven—and yet it supports rock climbing and hang-gliding for the daring. Just 35 kilometers south of Caen, Clécy is in the heart of enchanting Swiss Normandy.

The bedrooms in the mill are smallish, but comfortable, each furnished in a specific style—from the rustic 11th-century decor of William the Conqueror, to the elegance of Louis XV. Below the windows, the singing river and the sound of the turning mill wheel soothe the guests. (Not so for the seven rooms in an annex three kilometers from the inn, which are a bit noisy.)

The dining room occupies a converted barn, next to the mill. And there's a large waterside terrace for fair-weather dining.

FOOD & WINE

Chef Michel Choplin, son-in-law of the owner Mme Denise Léduc, offers polished versions of traditional Norman dishes. For example, *La Nonette de saumon au beurre de cidre* (salmon rolls with cider butter—see recipe); and *Pigeon roti au miel et à la poire* (honey-roasted squab with pears). Other specialties: *Coquilles Saint-Jacques feuilletées Nantais* (scallops with puff pastry and cream sauce); and *Ris de veau au vouvray* (sweetbreads with Vouvray wine sauce). The less-expensive menus offer excellent value.

The wine selection is good, with fine Muscadet and numerous Loire wines to consider. And there's a true *trou normand*—a glass of Calvados precedes the main course.

SIGHTS & SUCH

There's much to do at the inn. You can fish, hike, row boats or canoes, hang-glide, and go rock climbing. Within a kilometer you can swim, ride, play tennis, or miniature golf. Real golf is only three kilometers away. Or, you can sit, rest, read, or watch others get their exercise.

Across the river, accessible by a nearby stone bridge, is a small café/crêperie, with a wooden terrace overhanging the river. Friday nights you can enjoy live jazz, or other music. In Clécy visit the Manoir de Placy, a rich museum of Norman antiquities. There is also a locomotive museum. For other sights, see the Michelin green guide *Normandie Cotentin.*

SALMON ROLLS WITH CIDER BUTTER
La Nonette de saumon au beurre de cidre

1 lb. (400 g.) salmon filets	1 carrot, cut in julienne
1 lb. (400 g.) white fish filets	1 small onion, chopped
(sole, halibut)	5 mushrooms, cut in julienne
1 leek, white only, in julienne	1 cup (2 dl) fish stock
	or clam juice)
Cider butter:	
2 shallots, chopped	½ cup (1 dl.) cider vinegar
2 tablespoons cream	4 oz. (120 g.) cold butter
½ cup (1 dl.) hard cider	thyme, bay leaf, salt and pepper

Cut the fish filets in eight 1-in. (2 cm.) strips ½-in. (1 cm.) thick.
Cook carrot, onion, mushrooms and leek in 1 tablespoon butter.
Layer the two fish with the vegetable mixture between them.
Roll the fish up, as for a jelly roll, and place in refrigerator until
ready to cook.

The cider sauce: add the cream, vinegar and cider to the chopped
shallots, thyme and bay leaf. Reduce this for a few minutes. Add the
cold butter cut in pieces, to the sauce to thicken and enrich it. Add
salt and pepper to taste. Keep warm.

Poach the circles of salmon and white fish in the fish stock for
5 to 10 minutes. Remove and keep warm. Reduce the stock by two
thirds and strain into the cider sauce.

To serve, pour sauce on warmed plates and place the salmon
"nonettes" on one side of the plate. Decorate the opposite side with
small pared vegetables (potatoes, carrots, green beans, etc.) placed in
a circle. Top with a small tomato rose. A very pretty dish.

Serves 4.

★ ★ ★ HOSTELLERIE DU MOULIN DU VEY, Le Vey 14570 Clécy.
    Tel: 31 69 71 08. Fax: 31 69 14 14.
OWNER: Mme Denise Léduc. CHEF: Michel Choplin
ROOMS: 22 plus 3 suites (half at the mill site, half in annexes 0.4 and 3 km. away),
    all with bath, direct telephone, and TV. (Mill location is preferred.)
PRICES: Rooms: 380–500 F ($76–100); Breakfast: 50 F ($10). Menus: 135–360 F
    ($27–72); ½-pension: 440–475 F ($88–95). Credit cards: AE, DC, EC, MC,
    Visa.
AMENITIES: Bar, lounge, terrace, river, fishing, hiking, rock climbing. Parking.
    Boats, canoes for rent. Tennis, riding, hang-gliding, miniature golf 1 km. Golf
    3 km.
ASSOCIATIONS: Châteaux et Hôtels Indépendants; Chefs de la Suisse Normande.
MARKET DAYS: Caen: Tue to Sun.
DIRECTIONS: From Caen: S 35 km on D562 to Clécy, E on D133A 1.6 km, left
    over bridge 0.2 km, right to mill.
OPEN: Dec 30–Oct 29.

6. HOSTELLERIE DU MOULIN DU PRÉ
Cabourg-Bavent, Calvados, Normandy

The Vallée d'Auge, a gastronomically rich region of Normandy, is also scenically rich, with its green meadows, manor houses, and thatched cottages. The ancient Moulin du Pré sits at the edge of this Auge Region—less than three miles from the sea—and is the pride of the Hamchin-Holtz families: Jocelyne, daughter of the Hamchins, married Claude Holtz, a poet, and they stayed on—he to help M. Hamchin operate the inn, and she to run the kitchen.

Rooms are very small, but pleasant, and all with antique furnishings. The showplaces of the inn are the comfortable salon, the large, beamed restaurant with huge fireplace—and the countryside. Peaceful meadows (the *prés*) surround the mill and its grounds, which include a millpond, stream, and small wood. But the Moulin du Pré is best known for its food.

FOOD & WINE
As with many fine women chefs in France, the charming and inventive Jocelyne is self-taught. Her menu is large, with seafood

in almost half of the dishes. She prepares four scallop dishes, including a novel *Flan de coquille Saint-Jacques* (scallop flan—see recipe), and sole stuffed with scallops and saffron butter *(Turban de sole farci aux Saint-Jacques au beurre de safran)*. Other early-course specialties: *La terrine chaude aux coquilles Saint Jacques,* served warm in a luscious loaf that points up the scallop flavor. If you've had enough scallops and it's springtime, try the exceptional *Pâté de pleurotte au vinaigre de xérès,* an oyster-mushroom loaf with sherry vinegar sauce, served with oyster mushrooms.

True to Norman tradition, a *trou normand* (Calvados break) precedes the main course—in this case, a Calvados sorbet. An excellent main course is *Le lapin au cidre, aux pâtes fraîches* (rabbit cooked with cider, and served with fresh noodles). Another is *Le croustillant de saumon frais, au fumet de vin rouge de Bordeaux* (crusty fresh salmon, with Bordeaux red wine sauce—an excuse to drink red wine with your fish!); and *Ris d'agneau au morilles* (lamb sweetbreads with morel mushrooms).

The cheese platter is a tour of Normandy. From the Auge region, the *Pont-l'Éveque, Livarot, and Camembert*; from the Bray region, the fresh *Suisses, demi-sel* double cream, and *bondon* and other *Neufchâtel* farm-house cheeses; and *Brillat-Savarin*. For dessert you might try the excellent *Parfait au chocolat et aux amandes grillées* (home-made chocolate ice cream, with toasted almonds).

The wine cellar harbors a good selection of Loire wines, and several Beaujolais and Bordeaux—the Loires offering best value.

SIGHTS & SUCH

The channel coast from Cabourg to Honfleur is sprinkled with luxury resorts and picturesque fishing villages, and the Seine Valley from Le Havre to Rouen is well worth a journey. See the Michelin green guide *Normandy-Seine Valley* for suggested sights.

SCALLOP FLAN
Flan de coquille Saint-Jacques

12 oz. (350 g.) scallops
3 egg yolks
3 eggs
3 tablespoons crème fraîche
(or whipping cream)

2 cups (50 cl.) milk,
boiled and cooled
6 tablespoons (40 g.) flour
salt, pepper and nutmeg

Purée 7 oz. (200 g.) of the scallops in a blender. Add flour, eggs, cream and milk, and blend. Season with salt, pepper, and nutmeg according to taste.

Butter 8 custard cups and fill with scallop mixture. Set cups in a baking dish and pour boiling water around them. Bake 30 minutes at 350°F (175°C).

Leave in hot water bath until ready to serve.

Melt butter in a frying pan. Cut the remaining scallops in slices and sauté very quickly. If available, sauté the scallop coral also.

Unmold the custard on heated plates, surround with scallop slices and coral.

Serve with a beurre blanc sauce.

Serves 8.

★★ HOSTELLERIE DU MOULIN DU PRÉ, Rte de Goneville-en-Auge, 14860 Ranville. Tel: 31 78 83 68. Fax: 31 78 21 05.
PROPRIETORS: MM. Hamchin and Holtz. CHEF: Jocelyne Holtz.
ROOMS: 10, all with bath or shower, direct telephone; 5 with WC.
PRICES: Rooms: 215–330 F ($43–66). Breakfast: 40 F ($8). Menus: 250–310 F ($45–62). Credit cards: AE, DC, EC, MC, Visa.
AMENITIES: Lounge, terrace, pond, river, parking. Tennis 5 km, riding 1 km, golf 7 km. Beach and water sports 5 km.
MARKET DAYS: Caen: all but Mon; Deauville: all but Tue; Trouville: Wed, Sun; Cabourg: Wed; Dives-sur-Mer: Sat.
DIRECTIONS: From Caen, 15 km. NW on D513 to D95A, N 200 m. to the Mill.
OPEN: Nov 1–Feb 28, Mar 16–Sep 30; Restaurant closed: Sun dinner, Mon (except Jul–Aug).

7. LE MOULIN D'ORGEVAL
Orgeval, Yvelines, Île-de-France

An oasis of serenity, beauty, refinement, and enchantment, only 20 minutes from Paris—this describes the Moulin d'Orgeval. In the 12th century, monks of the Abbaye d'Abbecourt selected the site for just these qualities. The mill provided the abbey flour for 700 years, until the excesses of 1789 destroyed the abbey. But no one destroys a mill.

Part of the original mill is adjacent to the hotel-restaurant building, which dates from 1926, and was completely refurbished in 1986. The mill sits in the middle of a forest. In front blooms a large formal garden. The rear of the mill is washed by the Rû d'Orgeval, a stream which runs through an ornamental lake, and past two islands. Small bridges cross to the islands, one of which is reserved for birds.

Paths wander through the surrounding woods, passing an occasional small clearing furnished with tables and chairs. The silence is complete, except for the songs of the birds.

Bedrooms are large, modern, well-equipped, and comfortable, with views of garden or river. Your gracious and friendly hostess, Mme Douvier, recommends the third-story rooms as having the best views, and regrets that there is no elevator.

An open-beamed ceiling, mullioned windows, and Queen Anne chairs give the dining room a classical atmosphere. At one end of the room a fireplace takes up a third of the wall. Outside the dining room a waterside dining terrace, completely canopied, runs the length of the rear of the mill, overlooking river and woods.

FOOD & WINE

Chef Alain Caillot prepares regional dishes according to the season. A typical menu: *Minute d'empereur aux petit oignons confits* (fish in a cream sauce, with caramelized onions); *Noisette de lapin à l'ail doux et aux amandes grillées* (boned rabbit with garlic, artichokes, and grilled almonds—one of the best rabbit dishes we've tried—see recipe); and *Poêlée de pommes au miel et Calvados* (golden apples with honey, flamed with Calvados—see recipe).

Caillot makes his own terrines, smokes his own Norwegian salmon, and keeps his Breton lobster in an aquarium. You can have lobster roasted whole in the oven, poached, served cold in a salad, or made into a velvety cream soup. Meat dishes include *Filet de chevreuil sauce venaison* (venison filet with sauce), *Filet d'agneau au jus de truffe et foie gras* (lamb filet with truffle juice and foie gras), and *Pavé de charolais Marco Polo* (charolais beef "Marco Polo"). The food is excellent, but a bit expensive—for example, the cheese tray costs 70 F ($14), and lobster is priced by weight: 550 F per kilogram, or $50 per pound live weight. The less-expensive menus provide good value.

SIGHTS & SUCH

On the premises you can walk in the woods, swim in the heated pool, fish, play tennis or ping-pong, pedal or row in the lake, and enjoy the solarium and sauna. Golf and riding are nearby.

The mill makes a good spot from which to visit Monet's home at Giverny, Zola's home at Médan, and Ravel's home at Monfort l'Amaury. Then there's Louis XIV's home at Versailles, and the home of Henri IV and 12 of his children (by five wives) in Saint-Germain-en-Laye. Orgeval has one of the region's most beautiful churches, built in 1152—about the time the monks were building the Moulin d'Orgeval. See the Michelin green guide *Île de France* for other sights.

RABBIT NUGGETS WITH GRILLED ALMONDS AND GARLIC
Noisettes de Lapin à l'Ail et aux Amandes Grillées

1 rabbit	5 artichokes
1 head garlic	juice of ½ lemon
2 carrots	¾ cup (50 g.) sliced almonds
2 onions	¼ bunch of chives
bouquet garnie	

For the vinaigrette:
½ teaspoon Dijon mustard   2 tablespoons olive oil
2 tablespoons red wine vinegar   salt and pepper

Bone the rabbit, and cut the meat into small pieces.

Make a stock: Put the rabbit bones in a large casserole and add 2 quarts (2 l.) of water. Bring to a boil, skim, and add the whole carrots and onions, the bouquet garnie, and half the head of garlic. Cook over a low fire about 2 hours. Strain.

Cook the artichokes whole, starting with cold water, salt and lemon juice. Cook about 45 minutes. When the artichokes are tender, drain and cool. Remove the leaves and choke from the artichokes. Cut the hearts into 10 slices. Blend with the vinaigrette. Just before serving, heat in the oven.

Cook 4 garlic cloves in water for 15 minutes.

Toast the almonds in the oven.

Heat some butter and oil in a sauté pan. Add the rabbit meat, brown, and season with salt and pepper and the cloves of garlic.

Put the rabbit stock in a sauce pan, add a little butter, and reduce for 15 to 20 minutes. The stock should be a rich sauce.

Chop the chives and add to the warmed artichokes and vinaigrette. Place this mixture around the serving plate. In the center, place the rabbit and some sauce. Sprinkle with the toasted almonds.

Option: after reduction of the rabbit stock, add ½ cup (1 dl.) cream with 1 tablespoon cornstarch. Cook to thicken.

Serves 6.

CARAMELIZED APPLES WITH HONEY AND CALVADOS
Poêlée de Pommes au Miel et Calvados

4 golden apples	1 branch of fresh mint
2 oz. (5 cl.) honey	2 tablespoons (20 g.) butter
1 oz. (3 cl.) Calvados	sugar

Peel and core the apples, and cut into eighths. Melt the butter in a sauté pan. Add the apples and lightly powder them with sugar. Brown the apples on both sides. Add the honey and then flame with the Calvados.

To serve, place the apples in a fan shape on each plate. Pour the honey-Calvados sauce over the slices. Decorate with a leaf of mint.

Serves 4.

★ ★ ★ ★ LE MOULIN D'ORGEVAL, rue de l'Abbaye, 78630 Orgeval.
   Tel: 39 75 85 74 Fax: 39 75 48 52.
PROPRIETORS: M. & Mme Douvier. CHEF: Alain Caillot.
ROOMS: 14, plus 2 suites, all with bath or shower, WC, direct telephone, TV.
PRICES: Rooms: 450–800 F ($90–160); suites: 1200–1400 F ($240–280); ½-pension: 700–750 F ($140–150). Breakfast: 50 F ($10). Menus: 180–510 F ($36–102); children: 125 F ($25). Credit cards: AE, DC, EC, MC, Visa.
AMENITIES: Bar, lounge, heated pool, sauna, solarium, ping pong, pedalos, punts, 12-acre wooded park. Fishing (no permit needed). Parking, heliport. Dining inside, on the terrace, or in the garden. Tennis 2 km, golf 3 km, riding 2 km.
ASSOCIATIONS: Châteaux et Hôtels Indépendants.
MARKET DAYS: Chatou: Tue–Sun; Marly-le-Roi: Tue, Fri, Sun; Poissy; Tue, Thu, Fri; Rueil-Malmaison: Tue, Fri, Sat; St.-Germain-en-Laye: Tue, Fri, Sun; Versailles Tue, Thu–Sun.
DIRECTIONS: From Paris, A13 W to Poissy exit; N13 W to Orgeval, D45 S (follow signs to the mill).
OPEN: All year; Restaurant closed: Dec 20–31.

8. LE MOULIN DE VILLERAY
Condeau, Orne, Normandy

This superb mill is worth a detour for lunch, even if you don't plan to spend the night. It spans the Huisne River—three stories of stone walls, set in a wooded 2.5-acre private park. Built in 1879 for crushing grain, it worked until 1940, then was abandoned until 1973. Roland Coldeboeuf refurbished and enlarged it, creating a luxurious inn that became one of the prestigious Relais & Châteaux group. Muriel and Christian Eelsen recently took over from Coldeboeuf, and maintain the same standards of comfort. Their smiling welcome will make you feel at home.

The sixteen large, well-furnished rooms, and two suites, have views of the river, the park, or an ancient castle. Soundproofing reduces the noise from the mill wheel to a pleasant background hum. Each room is in a different style—some complain that they are over-decorated or "fussy," but that's a matter of taste.

FOOD & WINE

Speaking of taste, the most luscious room of the inn is its dining salon. Built in the old machine room, some mill gears remain, as well as a huge fireplace, and a view through windows in the end wall of the churning mill wheel. The old carved beams, clay-tiled floor and tapestry chairs lend a feeling of rustic elegance. The excellent breakfasts are worth the expensive tab.

Coldeboeuf's fine cuisine had earned a toque from GaultMillau. Christian Eelsen's excellent, innovative cuisine should shortly recapture this honor. He offers classic Norman dishes with a modern twist. We particularly liked the foie gras, followed by the *Civet de cuisses de canard, celeri à la crème* (savory salmi of duck, served with creamed celery—see recipe). Old-fashioned apple fritters *(Beignets de pommes)* follow a well-selected cheese platter.

A terrace borders the river, great for tea or an apéritif.

SIGHTS & SUCH

The mill has a swimming pool, and a helicopter pad. The trout stream offers private fishing, and fishermen will delight in knowing that it's a *rivière première categorie.* Or take a pleasant walk along the river, with an interesting island, and to medieval Villeray.

Villeray is in the heart of the picturesque Normandy Perche region: wooded hills, undulating pastures, and green valleys with burbling streams. (The region gave its name to the percheron horse.) In Nogent-le-Rotrou, the Château Saint-Jean, with its Perche Museum, is worth a visit, as is the Saint Martin church. See Michelin's green tourist guides *Normandy-Seine Valley* and *Châteaux of the Loire* for recommended routes to other principal sights. and tiny villages.

SALMI OF DUCK, WITH CREAMED CELERY
Civet de cuisses de canard, celeri à la crème

A civet is traditionally a meat stew thickened with the blood of the animal. Since most American cooks will find it difficult to obtain duck blood, you can thicken the sauce of this dish by puréeing the vegetables used in the marinade, or by using a beurre manié.

Marinade:
4 duck legs	thyme, bay leaf
1 large onion, coarsely chopped	1 bottle good red wine
1 carrot, coarsely chopped	¼ cup (5 cl.) wine vinegar
2 cloves garlic	¼ cup (5 cl.) vegetable oil
1 tablespoon (10 g.) juniper berries	salt, pepper

Garnish:
1 bulb celeriac	1 lemon
¾ cup (2 dl.) thick cream	salt
5 ounces (150 g.) lean bacon	nutmeg

Sauce:

2 tablespoons (20 g.) butter   1 teaspoon tomato paste
duck blood (see note above)

The night before cooking, cut the duck legs apart at the joint. Combine the ingredients of the marinade and marinate the legs overnight. The next day, drain the marinade, reserving the vegetables and seasonings, and the liquid.

Season the duck with salt and pepper and brown in a sauté pan. Set aside in a casserole. Brown the vegetables from the marinade and add the reserved liquid. Pour the mixture over the browned duck and bake at 375°F (190°C) for 1½ hours.

Meanwhile prepare the celeriac garnish. Peel the celeriac and rub with lemon. Cut it in quarters and cook in salted water until tender. Drain. Cut the bacon into small pieces and blanch in boiling water. Sauté until crisp. Before serving, mash the celeriac, mix with the cream, seasonings and bacon, and press into timbales.

Remove the duck from the cooking liquid, and strain the liquid. Thicken the liquid with the duck blood, heating it very carefully so it won't boil and curdle (or put the vegetables and some liquid in the blender or food processor to purée). Season with salt and pepper and blend-in the butter and tomato paste.

To serve, place two pieces of leg on each plate. Pour sauce over, and garnish with the timbale of celeriac.   Serves 4.

★★★★ MOULIN DE VILLERAY, 61110 Condeau. Tel: 33 73 30 22. Fax: 33 73 38 28.

PROPRIETORS: Muriel and Christian Eelsen. CHEF: Christian Eelsen.

ROOMS: 16, plus 2 suites, all with bath or shower and WC, direct telephone, TV, mini-bar; soundproofing.

PRICES: Rooms: 490–950 F ($98–190); suites: 750 and 1150 F ($150, 230); ½-pension: 560–915 F ($112–183). Breakfast: 70 F ($14). Menus: 145–320 F ($29–64). Credit cards: AE, DC, MC, Visa.

AMENITIES: Bar, lounge, terrace, swimming pool, 2.5-acre park, river, island. Parking, heliport. Private fishing (trout, grayling). Tennis, riding, canoeing: 1–2 km. Golf: 15 km.

ASSOCIATIONS: Moulin Étape; Relais du Silence; Châteaux et Hôtels Indépend.

DIRECTIONS: From Chartres: N23 W 47 km. to D203 (7 km before Nogent-le-Rotrou); D203/D10 NW 5 km. to Villeray.

OPEN: All year; Restaurant closed: Jan 10–Feb 8.

9. LE MOULIN FLEURI
Montbazon, Indre-et-Loire, Loire Valley

In the heart of the châteaux country, in a verdant valley on the Indre River, hides the Moulin Fleuri. The name means "flowered mill," and flowers are everywhere. They crowd the river bank, they spill over large boxes on the terrace, they fill boxes on window sills, and they surround the little garden, or "park." From the rear terrace, you look across the flowers, the mirror-smooth millpond, and a small meadow to the graceful Château d'Artigny, floating above the trees.

The Rohan-Guéméné family, Dukes of Montbazon, built the Moulin Fleurie more than 500 years ago. It operated as a gristmill until 1950, then became an inn. An ambitious young couple, Martine and Alain Chaplin, acquired it a quarter century later, increased the 10 small bedrooms to 12, and furnished them in French eclectic using family heirlooms. Eight rooms provide showers and toilets, and three of these are doubly blessed: rooms 4, 5, and 6 overlook the terrace and millpond, with a view of the Château (illuminated at night). The Chaplins offer simple, comfortable rooms, and excellent food, at modest prices.

The terrace spans the width of the building, and touches the millpond, river, and garden. Several umbrella tables permit guests to take coffee or apéritifs there. From the terrace, you pass through large double doors into the rustic dining room. It's a friendly room, big enough for a dozen tables, each with four third-empire wooden chairs. Hand-hewn beams and supports, wooden wainscoting, and parquet floors combine with pale blue walls for a somber, but pleasing, effect. A large fireplace with raised hearth fills much of one end of the room. At the opposite end, a large picture window looks out at the Indre River and an old stone bridge. Paintings and copper pots adorn the walls. The informal and homey atmosphere encourages conversation with guests at neighboring tables, to comment on impressions of the day or exchange fish stories.

Guests can fish in the river or pond, without license or fee. Chaplin may prepare and cook the catch.

FOOD & WINE

Slender, attractive Martine greets guests with a friendly smile, and makes them feel at home. She's a gracious hostess, unobtrusive but ready to help. Master chef Alain, a bit shy, hides in his remodeled kitchen, preparing Tourangelle cuisine—a traditional cuisine with true country flavor.

Tourangelle cuisine means salads and desserts from local fruits and vegetables, local fish and game according to the season, and filling in with chicken, duck, veal, and pork. A typical tourist menu: *Oeufs en cocotte à la crème et aux crevettes roses* (eggs in a casserole with tiny shrimp and cream); *Suprême de canette grillée et ses cerise à l'Armagnac* (grilled duck breast with cherry and Armagnac sauce); a choice of cheeses, or *Sainte-Maure rôti sur toast* (goat's milk cheese roasted on toast); and a selection of desserts.

We found three of his specialties outstanding: *Escalope de saumon d'Ecosse au fumet de moutarde à l'ancienne* (filets of Scotch salmon with mustard, in the style of the ancients—see recipe); *Carré d'agneau à la crème d'ail et petits legumes* (lamb chops with garlic sauce and little vegetables—see recipe); and *Pancake aux fruits rouges d'été, glace vanille* (pancake with red summer fruits and vanilla ice cream). Other delights: *Pigeonneau rôti au miel d'acacia* (roast squab with acacia honey); and an excellent luncheon dish, a salad of melon and smoked goose breast: perfect for the terrace on a sunny afternoon. The impressive cheese platter offers perhaps 20 different, delicious varieties, many from local farmers.

Chaplin's cellar has a superb collection of Loires, Burgundies and Bordeaux, with vintages from 1891 until the last year or so, and at reasonable prices. Local wines (white Saumur, Vouvray, Muscadet, and Sancerre; red Chinon and Bourgueil) provide exceptional value. The Vouvray, made from the chenin blanc, has a hint of sweetness; the others are dry.

Thirty restaurants in the Touraine gave recipes for a regional cookbook, *La Cuisine Tourangelle, d'Amboise à Chinon.* Chaplin offers the book for sale—it contains four of his recipes, which now and then appear on his menu.

SIGHTS & SUCH

Montbazon makes an ideal base for visiting the châteaux of the Loire. Eighteen lie within 30 minutes of the Moulin Fleurie (see the Michelin green guide *Châteaux of the Loire*). Be sure to visit Azay-le-Rideau, with perhaps the loveliest château in the Valley of Kings. While in Azay, lunch on the garden terrace of the Hôtel du Grand Monarque—so friendly and comfortable, you'll think you're at a mill. (They also contributed recipes to *La Cuisine Tourangelle*). Another favorite: the medeival village and château of Loches.

Other sights include the wine caves at Vouvray, just east of Tours, and caves for mushroom culture—e.g. on D751, opposite the Vienne River, about 12 kilometers west of Chinon. And of course, visit a village market. In French village markets everyone has a good time, especially the vendors. And the Touraine has some of the most colorful markets in France. Nona and I particularly like those at Saumur, Montbazon, and Meung-sur-Loire (the retirement village of Simenon's Inspector Maigret).

You can swim, ride and play tennis within a few kilometers of the mill, and golf a bit farther (12 kilometers). When weary of sight-seeing or other activities, return to the Moulin Fleuri and relax in the garden with a book or a fishing pole. Or sit on the terrace with an apéritif and watch the prattling ducks.

SCOTCH SALMON WITH MUSTARD, AS PER THE ANCIENTS
Escalope de saumon d'Ecosse au fumet de moutarde à l'ancienne

Basic recipe:
   2 lb. (900 g.) salmon filet   6 egg yolks
   1 tablespoon mustard (Dijon or Meaux)

Garnish:
    2 red peppers   1 cucumber
    4 egg yolks   1 lb. (500 g.) butter, softened
    2 tablespoons thick cream   parsley
    salt and pepper

Remove the skin from the salmon filets. With tweezers, remove any small bones remaining. Cut the filet into 12 slices, cutting on the bias. Place in refrigerator.

In a saucepan (copper, if possible) put a tablespoon of mustard and 6 egg yolks and whip with a whisk. Add 2 tablespoons water and whisk again. Set aside.

Char the red peppers and remove the skin. Cut in half, remove the seeds and membrane and cut in slices. Cook in salted water until tender. Drain and purée in blender along with 4 egg yolks, cream, salt and pepper. Put red pepper mixture in buttered custard cups and place in baking dish. Add boiling water to dish coming halfway up custard cups. Bake at 350°F (175°C) until done (about 30 minutes). Leave in baking dish to keep warm.

Peel and seed the cucumber. Carve into 30 ovals the size of a large olive. Cook cucumbers by steaming or in the microwave, and keep warm.

To make the sauce, take the saucepan of egg yolk and mustard and cook over a low fire, stirring constantly, until it resembles an hollandaise. Remove from the heat and add the softened butter, piece by piece until all is incorporated. (If the sauce separates because it gets too hot, add a teaspoon or so of cold water and whisk it again.) Set aside and keep warm.

And now the fish: salt and pepper the salmon and place the slices on the buttered surface of a frying pan or baking sheet. Place under a very hot broiler and cook so that the surface of the fish is cooked but the inside is rare.

To assemble Warm the plates. Place a bunch of parsley at the top of each plate, a flan of red pepper on the right side, 5 cucumber ovals on the left. At the bottom of the plate, spoon some sauce and place 2 scallops of salmon. Serve very warm.

Serves 6.

LAMB CHOPS WITH GARLIC SAUCE AND LITTLE VEGETABLES
Carré d'agneau à la crème d'ail et petits legumes

4 racks of lamb, about 1½ lb. (675 g.) each
1½ lb. (675 g.) garlic, peeled   4 zucchini squash
salt and pepper   4 carrots
4 cups (1 l.) whipping cream   6 turnips
1 head cauliflower   1 or 2 stalks broccoli
24 small red or white rose potatoes   parsley

Put garlic into a sauce pan and cover with water. Add a little salt and cook until tender.

Place the garlic and a little of the cooking liquid into a blender and purée. If too thick, add more liquid so that it is smooth. Return it to the sauce pan, add cream, and cook until reduced by a fourth. Season with salt and pepper.

Peel the carrots, zucchini, potatoes and turnips and cut into small, egg-shaped pieces. Separate the cauliflower and broccoli into small flowered heads. There should be three pieces of each vegetable per person. Blanch the cauliflower and broccoli in boiling salted water (about 3 minutes), and drain. Cook each of the other vegetables separately, in boiling, salted water until they are almost tender. Drain and place on an ovenproof dish. Dot with butter, salt and pepper, and set aside until end of cooking.

Prepare the racks of lamb, seasoning with salt and pepper and brushing with a mixture of melted butter and oil. Bake to desired doneness in an oven preheated to 400°F (200°C). Ten minutes before the end of baking, add the vegetables to rewarm them. Remove the lamb and cut the chops apart (there should be 5 chops per person).

To serve, place the meat attractively at the bottom side of each plate. Around the rest of the plate, place the vegetables beginning with the cauliflower, then the zucchini, potatoes, carrots, turnips, and lastly, the broccoli. In the center of the plate place a bouquet of parsley. Spoon a ribbon of the garlic cream on the lamb. Serve the rest of the sauce in a side dish.

Serves 8.

★★ LE MOULIN FLEURI, 37250 Montbazon. Tel: 47 26 01 12.
PROPRIETORS: Martine and Alain Chaplin.
ROOMS: 12, all with WC, direct telephone; 10 with TV and minibar; 8 with shower.
PRICES: Rooms: 180–275 F ($36–55); ½-pension: 240–330 F ($48–66). Breakfast: 44 F ($9). Menus: 170 F ($34), children 50 F ($10). Credit cards: AE, MC, Visa.
AMENITIES: Bar, lounge, terrace by millpond/river, garden by river, woods. Free trout and perch fishing. Tennis, swimming, riding 3 km; golf 12 km.
ASSOCIATIONS: Châteaux et Hôtels Indépendants; Restauranteur de Métier; Chaine des Rôtisseurs; Touraine Gourmande en Val de Loire; Logis de France.
MARKET DAYS: Montbazon: Tue, Fri; Montrichard: Mon, Fri; Saumur: Thu, Sat; Meung-sur-Loire: Thu, Sun; Chinon: Thu; Tours: every day—best on Sat, Sun.
DIRECTIONS: From Tours, 6 km. S on N10, right on D87, then follow signs to the mill.
OPEN: Mar 10–Jan 31. Restaurant closed: Mon.

10. AUBERGE DU MOULIN DE CHAMÉRON
Bannegon, Cher, Center

This is the ultimate in converted water mills—a rustic 18th-century grain mill, beautifully restored, in a tranquil rural landscape beside the Auron River. A mill was in place here in 1469, but the present building dates from 1767. It stopped grinding more than a century ago, to be converted into an inn in 1972. The old building houses a one-toque restaurant (should be two!) and a mini-museum of milling.

While waiting for your table, visit the three floors of mill machinery: in perfect shape, with diagrams to show how the mill worked, and how the grain was moved from floor to floor and process to process. They display a museum's worth of molinological tools. At the end of the building sits the rebuilt 16-foot mill wheel. One night as we left the restaurant, we found a photographer recording the scene in the misty moonlight—"A photographer's dream," he said, "it's incredibly picturesque."

Jacques and Annie Candoré own the hotel and grounds; the chef, Jean Mérilleau, the restaurant. For seven years, Jacques was manager of Jack's, a well-known restaurant in San Francisco's financial district. He and Annie returned to France after a bout of homesickness, longing for the more simple village life. They are happy with the change. Naturally friendly people, they can now enjoy their guests and themselves. Jacques also was director of the two-toque Château d'Artigny in Montbazon.

Less sumptuous than the Château d'Artigny, the hotel is no less pleasant. Two separate buildings house the 13 charming bedrooms. All are calm and comfortable, each differs in size and style. One building, the older, has rooms furnished with antiques, and small private terraces where breakfast can be served. The other, newer building is less distinctive. Rooms on the ground floor open onto a shared terrace.

You can dine inside the mill, or on a canopied terrace by the pond and bridge, just in front of the mill. Inside, you find a comfy bar and two small dining rooms (about eight tables each), romantic and intimate, with thick walls, heavy beams, fireplace, and indirect lighting. A few small pictures (some for sale) decorate the white walls, and fresh flowers and candles decorate the tables. Soft, pleasant music adds to the mood. One evening the lights went out for a short time. No problem: with all of the candles, it was light enough, and had a cozy, romantic atmosphere.

FOOD & WINE

Chef Jean Mérilleau worked with Marc Meneau at l'Espérance, and learned his craft well. He improved and modernized old recipes of Berry and the Cher. He gave us recipes for two of our favorite dishes: *Émincé de foie de veau au caramel de vin poivré* (thinly sliced, caramelized calves liver in a peppery wine sauce) and *Fondant au chocolat au café* (chocolate and coffee fondant).

Other dishes: *Terrine de légumes au saumon fumé au coulis de tomate* (smoked salmon and vegetable loaf with fresh tomato sauce); *Râble de lapin Farci aux morilles aux pâtes fraîches* (saddle of rabbit stuffed with morel mushrooms, served with fresh noodles); and *Crêpes farcies à l'ananas au rhum* (crepes stuffed with pineapple and rum sauce). Service is excellent.

Mérilleau has a fine cellar, with well-selected local wines: Menetou-Salon, Quincy, Sancerre, and fine wines from other regions. And they're not overpriced.

SIGHTS & SUCH

You can swim in the solar-heated pool, explore the river banks and the local forests, or just relax in the calm, quiet countryside.

The inn is near the *Route Jacques Coeur* and amid several interesting churches and châteaux. The Cathedral of Saint-Étienne in Bourges provides one of the finest examples of the use of "flying buttresses." On our last visit, we found a rock group rehearsing in the cathedral, preparing for the annual music festival. With the amazing acoustics in the cathedral, we actually enjoyed the music!

Local châteaux and churches: the Château Meillant (25 kilometers) and Ainay-le-Vieil; Noirlac Abbey (30); the Château and Basilica at Châteauneuf-sur-Cher, and the church of Saint-Amand-Montrond. Local villages merit a detour, especially Apremont-sur-Allier. See Michelin's green guide *Berry Limousin*.

Return to the Moulin de Chaméron for an apéritif and unusually fine dinner.

CARAMELIZED CALVES LIVER IN A PEPPERY WINE SAUCE
Émincé de foie de veau au caramel de vin poivré

Liver is that oft-maligned variety meat that many Americans avoid at any cost. Stop avoiding—this recipe is well worth the cost!

8 thin slices calves liver	1 teaspoon black pepper
2 cups (½ l.) red wine	1 cup (¼ l.) veal stock
2 cups (½ l.) wine vinegar	4 oz. (120 g.) butter cut in pieces
½ cup (50 g.) powdered sugar	

Sauté the liver very quickly, salt, and set aside in warm oven.

Put wine, vinegar, sugar and pepper in pan and bring to a boil. Reduce by three-fourths. Add stock, reduce again, then gradually add butter. Check the seasoning (may need more sugar).

Spread the sauce on the liver, add a bit of parsley, and serve.

Note: recipe is also excellent with baby-beef liver.   Serves 8.

CHOCOLATE & COFFEE FONDANT
Fondant au Chocolat au Café

Here is one of those marvelous chocolate desserts that is not only delicious, but keeps for several days (if by some rare and lucky chance there is some left). Your efforts will be well repaid.

6 eggs	½ cup (12 cl.) strong coffee
½ lb. (225 g.) unsalted butter	Chocolate Genoise*
½ lb. (225 g.) bittersweet chocolate	Coffee Cream Anglaise*

Separate eggs. Melt chocolate in a double boiler.

Soften the butter. Mix egg yolks, melted chocolate, softened butter, and half of the coffee.

Beat egg whites until stiff, and fold in the chocolate mixture.

Place the Genoise in the bottom of a spring-form mold. Moisten with remainder of the coffee. Fill mold with the chocolate and chill.

To serve, put crème anglaise on plates, put slice of fondant on top, and decorate with 2 mint leaves.

Serves 8 to 10.

* *See Appendix C.*

★ ★ ★ AUBERGE DU MOULIN DE CHAMÉRON, Bannegon, 18210 Charenton-du-Cher. Tel: Hotel 48 61 83 80; Restaurant 48 61 84 48. Fax: 48 61 84 92.

PROPRIETORS: (Hotel) Jacques and Annie Candoré; (Restaurant) Jean Mérilleau.

ROOMS: 12, plus 1 suite, all with bath or shower and WC, direct telephone. central heating, TV.

PRICES: Rooms: 350–500 F ($70–100); suite: 650 F. ($130). Breakfast: 50 F ($10). Menus: 145–195 F ($29–39), children 58 F ($11). Credit cards: AE, EC, EC, MC, Visa.

AMENITIES: Two sitting rooms, bar, 2 dining rooms, canopied dining terrace by pond, large garden, solar-heated outdoor swimming pool, river, pond and river fishing, mill museum, and ample parking. Canal and river walks. Tennis, riding, canoeing nearby.

ASSOCIATIONS: Moulin Étape; Châteaux et Hôtels Indépendants; Les Tables Gourmandes du Berry; Logis de France.

MARKET DAYS: Sancoins: Wed.

DIRECTIONS: From Bourges, 37 km. S on N76/D953 to Thaumiers; 5 km. on D41 to Bannegon; follow signs to mill.

OPEN: Mar 1–Nov 15; Restaurant closed: Tue in low season.

11–22. ADDITIONAL NORTHWEST FAVORITES

11. LE MOULIN DE VIA
Redon, Ille-et-Vilaine, Brittany

A pretty, rustic inn with large garden and terraces. Varied Breton cuisine—from spicy salmon or scallops on Belgian endive, to rabbit with a marmalade of wild thyme, or duck with elderberries—has earned a GaultMillau toque. Cheneau keeps a good selection of Loire wines. (Restaurant only.)

★★★ LE MOULIN DE VIA, Rte de la Gacilly, 35600 Redon. Tel: 99 71 05 16.
  Fax: 99 71 08 36.
OWNER/CHEF: Jean-Paul Cheneau.
PRICES: Menus: 150–280 F ($30–56). Children: 70 F ($14). Credit cards: Visa.
DIRECTIONS: From Rennes 66 km. SW on D177; 3 km. N on D873. 3 minutes
  from center of Redon
OPEN: All year; Restaurant closed: Sun dinner and Mon.

12. HOSTELLERIE DU VIEUX MOULIN
Hédé, Ille-et-Vilaine, Brittany

In the heart of the "Valley of the Seven Mills" you find a modest but comfortable inn with excellent restaurant, where Général de Gaulle and other notables have stopped.

Mme Piro graciously furnished the following recipe, which we particularly enjoyed:

WARM SCALLOP SALAD

Salade de Noix de Saint Jacques

12 large scallops
4 tablespoons thick cream
1 teaspoon tomato paste
1 teaspoon raspberry vinegar

1 bunch chives, finely chopped
1 cup (25 cl.) fish stock,
    clam juice or white wine
2 oz. (60 g.) mache, watercress,
    or other lettuce

Beat the cream. Incorporate the tomato paste, vinegar and chives. Add salt and pepper to taste.

Cut each scallop in two slices. Gently heat the fish stock in a frying pan. Add the scallops and poach for 1 minute. Set the scallops aside and keep warm.

Add the whipped cream to the stock. Reduce by half.

Put the lettuce on heated plates. Add the slices of scallop and top with the cream sauce.

Serve quickly.

Serves 4.

★★ L'HOSTELLERIE DU VIEUX MOULIN, 35630 Hédé. Tel: 99 45 45 70. Fax: 99 45 44 86.
PROPRIETOR & CHEF: Mme Piro.
ROOMS: 14, all with bath or shower and WC, direct telephone, TV.
PRICES: Rooms: 250-450 F ($50-90); ½-pension: 280-320 F ($56-64). Breakfast: 32 F ($6). Menus: 85-240 F ($17-48). Credit cards: AE, DC, MC, Visa.
AMENITIES: Bar, lounge, terrace, parking. Fishing, riding: 1 km. Tennis: 5 km. Swimming, golf: 15 km.
ASSOCIATIONS: Logis de France (3 chimneys).
MARKET DAYS: Hédé: Tue; Rennes: Sat.
DIRECTIONS: From Rennes, 20 km. N on N157.
OPEN: Feb 1 to Dec 19; Restaurant closed: Sun dinner, Mon.

13. HOSTELLERIE DU MOULIN FOURET
Bernay, Eure, Normandy

On the menu of the one-toque Moulin Fouret is the motto *"La cuisine et l'amitié sont les deux seules vertus capable d'unir les peuples du monde"* (food and friendship are the only qualities that can unite the peoples of the world). This devotion to food and friendship by proprietors François and Edwige Deduit pervades the mill and its staff, and even infects the guests.

★ ★ ★ HOSTELLERIE DU MOULIN FOURET, 27300 Bernay. Tel: 32 43 19 95
    Fax: 32 45 55 50.
PROPRIETORS: Edwige and François Deduit. CHEF: François Deduit.
ROOMS: 8, all with shower and WC. (Rooms are *very* modest, but food is great.)
PRICES: Rooms: 210–235 F ($42–47). Breakfast: 41 F ($8). Menus: 100–285 F
    ($20–57). Credit cards: AE, EC, MC, Visa.
AMENITIES: Bar, lounge. Dining inside, or on terrace. Large, shaded garden flanked
    by curving river, fishing in river. Parking. Golf 4 km.
DIRECTIONS: From Bernay, 4 km. S on D33 to St-Aubin-le-Vertueux; follow signs
    to the mill.
OPEN: All year; Restaurant closed: Sun dinner, Mon.

14. LE MOULIN DE CONNELLES
Connelles, Eure, Normandy

A half-timbered manor house and mill—decorated with copies of impressionist paintings—on an island on a fork in the Seine River. Some rooms span an arm of the river. The following recipe is typical of the excellent kitchen.

MONKFISH WITH CREAM, MOREL MUSHROOMS, AND PAPRIKA
Noisettes de lotte poêlées à la crème de morilles et paprika

1 lb. (500 g.) monk fish	4 shallots, finely chopped
fish bones	4 oz. (110 g.) cold butter
2 carrots, chopped	10 oz. (30 cl.) cream
¼ onion, chopped	½ bunch chives
12 morels, fresh or dried	salt, pepper, paprika
¼ cup (7 cl.) olive oil	

Make a stock using the fish bones, carrots and onion. Reduce this stock by two thirds.

Wash the morels in several changes of water (if dried, soak them in cold water for 30 minutes). Put the mushrooms in a pan of fresh cold water and bring to a boil. Retire the morels and combine the cooking liquid with the fish stock. Reduce this by two thirds.

Cut the fish into 12 slices. In a Teflon pan, heat the olive oil to a very high temperature (smoking). Add the slices of monk fish and cook quickly. Remove the fish from the pan and keep warm.

Degrease the pan used for sautéing the fish. Add the shallots and a nut of butter and let cook lightly. Then add to the morels and the strained fish stock. Reduce this liquid again.

Add the cream to the stock and heat for 5 minutes. Remove from the fire and gradually add the rest of the cold butter to finish the sauce. Season with salt and pepper.

Pour the sauce over the slices of monk fish. Sprinkle the dish with finely chopped chives and a little paprika.

Serves 4.

★★★ LE MOULIN DE CONNELLES, 27430 Connelles. Tel: 32 59 53 33.
Fax: 32 59 21 83.

PROPRIETORS: M. & Mme Petiteau. CHEF: Stephane Cavelier.

ROOMS: 7, plus 6 suites, each with bath or shower and WC, direct telephone, TV, mini-bar.

PRICES: Rooms/suites: 550–950 F ($110–190); ½-pension: 520–1000 F ($104–200). Breakfast: 65 F ($13). Menus: 135–280 F ($27–56), children 70 F ($14). Credit cards: AE, DC, EC, MC, Visa.

AMENITIES: Bar, lounge, terrace, park on the edge of the Seine River. Parking. Row boats, archery, swimming pool, tennis, fishing. Riding, four golf courses, sailing, and water skiing nearby.

MARKET DAYS: Vernon: Wed; Les Andelys: Sat; Louviers: Sat.

DIRECTIONS: From Paris, A13 W 104 km. to N15/Heudebouville; 4 km. N on N15 to Saint-Pierre-du-Vauvray; cross Seine River bridge to Andé; 2.5 km. N on D11/D19 to Connelles.

OPEN: Feb 1–Jan 1. Restaurant closed: Sun dinner and Mon (Oct–May).

15. MOULIN DE BALISNE

Balisne, by Verneuil-sur-Avre, Eure, Normandy

Picture a rustic, elegant inn amid peaceful ponds, rivers, and woods, plus exciting, inventive cuisine—and all less than 90 minutes from Paris. Set in the quiet countryside, the Moulin de Balisne is the joy of owner Michel Gastaldi, who describes it as "an old mill with new ideas." He bought it in ruins almost 30 years ago, restored it beautifully, and filled it with family antiques and bric-a-brac. It's as much an exquisite home as a rustic inn. This, together with his genial welcome, makes you feel you've come to visit an old friend. And the fishing is great!

★★★ MOULIN DE BALISNE, Balisne 27130 Verneuil-sur-Avre. Tel: 32 32 03 48. Fax: 32 60 11 22.
OWNER: Michel Castaldi.
ROOMS: 8, plus 2 suites, all with bath or shower and WC, direct tel; 9 with mini-bar, 6 with TV.
PRICES: Rooms: 400–450 F ($80–90); suites: 500 F ($100). Breakfast: 50 F ($10). Menus: 100–200 F ($20–40). ½-pension: 380 F. ($76). Full pension: 480 F ($96). Credit cards: AE, DC, MC, Visa.
AMENITIES: Bar, lounge, ping-pong, pétanque, archery. Supervised parking, helipad. Rowing and canoeing. Fishing in 2 lakes and rivers by mill. Bicycles

available to rent. Swimming, tennis, riding: 0.3 km. Golf: 7 km.
ASSOCIATIONS: Moulins Étape; Châteaux et Hôtels Indépendants; Hostelleries
d'Atmosphère; Hôtels Relais Saint Pierre.
DIRECTIONS: From Paris, W 113 km. on RN 12 to a private access road (4 km.
E of Verneuil-sur-Avre).
OPEN: All year. Restaurant closed: Mon lunch.

16. LE MOULIN DE LA REILLÈRE
Mantes-la-Jolie, Yvelines, Île-de-France

Lunch at an old mill next to its weir, with a pleasant terrace-garden. Traditional cuisine, well prepared. (One toque GaultMillau. Restaurant only.)

★★ MOULIN DE LA REILLÈRE, 171, route de Houdan, Mantes-la-Ville 78200
Mantes-la-Jolie. Tel: (1) 30 92 22 00.
PROPRIETOR/CHEF: M. Roland Ménard.
PRICES: Menus: 150–240 F ($30–48). Credit cards: AE, EC, MC, Visa.
AMENITIES: Bar, dining terrace, 15-acre park, woods. Parking.
DIRECTIONS: From Paris, 56 km. W on A13.
OPEN: Jan 1–Aug 13, Sep 1–Dec 31; Restaurant closed: Sun dinner; Wed.

17. LE MOULIN DE LA RENARDIÈRE
Osny, Val-d'Oise, Île-de-France

The old mill still has a millrace passing under one of the dining rooms. Two streams wash the mill: the Renardière, and the Vosne. Classic cuisine that has earned M. Ganier a GaultMillau toque, as you will understand when you try these recipes. (Restaurant only.)

WARM OYSTERS WITH JULIENNED VEGETABLES
Huîtres chaudes à la julienne de légumes

12 oysters	Salt and pepper
2 carrots	1 lemon
2 leeks (whites only)	1 tablespoon cream

1 turnip	2 stems Italian parsley
2 tablespoons (40 g.) cold butter	6 stalks chives

Wash, peel and cut the carrots, leeks and turnips in fine julienne. Dry in a towel. Put in a casserole over a low fire with 1 tablespoon butter, salt and pepper. Cook covered, shaking the casserole frequently until the vegetables are cooked but still crisp. Put vegetables on a cold plate to stop cooking.

Open the oysters, catching their liquor in a saucepan. Detach the meat and put into the oyster liquor. Wash the shells and place on a baking sheet (use coarse salt to hold the shells upright).

Heat the oven to 450°F (230°C). Place one-twelfth of the vegetables on each shell.

Add the juice of half a lemon to the saucepan containing the oysters and their liquor. Bring to a simmer over a low fire and cook 1 to 2 minutes. Remove the oysters with a slotted spoon and place one oyster on each vegetable-filled shell.

Add cream to the oyster liquor and reduce one-fourth. Add the cold butter, little by little to enrich the sauce. Remove from the fire and add the chopped parsley and chives. Do not add salt but do add a little pepper. Spoon the sauce on the oysters. Put the oysters into the oven for 3 minutes. Serve immediately.   Serves 4.

VEAL SWEETBREADS WITH ASPARAGUS
Escalopes de ris de veau aux pointes d'asperges

2 veal sweetbreads	2 tablespoons cream
bouquet garnie	½ cube veal or chicken bouillon
1 small onion	½ cup (120 g.) butter
1 clove	3 or 4 stems parsley
1 carrot (finely chopped)	10 stalks chives
1 leek (finely chopped)	1 lb. (500 g.) asparagus
½ cup (15 cl.) Madeira	salt, pepper

The night before, put the sweetbreads in cold water and soak overnight in the refrigerator.

The next day, drain the sweetbreads, place in a casserole and cover with cold water. Add the bouquet garnie, the onion pricked by a clove, chopped carrot and leek, salt and pepper. Bring to a boil and simmer 10 minutes. Drain, the sweetbreads, refresh in cold water, and trim off skin and fat. Wrap the sweetbreads in a towel and place a heavy weight on top of them. Leave this way for about two hours.

Sauce: put the Madeira into a saucepan and reduce by two-thirds over a low fire. Add the cream and bouillon. Add, the butter, little by little. Check the seasoning for salt the pepper, then add parsley and chives.

Trim and cook the asparagus in salted water, being careful not to overcook. Drain well and keep warm.

Cut the sweetbreads into thin slices. Salt and pepper the slices, then dip each side in flour. In a sauté pan, melt 1½ tablespoons butter and sauté the sweetbread slices two to three minutes per side.

To serve, place the sauce on warmed plates, arrange the slices of sweetbreads on this, and garnish with the asparagus.   Serves 4.

★★★★ MOULIN DE LA RENARDIÈRE, Rue du Grand Moulin, 95520 Osny.
   Tel: (1) 30 30 21 13. Fax: (1) 34 25 04 98.
PROPRIETOR/CHEF: Jean-Louis Ganier.
PRICES: Menus: 160–210 F ($32–42). Credit cards: AE, DC, EC, MC, Visa.
AMENITIES: Bar, lounge, terrace, garden. Parking. Dining inside, or on terrace.
DIRECTIONS: From Paris: 40 km. NW on A15 (near Pontoise).
OPEN: All year except Aug; Restaurant closed: Sun dinner; Mon.

18. LE MOULIN D'IVRY

Ivry-la-Bataille, Eure, Normandy

An ancient mill in a drowsy village—the mill isolated on an island in the Eure River. In summer, the country meals are served on a balcony overhanging the water. Try the Normandy duck; game. (Restaurant only.)

★★★ LE MOULIN D'IVRY, 10 rue Henri IV, 27540 Ivry-la-Bataille, Eure, Normandy. Tel: 32 36 40 51. Fax: 32 26 05 15.
PROPRIETOR/CHEF: Michel Guy.
PRICES: Menus: 165–300 F ($33–60). Credit cards: AE, EC, MC, Visa.
AMENITIES: Bar, garden, terrace. River runs around and under mill.
DIRECTIONS: From Paris: 61 km. W on A13 to Mantes-la-Ville, then 24 km. SW on D928/D933.
OPEN: Mar 1–Oct 1, Oct 10–Jan 31; Restaurant closed: Sun dinner; Mon.

19. LE VIEUX MOULIN

Neuville-sur-Sarthe, Sarthe, Loire

There's a dining room in the rustic mill, and another on an island terrace. Large weir and pond. A mill wheel still operates, to furnish electric power to the inn. (Restaurant only.)

★★★ LE VIEUX MOULIN, 72190 Neuville-sur-Sarthe, Sarthe. Tel: 43 25 31 84. Fax: 43 25 50 80.
OWNER: Mme J-P. Sivadier
PRICES: Menus: 140–320 F ($28–64), children 80 F ($16). Credit cards: AE, DC, MC, Visa.
AMENITIES: Bar, lounge. Dining terrace on an island in the Sarthe River. Parking.
ASSOCIATIONS: Moulin Étape.
DIRECTIONS: Le Mans is 190 km. SW of Paris, on A11. From the exit at Le Mans, N 1 km. to D197, cross river to Neuville-sur-Sarthe.
OPEN: Feb 1–Oct 9, Oct 30–Jan 1. Restaurant closed: Sun dinner and Mon.

20. LE MOULIN DES EAUX VIVES
Tendu, Indre, Loire

Dine well on the terrace, or in a dining room furnished with antiques. The less-expensive menus offer excellent value. Wines very good, but a bit pricey. (Restaurant only.)

★★★ LE MOULIN DES EAUX VIVES Tendu, 36200 Argenton-sur-Creuse. Tel: 54 24 12 25. Fax: 54 24 34 62.
PROPRIETOR/CHEF: Philippe Vergotte.
PRICES: Menus: 89–280 F ($18–56). Credit cards: AE, Visa.
AMENITIES: Bar, lounge, terrace. Parking.
DIRECTIONS: Tendu lies on N20, 8 km. N of Argenton-sur-Creuse, or 23 km. S of Châteauroux (292 km. S of Paris).
OPEN: Feb 9–Oct 8, Oct 14–Jan 11; Restaurant closed: Mon dinner and Tue (except for Jul–Aug).

21. AUBERGE DU MOULIN BUREAU
La Châtre, Indre, Loire

Enjoy simple regional cooking in an 18th-century, ivy-covered mill on the Indre River. You can also enjoy homemade pastries, ice cream, and drinks all afternoon, on an island. (Restaurant only.)

★ AUBERGE DU MOULIN BUREAU, 53, rue du Faubourg-Saint-Abdon, 36400 La Châtre. Tel: 54 48 04 20.
PROPRIETORS: Gilles and Marie. CHEF: Michel Carrat.
SPECIALTIES: Freshwater fish, duck, terrines.
PRICES: Menus: 98–188 F ($20–38). Credit cards: EC, MC, Visa.
AMENITIES: Bar, lounge, island terrace, children play area, picturesque village.
DIRECTIONS: La Châtre is 33 km. SE of Châteauroux on D943.
OPEN: Dec 16–Oct 31; Restaurant closed: Wed (Oct–Apr).

22. LE MOULIN

Saint-Jean-Saint-Germain, Loches, Indre-et-Loire, Loire

On a small island in the Indre River, this 19th-century mill is modest, and delightful. Chef Andrew Page and partner Susan Hutton are English (Page is French-trained). Most menus involve fish or fowl. (Vegetarian food on request.)

★★★ LE MOULIN, St-Jean-St-Germain, 37600 Loches. Tel: 47 94 70 12. Fax: 47 94 77 98.

PROPRIETORS: Susan Hutton and Andrew Page. CHEF: Andrew Page.

ROOMS: 5, all with bath or shower and WC, central heating.

PRICES: Rooms: 300 F ($60), incl. breakfast. Menus (dinner only): 110 F ($22). No credit cards.

AMENITIES: On private island in Indre River. Two salons, terrace, garden. Free fishing. Bathing beach. Rowboats.

ASSOCIATIONS: Moulin Étape.

MARKET DAYS: Loches: Wed, Sat.

DIRECTIONS: From Paris, 237 km. SW on A10 to Tours, then 41 km. SE on N41 to Loches. St-Jean-St-Germain is 7 km. S on N143. Follow D992 over first bridge, swing immediately left into the private drive to Le Moulin.

OPEN: All year except Christmas and Jan.

II. NORTHEAST FRANCE

The Northeast provinces are as diverse as the Northwest. Burgundy is thoroughly French, and perhaps the finest gastronomic region in the country. Farther north, Champagne is French, but with less of an epicurean tradition. Picardy and Flanders, Alsace and Lorraine have their own dialects, traditions, and foods, and drink more cider or beer than wine. The Franche-Comté and Jura, more definitely French, are influenced by their proximity to Germany and Switzerland. All of these lands have in common the appreciation of "the good life," even if defined differently.

BURGUNDY: For centuries, Burgundy has been rich and powerful. As an independent duchy, its holdings included most of Northern France, Belgium, Holland, and Luxembourg. The dukes enjoyed the good life as well as, if not better than did the kings of France. The monastery at Cluny was the high point of medieval Christendom, with an immense influence on all aspects of life throughout the West, amplifying further the importance of this province.

Burgundy is unparalleled in its natural resources: green meadows full of Charolais, other cattle, and pigs; forests full of game; rivers full of delectable fish (pike, shad, salmon, trout); and slopes full of vines for the finest of wines. The Lyonnais to the Southeast and the Dijonais in the Northeast each believe their city to be the gastronomic capital of the world.

When you think of Burgundy, you probably think first of great wines—Burgundy produces reds that rival the best in Bordeaux, and the finest dry white wines in the world. Then the food: Dijon mustard, and typical Burgundian dishes *(boeuf Bourguignon, coq au vin)*.

If you have travelled a bit in Burgundy, you may also think of the lesser, but still fine, wines of regions such as the Auxerrois, the Yonne, the Côte Chalonnaise, and the Côte Mâconnaise. And such

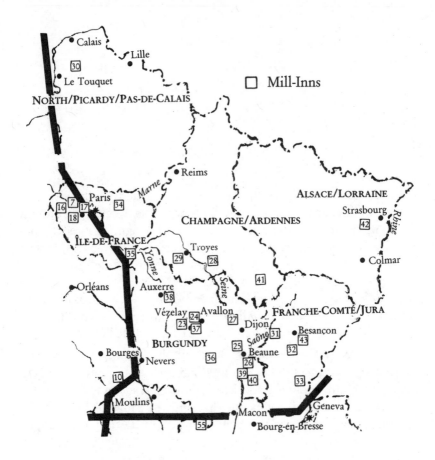

Northeast France

dishes as *jambon persillé* (parsleyed ham), *gougère* (cheese puffs), and *saupiquet* (ham in wine and cream sauce) come to mind. Also *quenelle de brochet* (pike dumplings in a rich cream sauce), *pochouse (fresh-water* fish stew), potatoes and other things *en meurette* (with a red wine sauce), *escargots Bourguignons* (fat snails from the grape vines) . . . the list is too long. The only Burgundian specialty that we have failed to appreciate is *andouillette,* a tripe sausage, usually served grilled. Some writers find it "rich and satisfying"—we have found it rich and malodorous.

Burgundian cheeses (the powerful, creamy Epoisse and the similar Soumaintrain; the Charolais, Saint Florentin, and Montrachet) are less well-known than other French cheeses, but no less delicious.

CHAMPAGNE-ARDENNES: La Champagne (the province) is famous for le Champagne (the wine), and for Reims' Cathedral of Notre Dame, where many French kings were crowned. It's famous for little else—but that's enough.

Four vineyard regions contribute to le Champagne: the Reims Mountain, the Marne Valley, the Côte des Blancs, and the Aube vineyards. The first three produce the finest crus, which are stored in miles of caverns under the cities of Reims, Epernay, and Ay. The grapes used almost exclusively are the Chardonnay, Pinot Noir, and Pinot Meunier.

When recipes in la Champagne call for le Champagne, it usually means a still, white Champagne, called Coteaux Champenoise (this also covers still red and rosé wines). No need to spend $20 or so for a sparkling wine whose bubbles would soon disappear—just select a good white with suitable dryness.

The most-famous Champagne dish is *potée Champenoise*, a stew of cabbage, pork, Ardennes smoked ham, bacon, sausage, andouillette, potatoes and other vegetables, and the famous pigs' feet from Sainte-Menehould. Other specialties include *cevelas*, a fine sausage made from pike and potatoes. The traditional snack with a glass of Champagne is a macaroon: the *biscuit de Reims*. Cheeses include brie and the soft, creamy Chaource.

The Ardennes region, with its forests, is the source of game (wild boar and venison) and fish (trout and pike). Specialties include *boudin blanc* (sausage made with pork); *grives* (thrushes) roasted in sage leaves; and pike in *quenelles* (see Burgundy) or in *matelote* (fish stew).

PICARDY/FLANDERS: The North has several pleasant white-sand beaches, the delightful towns of Le Touquet and Boulogne-sur-Mer; and the Parc Ornithologique du Marquenterre. It also has the largest industrialization, and the greatest number of military cemeteries. It once had 600 to 700 windmills, but only a handful of water mills.

The food tends to be heavy. For example the Flemish *carbonnade*—beef stewed in beer. The *hoche-pot* is a rich meat stew. *L'étouffée* is a potato-and-onion pie. *Flamiche aux poireaux* is a leek quiche. Much seafood is served, and many pâtés, including those made with snipe or woodcock. The pungent Maroilles cheese (and its several variants) are almost worth the journey. With it you sip beer or gin.

ALSACE: Of the several parts of France which have a separate regional identity—such as Brittany, Flanders, and the Basque region— none is more completely different from the rest of France than is

Alsace. From the Roman era until 1945, Alsace and Lorraine were under German occupation most of the time. The Alsatians speak a German dialect, drink German-like beer and wine, and eat German food, but they often dislike the Germans, and are firmly pro-French.

Like Burgundy, Alsace is a great French gastronomic region—but serving dishes uniquely Alsatian. These include: *choucroute* (sauerkraut) with ham and sausages, or a pork chop, or a piece of goose; *Pikefleisch* is smoked brisket of beef. Quiches are custard pies: with bacon or ham and cheese (quiche Lorraine), onion, or leeks. My favorite: the *tarte flambée*, wafer-thin bread dough topped with bacon, eggs, and onions, then cooked crisp.

In Alsace the pig and goose are king and queen, yielding a rich charcuterie and foie gras. Alsace's best-known cheese is the pungent Munster. For dessert, *Kugelhopf*, a light yeast cake with a hole in the middle, is one of many unusual bakery sweets.

Alsace produces nearly 20 percent of the A.O.C. (Appellation d'Origine Controlée) white wines of France. These wines are made from the Gewurztraminer (spicy Traminer), the Riesling, Sylvaner, Pinot Gris or Alsatian Tokay, Chasselas, and Muscat d'Alsace. Alsatian vintners have the right to the "Grand Cru" appellation, similar to the Burgundy classification, to help consumers distinguish the great wines from others.

JURA/FRANCHE-COMTÉ: This province runs from Alsace and the Vosges Mountains, south to Savoy and the Alps, separating Burgundy from the German and Swiss borders. The region has been under Austrian, French, Burgundian, Holy Roman Empire, Spanish, and French rule. Since 1674 it has been part of France (with occasional occupation by German troops).

The Jura Mountains form a crescent between the Rhône and Rhine Rivers, 300 kilometers long and up to 70 wide. Their crest forms much of the Franco-Swiss border, and reaches a height of 1718 meters (5722 feet)—higher than the more-rounded Vosges, but much lower than the craggy Alps. Each valley forms a little world apart, its inhabitants grouped by a water source—spring, river, or lake. A wry saying is that in the mountains you find "eight months of snow, two months of high winds, and the rest of the year the weather is so nice you can't believe it." To occupy the winter, the people have cottage industries such as the making of wooden toys and boxes.

If you come during summer or fall, the mountains and forests are incredibly beautiful, with many rivers, lakes, cascades, caverns and underground rivers.

Typical of mountainous regions, pork is plentiful, hence smoked ham, sausages, and cold cuts. Cattle graze in the high meadows, producing dairy products and beef. The forests yield game and mushrooms: morels, cèpes, and chanterelles, and numerous others, all used in local fish and meat dishes.

The poulet de Bresse is a high-quality chicken—raised to exacting standards, since it has its own A.O.C.—said to be the best chicken in the world.

Cheeses include the Morbier, a tangy cows' milk cheese—with a streak of fir and spruce ash running through the center—from near the mountain village of Morbier. Another is the Bressan, a strong, soft, goats' milk cheese. They make cheeses similar to gruyère, and have a local version of *la fondue*, or melted cheese dip.

Jura wines deserve to be better-known. Their vineyards occupy a narrow band, about five kilometers wide, along the western slopes of the Jura Mountains. They make not only red, white, and rosé wines, but also *vin jaune*, or "yellow wine." It is made from the Savagnin grape, harvested late with a maximum of sugar, and pressed. After several months of fermentation, the wine is racked and put in small oak barrels for six to ten years. A very unusual wine, with a unique nutty flavor, they say it can be aged forever and never spoil.

23. L'ESPÉRANCE
Saint-Père-sous-Vézelay, Burgundy

Ask a Frenchman to name the three finest restaurants in France, and he's likely to include Espérance—with three Michelin stars and four GaultMillau toques, it has had few peers (in 1996, GaultMillau reduced the number to three). Then ask him about the water mill, and you'll get a Gallic shrug. Espérance bases its reputation on the cuisine of Marc Meneau. The mill, recently converted and separate from the restaurant, is not well-known. But Espérance is now much more than a fine restaurant, and the mill is a more-charming place to stay than are the manor house or Meneau's new, modern inn, Le Pré de Sainte Marguerite.

In 1985, the Meneaus bought and restored the ivy-covered, 17th-century mill. Mullioned windows, with crisp white shutters, look out on a cozy courtyard enclosed by ancient stone walls. The millstream slips silently along one wall. White tables with white umbrellas, and white chaises longues tempt you to relax with a drink or a book. Banks of red and pink geraniums and hydrangeas relieve the white. The four large rooms and four suites have hand-hewn open-beam ceilings, oriental carpets to warm the stone floors, and well-kept antiques. To this, they've added a few modern touches: color television, direct telephones, mini-bars, and luxurious bathrooms.

The mill is about 200 meters from the restaurant. On our first visit to the mill, we reached the restaurant by strolling three minutes along a narrow, tree-shaded path. Old stone walls rise on the right, and the millstream slides along the left. Behind the walls grew well-tended gardens of vegetables grown for Meneau's kitchen. Beyond the stream, meadows with a few cows and ducks. White boxes, with more pink geraniums, perched on the railing by the stream. Soft lights illuminated the path at night—a lovely walk any time, but especially in the evening. Alas, since 1993, the meadows have been occupied by the Pré de Sainte Marguerite—more of this later.

The Espérance restaurant and reception occupy a three-story manor house that straddles the millstream. On the edge of the village, set back from the road in its own park, it's as pleasant a haven as the mill. The house contains 18 rooms and suites. The rooms are smaller than the mill's, but equally elegant, and also furnished with antiques.

The rear of the house, containing the bar and the restaurant, resembles a greenhouse. Clear glass flows up from the floor, and curves into the ceiling. Diners look out across the terrace to flowers, grass, trees, and brooks. Some like to eat at Espérance at midday, when they feel they're sitting in the garden; others prefer the evening, when lights in the trees make the garden a fairy-land.

This garden was made for wandering. From the terrace, with its cluster of tables and chairs, a tree-shaded path on the left leads to a large herb garden, the "Potager Meneau." Signs label each herb and benches invite you to linger. From the right of the terrace, another path—a tree-covered walk along the millstream—leads to a bower with old stone benches and stone statuary. Between the paths lies a large lawn, with more paths and benches. We could happily spend a weekend in the mill and gardens, with periodic visits to Meneau's dining room.

FOOD & WINE

"Neither noble nor common, neither home-style nor regional, neither old nor new, the cuisine of Marc Meneau is, above all, cunning." This from GaultMillau's *France 1990*, as they explain why they gave Meneau four toques and their highest rating, 19.5 of 20 points. Meneau's wildly inventive cuisine results from a passion for creating clever new dishes, unusual combinations of ingredients and flavors. For example: lobster tail with squash, warm asparagus and foie gras pie, and veal chops with pistachio nuts.

Other original dishes include *Huîtres à la gelée de mer sur échalotes et cresson* (raw oysters on a bed of creamed shallots and watercress, in a sea-water aspic); and luscious, crunchy fritters filled with liquid foie gras (*Cromesquis aux parfums de foie gras et de truffe en serviette*). Eat the *cromesquis* carefully—they may explode in the mouth, posing a hazard to shirt fronts.

Marc Meneau was born in the village of Saint-Père-sous-Vézelay, where his father made harnesses, and his mother ran a small café. Marc took over the café, found he had a culinary talent beyond his mother's pancakes, and Espérance was born. His first Michelin star came only three years later, and he then increased the stars to the maximum three. His fame is international, and even extra-terrestrial. The Soviets selected Meneau to design menus for their cosmonauts.

On arrival for dinner, you climb one of two curved stairways to the main entrance, and enter a large vestibule. The reception desk is to the right. On the left, a sparkling boutique sells small assortments of fine Burgundies and champagnes, in attractive wooden boxes.

A hostess leads you to the lounge and bar, where you relax in soft leather chairs, with an apéritif and a menu. While you plot the evening's culinary adventures, hors-d'oeuvres arrive—perhaps the *cromesquis*, or some wafers with thin slices of scallop and truffle. As if by magic, the white player-piano begins to perform. The elegant, blond Françoise Meneau drifts in to help with the food selection. (Her son may escort her. When he was five, he wore a chef's apron, and acted as host.)

Your hostess next takes you to the dining room, to a discreetly spaced table with pastel linen, bright flowers, and gleaming silver and crystal. The head-waiter takes the order, possibly with Mme Meneau looking on. She's in charge of the dining room staff, and bustles about all evening, greeting, inviting comments, and helping serve.

The sommelier offers an extensive wine list, devoted primarily to fine Burgundies, with many in half-bottles. He has some Bordeaux, and you can order Sauternes by the glass to accompany foie gras.

Order à la carte, or select one of two fixed-price menus, which change often (the less-expensive menu may be for lunch only). Nona and I return here on special occasions, most recently on our wedding anniversary. At this dinner, we chose the evening menu. It started with savory tarts, then a terrine of foie gras and *cèpes* (boletus mushrooms). Glasses of sauternes accompanied this course. Nona then had a filet of turbot with a celeriac sauce, while I had a filet of sole with a velvety hazelnut butter. With this, they served a Meursault

"Charmes." The main course was a *Canette de Challans, sauce à la pêche* (Challans duckling, with peaches).

"Challans is to duck as Bresse is to chicken," the waiter explained, "and the *canette*, a female duckling, is better than the male." This earned from Nona a shrug, a sweet smile, and "of course." The peach sauce was rich but not too sweet—caramelized, and balanced by a bit of sherry vinegar. A half-bottle of Corton complemented the duck. Next came a crisp green salad, followed by an impressive selection of local cheeses, then dessert. We particularly enjoyed the *Pain perdu aux pommes, crème anglaise* (sautéed apples on fried bread, with caramel sauce and crème anglaise—see recipe).

We moved to the lounge for coffee, served along with a tasty, gooey, warm chocolate tart, and an assortment of cookies. Marc Meneau wandered in. He greeted the gratified diners with a pleased smile, as though his greatest reward is a contented guest. From hors-d'oeuvres to coffee, every bite, every sip, and every personal touch had been perfect.

As we sipped our coffee, the waiter asked when and where we wanted breakfast. We could return along the path and breakfast in the comfortable lounge, but we chose to stay at the mill, warmly wound up in the terry-cloth bathrobes.

Their breakfast is exceptional, both in variety and quality. The staff prepares everything. Again: expensive, but worth it.

Meneau added a functional-style inn in 1993, "Le Pré des Marguerites," mentioned earlier. At this time, Nona and I lived near Corbigny, 30 kilometers away, and looked forward eagerly to the opening of its restaurant and a chance to enjoy Meneau's food at lower prices. We found that while the food was excellent, the atmosphere in the huge dining room was uninspired, the service slow, and the staff insisted on practicing their English, rather than enduring our French. And the path from the mill, no longer well-maintained and flanked by the motel, had lost its magic (the walk, not the mill).

SIGHTS & SUCH

Saint-Père, a village of 356, sits on the banks of the Cure River at the foot of the hill of Vézelay. Most find the village itself interesting, and there are several pleasant walks. For example, walk a mile south of town on D958, and off to the left find the *Fouilles des Fontaines Salées* (Excavations of the Salty Fountains). These mineral springs preserved many Roman and Gallic relics from a century or more before Christ. The Archeological Museum in town displays items found in the excavations (the same ticket admits you to the site as well as the museum).

A surprising local activity: wine tasting. A wine merchant from Corbigny, M. Spanoudakis, introduced us to Saint-Père-sous-Vézelay wines. He took us to a tasting at the caves de La Vézelienne. Grapes grown include the pinot chardonnay, melon, and pinot noir. The whites were quite pleasant (from stainless tanks only; no barrels are used). All of the vines are young, although vines were planted here as early as the 15th century.

The principal local sight is the picturesque village of Vézelay, on top of the hill, and in particular the striking 12th-century Basilica of Sainte-Madeleine. This romanesque church crowns the hill at its highest point. And it's even more impressive inside than out.

Saint-Père lies only 18 kilometers from the Yonne River and the Canal du Nivernais, which has the finest barging in France. Two of the most-delightful old villages on this waterway are Châtel-Censoir, about the same size as Vézelay, and Clamecy, much larger but equally picturesque.

Drive along the right bank (east side) of the river/canal for the best views. Visit a lock or two to watch the boats and mini-barges. The crews often speak English, and love to chat about their trips as they wait for the lock to fill. Visitors with some French enjoy talking to the friendly lock-keepers. Theirs is a different way of life, which—except for the television set in their little house—hasn't changed for more than a century.

East of Vézelay is Avallon, and the verdant valley of the Cousin River. Southeast lies the Morvan Regional Park with its forests, lakes and streams. For more information, see Chapter 24.

At check-out time, the concierge may hand you a bag of candies or cookies, and a souvenir menu to help you plan the next visit. And, God and fortune willing, a next visit will surely come.

SAUTÉED APPLES ON FRIED BREAD,
WITH CREME ANGLAISE AND CARAMEL SAUCE
Pain perdu aux pommes, crème anglaise

While this is not an official recipe from Meneau—rather, Nona created it just after we enjoyed the dish at Espérance—we both think that it's a faithful version.

4 1½-in. (4-cm.) slices french bread	1 egg
(not sour dough)	¼ cup (60 g.) sugar
crème anglaise (see Appendix C)	1 cup (25 cl.) cream
4 apples	½ teaspoon vanilla

Caramel sauce:
2 tablespoons butter   ½ cup (12 cl.) cream
½ cup (125 g.) sugar

Make the crème anglaise, set aside and keep warm.

For the caramel sauce, put the butter and sugar in a saucepan and cook over medium heat until it begins to turn brown. Add the cream all at once, and cook, stirring until the sauce is smooth. Set aside.

Peel and slice the apples into eighths. Sauté in butter until tender. Mix the apples with the caramel sauce and keep warm.

Combine the egg, sugar, cream and vanilla. Dip the bread slices into this mixture and sauté in 2 tablespoons butter until nicely browned.

To serve, place a slice of the fried bread on each plate. Top with the apples from the caramel sauce. Spoon the caramel sauce around the bread and the crème anglaise around that.   Serves 4.

★ ★ ★ ★ L'ESPÉRANCE, 89450 Saint-Père-sous-Vézelay. Tel: 86 33 39 10
Fax: 86 33 26 15.
PROPRIETORS: Marc & Françoise Meneau.
ROOMS: 34, plus 6 suites, all with color TV, bath or shower and WC, mini-bar, direct telephone, TV. Four of the rooms are in the old mill.
PRICES: Rooms/suites: 400–1500 F ($80–300); ½-pension: 1400 F ($280). Breakfast: 120 F ($24). Menus: 350 F (lunch), 630–850 F ($70, 126–170). At Le Pré des Marguerites: Menus 98 F (Lunch, incl. wine), 190 F ($19, $38). Children: 70 F ($14). Credit cards: AE, DC, EC, MC, Visa.
AMENITIES: Bar, sitting room, large garden/park, 3 rooms for handicapped. Ample parking, heliport. Tennis: 0.5 km. Golf: 5 km. Fishing: in Cure River.
ASSOCIATIONS: Relais & Châteaux.
MARKET DAYS: Avallon: Thu, Sat; Clamecy: Sat.
DIRECTIONS: From Paris A6 to Auxerre, 42 km. S on N5 to D951, 10 km. to Vézelay, D957 3 km. to St-Père.
OPEN: Mar 1–Jan 31; Restaurant closed: Wed lunch; Tue.

24. HOSTELLERIE DU MOULIN DES RUATS
Avallon, Yonne, Burgundy

Here we have a 17th-century flour mill with flower-decked balconies, hidden in a steep lush green valley alongside the little Cousin River. In summer you can eat on a gravel river-bank terrace within casting distance of the trout. The old mill building, with a refurbished wheel and the millrace flowing underneath, has a lounge, bar, and several bedrooms. A more modern, vine-covered building was attached to provide the restaurant, and more rooms. The rooms are modest but quite comfortable. The restaurant is not modest, but elegant.

FOOD & WINE

It's not only the food, but the setting. The dining room features an intoxicating view of tree-lined river, garden and terrace. GaultMillau's *France 1995* says it best: "The Cousin coos lazily and steadily, practically under the tables, and the luminous rosé decor, the sylvan surroundings, invite you to linger long amid peace and sensuality."

But the food counts too. For many years the Moulin des Ruats had a good restaurant, popular with the Avallonais, but unexceptional. It then became outstanding, meriting two toques from Gault-Millau. The new owners had not only refurbished the mill, they also had hired Gérard Fillaire. His cuisine was modern, original, and eclectic. I say "was" because he has recently been replaced by new owner-chef Jean-Pierre Rossi. Given the new owner's desire for an exceptional table, no doubt he will do as well as Fillaire.

We haven't had an opportunity to sample Rossi's fare, but to judge by a recipe which he shared with us, it is very good: *Rognons de veau braisés au vin d'Épineuil* (veal kidneys braised with Épineuil, a red wine from the Auxerrois).

Rossi offers other regional wines, including a Vézelay white as well as a selection of more-traditional Burgundies.

SIGHTS & SUCH

Activities include walks along the river bank, fishing in the river, dozing in the meadow, reading in the garden, and sipping on the terrace. If you need more action, drive six kilometers to Avallon for tennis, swimming, riding, canoeing, and golf.

This is the Morvan, the northern part of the Massif Central. Forests of beech, oak, and pine border swift streams, cataracts, and sapphire lakes. The region extends from Avallon about 70 kilometers south to Beuvray, and from Corbigny about 50 kilometers east to Saulieu. When Nona and I lived near Corbigny, at the edge of the Morvan, we found in the spring incredibly brilliant flowers, of every color, carpeting the forest floor.

As with most poor areas, the Morvan has seen an exodus of peasants. Then in 1970, most of the Morvan became part of the *Parc naturel régional du Morvan*. The region enjoys an increasing tourist flux, and the remaining residents are beginning to prosper. See Michelin's *Burgundy/Morvan*.

Avallon, an old fortified city is well worth a visit, as are Vézelay (Chapter 23), and the charming villages[34] of Noyers, Époisse, Sémur-en-Auxois, and Flavigny, a few kilometers north and east.

VEAL KIDNEYS BRAISED IN WINE FROM ÉPINEUIL
Rognons de veau braisés au vin d'Épineuil

4 veal kidneys	5 tablespoons Armagnac
1 carrot	1 bay leaf
1 onion	1 branch thyme
3 stalks celery	1 bottle red wine of Epineuil
1 leek (white only)	½ cup (1 dl.) white port wine
2 cloves garlic: peeled, crushed	½ cup veal (or chicken) stock
4 tablespoons butter	2 tablespoons white mustard
salt and pepper	

In a casserole that can go in the oven as well as on top of the stove, brown slowly the carrots, onion, celery, leek and garlic in 3 tablespoons of butter (have casserole covered).

While the vegetables are cooking, salt and pepper the kidneys and brown in 1 tablespoon of butter in a frying pan.

When the kidneys are brown, place on top of the browned vegetables, cover and cook slowly for 5 minutes.

Flame the kidneys with armagnac and add the thyme and bay leaf. Add the port and deglaze the casserole. Add red wine and let it all reduce for 5 to 10 minutes. Add the stock, cover again and bake in the oven at 375°F (180°C) for 1 hour.

Remove the kidneys from the casserole and skim off any fat from on top of the sauce. Remove the bay leaf and thyme branch. Purée the sauce in a blender and add the mustard.

Put the kidneys in an earthenware casserole and pour over a little more port wine. Cover casserole and seal with a rope of pastry or a paste of flour and water. Place casserole in a baking dish with hot water and bake for 20 minutes at 350°F (170°C).

Open earthenware casserole and remove and slice kidneys. Serve with sauce. Scalloped potatoes are a good dish to accompany this.

Serves 4.

★★★ HOSTELLERIE DU MOULIN DES RUATS, Vallée du Cousin, 89200 Avallon. Tel: 86 34 07 14. Fax: 86 31 65 47.

PROPRIETORS: Jean-Pierre & Jocelyne Rossi. CHEF: Jean-Pierre Rossi.

ROOMS: 24, plus 1 suite. Some rooms with bath, 14 with color TV, all with WC, direct telephone.

PRICES: Rooms: 320–650 F ($64–130); suite: 850 F ($170); ½-pension: 430–590 F ($86–118). Breakfast: 50 F ($10). Menus: 150–230 F ($30–46). Credit cards: AE, DC, EC, MC, Visa.

AMENITIES: Bar, lounge, garden, terrace on river. Dining inside, or on terrace. Heliport, parking. Fishing in river by mill. Tennis, swimming, riding, golf, canoeing: 4 km.

ASSOCIATIONS: Châteaux et Hôtels Indépendants.

MARKET DAYS: Avallon: Thu, Sat.

DIRECTIONS: From A6, exit at Avallon. From Avallon, D957 to Pontaubert, D427 2 km. to mill.

OPEN: Feb 1–Nov 14; Restaurant closed: Mon.

25. HOSTELLERIE DU VIEUX MOULIN
Bouilland, Côte-d'Or, Burgundy

The village of Bouilland lies in the little valley of the Rhoin River, only six kilometers northeast of the frantic A6 *"Autoroute du Soleil,"* which carries freight and tourists from Paris to Lyon and the French Riviera. It's a mere 15 kilometers north of bustling Beaune, and ten kilometers east of the beautiful *Canal de Bourgogne.* Yet it's so secluded and quiet, you'd think you're in the Jura. At the village edge sits the Vieux Moulin, with luxurious accommodations and exceptional restaurant.

Nona and I first visited this inn while on a wine-buying trip to Burgundy. The then owner/chef was Mme Lebreuil, who had no menu—only a delicious *truite a à la crème*, and some sausages for the visitor who didn't like trout. Not a true restaurant, except in the original meaning of the term.

Two years later, we drove to Nuits-St-Georges to meet Marc Misserey, a wine merchant, grower, and friend, who greeted us with: "I have a real treat for you this time." You guessed it—the Vieux Moulin at Bouilland. Mme Lebreuil had sold the mill to Raymond

Hériot and his father. This was our first water-mill inn, and we had the pleasure of watching it from its modest inception, through a rustic period under Hériot (he earned a Michelin star and increased the rooms from eight to 12), to its present elegance and renown under Jean-Pierre and Isabelle Silva (three toques GaultMillau, and one or two stars Michelin, depending on the mood of the inspector).

We have traveled in France many times since, frequently seeking-out mills, and still have a special fondness for this one. In 1990, it received its second Michelin star, and by 1993 the 12 rooms had become 24—the Silvas built a new hotel annex 50 meters from the mill amidst apple trees, and added additional rooms to the mill, with three overlooking the river. The well-furnished bedrooms include an intercom for anxious parents, who can monitor their children without diverting their attention from dining. Rustic simplicity has been replaced with elegant formality, and the prices rival a Relais & Châteaux inn. Most of the "millness" has disappeared. But we still love it, and recommend it highly.

FOOD & WINE

Three tables in the large, modern dining room look out through huge picture windows to the stream, garden, and wood, all dramatically illuminated at night. Silva's cuisine is limited, for the most part, to local products—all of his suppliers are within 40 kilometers of Bouilland—but there's no limit to his imaginative and audacious use of these products. Consider split-pea soup with sautéed oysters and smoked salmon strips, or guinea fowl with an infusion of tea, orange peel, and wild rice, or crêpes with apricot jam, chocolate sauce, and pistachio ice cream.

Most of his menus are excellent versions of regional dishes, but the unusual is a mark of his genius. Which reminds me of an anecdote of Eunice Fried's[10]: One afternoon she arrived to share an apéritif with Isabelle and Jean-Pierre. He had been working in the herb garden, and ". . . was wearing a sweatshirt and jeans. Across the sweatshirt was a Snoopy, sitting in front of a rainbow and saying:

> *Ne negligeons pas*
> *Le fait que je suis*
> *Peut-être génial.*"

(Let's not overlook the fact that I am perhaps a genius.)

This culinary genius shared with us recipes for the odd but delicious soup mentioned above, and a more-conventional dish: *Noisettes de biche, sauce cremeuse à la tomate sechée, rissolée d'endives à la coriandre* (venison medallions with creamy dried-tomato sauce and sautéed endive with coriandre).

The menus at 200 and 320 francs offer four or five courses, with two or more choices in each course. The 470-franc *Menu Surprise* is composed at your table, where the hostess will propose several dishes, to be shared by all members of your party.

The Silva cellar comprises about 400 wines, 85 percent of which, appropriately enough, are Burgundies—all carefully selected by Jean-Pierre and Isabelle.

SIGHTS & SUCH

You can use the mill's swimming pool and exercise facilities, and fishing, tennis, and golf are nearby. Best, though are the many well-marked little walking trails—to the ruins of the Abbey of Sainte Marguerite, for example, or just in the forests, and along the narrow valley of the Rhoin River.

For sightseeing, the village church is over 900 years old, and Beaune, with a Wine Museum and the famous Hospice de Beaune is rewarding, as are the picturesque wine villages between Chagny and Dijon. Wine tastings are available everywhere. See Chapters 26 and 27, and Michelin's green guide *Burgundy.*

SPLIT-PEA SOUP WITH SAUTÉED OYSTERS
AND SMOKED SALMON STRIPS
*Soupe de pois cassés, aux huîtres
et petits lardons de saumon fumé*

7 oz. (200 g.) dried split peas	1 cup (25 cl.) chicken stock
1 carrot	20 oysters
2 shallots	4 oz. (100 g.) smoked salmon
thyme, bay leaf	chives
7 oz. (200 g.) crème fraîche or whipping cream	

The night before, put the split peas to soak in water.

The next day, drain and cook the peas in fresh water with a carrot cut in rounds, 2 shallots, chopped, a branch of thyme and a bay leaf. When the peas are cooked, remove the thyme and bay leaf and purée the rest. Thin with chicken stock and cream. Salt and pepper to taste and keep warm.

Shuck the oysters and sauté them in a buttered teflon frying pan for 30 seconds—just enough to slightly brown one side, not cook them. Remove from heat.

To serve, pour the soup into flat soup bowls. Top with the oysters and sprinkle with the smoked salmon cut in thin strips, and chopped chives.

Serves 4.

VENISON MEDALLIONS WITH CREAMY DRIED-TOMATO SAUCE
SAUTÉED ENDIVE WITH CORIANDER

*Noisettes de biche, sauce cremeuse à la tomate sechée,
rissolée d'endives à la coriandre*

1¼ lb. (600 g.) filet of venison	8 Belgium endives
6 dried tomatoes	½ teaspoon ground coriander
4 oz. (12 cl.) game stock	1 tablespoon butter
2 oz. (6 cl.) heavy cream	salt and pepper

Chop the dried tomatoes and set aside.

Sauté the filets, browning them on all sides. Remove when still very rare, and put them on a plate in a low oven (140°F, 60°C) for 10 minutes, so they become rosy pink in the center.

To make the sauce, remove fat from the pan, and add the stock, cream, and tomatoes. Reduce over low heat.

Chop the endive finely, add salt and pepper. Heat the butter in a nonstick pan, and add the endive and coriander. Let the endive brown, stirring frequently. Keep warm.

Cut the meat into ¼-in. (½-cm.) pieces. Put remaining juice from the meat into the sauce and whisk rapidly.

To serve, place a mound of endive in the center of each of 4 heated plates. Arrange the meat pieces around it in a star, and coat with the sauce.

Serves 4.

★★★★ HOSTELLERIE DU VIEUX MOULIN, Route de Savigny, Bouilland
21420 Savigny-lès-Beaune. Tel: 80 21 51 16 Fax: 80 21 59 90.
PROPRIETORS: Jean-Pierre & Isabelle Silva. CHEF: Jean-Pierre Silva.
ROOMS: 24, plus 2 suites, all with TV, radio, telephone, bath or shower, WC,
   intercom to monitor children in rooms, while dining. Three rooms overlook
   river, some have terraces.
PRICES: Rooms: 390–800 F ($78–160); suites: 1200–1500 F ($240–300); ½-pension:
   580–1340 F ($116–268). Breakfast: 75 F ($15). Menus: 190–470 F ($38–94)).
   Credit cards: CB, EC, MC, Visa.
AMENITIES: Bar, lounge, gardens, terrace, Rhoin River, swimming pool, exercise
   room, sauna, parking. Dining inside, or on terrace. Fishing: 1 km. Tennis: 10
   km. Golf: 12 km. Riding: 1 km. Many little walking trails.
MARKET DAYS: Chalon-sur-Saône: Sun, Tue, Wed, Fri; Beaune: Sat; Nuits-St-
   Georges: Fri; Chagny: Thu, Sun.
DIRECTIONS: From Beaune: D18 N 4 km. to D2; then W 2 km. to Savigny-lès-
   Beaune; continue 10 km on D2 to Bouilland; then follow signs to the mill.
OPEN: Jan 26–Jan 1; Restaurant closed: Wed (except dinner May-Oct); Tue lunch.

26. MOULIN D'HAUTERIVE
Chaublanc, Saône-et-Loire, Burgundy

This is the perfect place to escape the burdens of city life, and re-learn how to live for the moment. And Paris lies only two hours away by car or train, or one by helicopter. Like most mill-inns, the Moulin d'Hauterive offers fine living and rural seclusion, but in one area it stands alone. It provides a *vast* variety of activities.

The list starts with a tennis court, exercise room, and heated pool. The pool has a massive solid cover, with heavy posts at its corners. Want to swim? Someone cranks the cover up on the posts, where it acts as a sunshade.

You can also fish, ride, play table tennis or billiards, and practice on the putting green. You can jog, walk, or stroll through the fields, or to Chaublanc and other nearby villages. After exercise, enjoy the Jacuzzi or sauna.

"One of my customers comes from Switzerland three times each year, by helicopter," our host, Michel Moille, said. "And many repeat guests come for a *forfait weekend"* (a fixed-price health-spa weekend with room and meals for two, from Friday evening until Sunday noon). "But don't think of the inn as an athletic club. Most come to escape, and to eat."

Monks of the Abbey of Citeaux built an oil mill here in the 12th century. Modified to a flour mill, it turned until 1962. Michel and Christiane Moille discovered and restored it, creating an Arcadian delight: eight acres of garden and park set in a sea of green meadows. The only sound is the soft murmur of the Dheune River, sliding over the weir and bathing the walls of the mill. Nine miles from bustling Beaune, it could be ninety.

Vines cloak every building, and in autumn the vine leaves turn red, setting the old stone ablaze. The main building has four stories, with tall, narrow windows and dormers—severe elegance, saved from austerity by the vines, and the brilliant boxes of flowers under each window.

Inside the mill, every room charms. Public rooms have stone walls and fireplaces, and open-beam ceilings. Christiane Moille filled them with antiques, and colorful hangings and flowers. She furnished the hallways and landings with armoires, settees, a spinning wheel, manual sewing machines, and old helmets. A stuffed hawk sits poised above the stairs to menace the guests as they descend. An atmosphere elegant yet rustic, and somehow gay.

The comfortably old-fashioned suites and bedrooms have beamed ceilings, mini-bars, color television, and direct telephones. Antique furnishings include some canopied beds. The carpeted bathrooms have all the modern amenities. Yet each room is different, in wall treatment, draperies, and decor.

The two dining rooms are each charming and intimate, but there the similarity ends. One, as old as the mill, has stone floors and walls, dark open beams and pillars, and antique tables, chairs, and artifacts. Colorful tablecloths and bowls of bright flowers lighten the room a bit. The large open fireplace makes it inviting on a crisp fall day.

The Moilles opened a new dining room in 1990, built as an extension on one side of the mill. Two walls of windows make it bright and airy; white and pale-green table cloths brighten it further. Palms, vines, and flowers, repeated in colorful pictures, illuminate the two stone walls.

Summer diners have four options: the ancient or the modern dining room, or the flowered front terrace, or a tiny wooded island in the river, with a footbridge from the mill.

FOOD & WINE

The cooking combines country with modern, lavish, yet light. Christiane's imaginative dishes have received accolades in food and restaurant publications, and in 1990 GaultMillau awarded her a second toque. Her confidence is improving. yet, she occasionally takes instruction in the kitchens of famous chefs, such as the frères Troisgros. Shy, she spends most of her time in the kitchen, but loves to please her guests. When I praised her *terrine de foie gras*, she glowed.

Michel wanders about the inn. A quiet, slender, bearded man, he helps in the reception, bar, dining room—wherever needed—or relaxes in the lounge and chats with his guests. When he learned that I come from California, he said:

"You must live near my son, Gerald. He went to Santa Rosa to learn English, to study wine making, and to find himself." When I suggested that Gerald might become sommelier and wine buyer for the Moulin d'Hauterive, his father shook his head a bit sadly.

"I think not," he said. "He interests himself primarily in sports, and may become a sports professional."

Asked about the food, M. Moille recommended first exploring the two fixed-price menus. Each offers a choice of two items for each course, the items determined by the season. The larger menu includes a starter, fish course, meat course, choice of salad with melted blue cheese or the cheese platter, and dessert. We started with a duck-liver terrine, served with toast points and a chilled glass of Sauternes. Next came two unusual and delectable dishes: *Salad de caille aux langoustines* (a salad of quail and crayfish), and, as main course, *Panaché de ris et rognon de veau aux pâtes fraîches* (veal sweetbreads and kidneys in a Burgundy sauce, served with freshly made noodles). A refreshing lettuce salad followed, with vinaigrette dressing and topped with toast and melted goat cheese *(Salad au crottin de Chavignol chaud)*. For dessert, *Soufflé glacé Marie Brizard au coulis de kiwis et basilic* (a delicate soufflé made with Marie Brizard liqueur and cream, served with a purée of kiwi fruit and basil—see recipe).

Our very favorite dish was the exciting: *Marmite de poisson en croute*, chunks of salmon and turbot in a deep bowl of creamy sauce, capped with a thick, crusty puff pastry. It spilled over the edges, looking like a fine souffle, or a huge mushroom (see recipe).

SIGHTS & SUCH

From the Moulin d'Hauterive, Chagny lies less than 20 kilometers to the west, and Dijon 55 to the north. Between these points range the slopes of the Côte-d'Or, with all of the great vineyards of Burgundy (excluding Chablis). Get a good guide to the vineyards, such as you find in the Michelin green guide *Burgundy*, and spend a day on the Route des Vins, from Santenay to Fixin. It's like leafing through the wine list at a Four Seasons restaurant.

Don't miss the Château de Vougeot, built by the same Cistercian monks that built the Moulin d'Hauterive. The wine, Clos Vougeot, ranks with the best—a *tête-de-cuvée*, like Le Chambertin and a few others. The Clos Vougeot is so good that in the 14th century, a cask sent to the Pope at Avignon gained an archbishopric for the Abbot. The 124 acres of Clos Vougeot have been parceled out to 54 independent proprietors, some of whom make better wine than others. Reliable proprietors, with five acres or more: J. Morin, Mme Veuve Noëllat, Louis Gros, G. Grivot, and Champy Père et Fils.

Using the mill's heliport, a pilot picks-up guests for sight-seeing flights over the Burgundy vineyards and the surrounding countryside. Moille can make the arrangements.

Visit the postcard village of Verdun-sur-le-Doubs, nine kilometers to the southeast on D183 and D184. If your car likes steep climbs on narrow mountain roads, try the Mont de Sène, near Santenay, for superb views. Beaune and Dijon each merit a visit—see Chapters 25 and 27, and Michelin's green guide *Burgundy*.

Return to the Moulin d'Hauterive for an apéritif on the little island, a chat with M. Moille, and dinner in the new dining room. And don't worry about calories—tomorrow can be an exercise day.

FISH IN CREAM SAUCE, COVERED WITH PUFF PASTRY
Marmite de poissons en croûte

We'd been out all day, sightseeing and visiting wine growers and returned to this lovely mill, cold and tired. We didn't feel like a full dinner, so when this dish was suggested we quickly agreed. It was perfect—simple, delicious and comforting. It remains one of our favorite food memories.

puff pastry	2 zucchini
2 lbs. (1 kg.) assorted fish –	1 tablespoon butter
salmon, halibut, sea bass, carp	3 cups (75 cl.) cream
fish bones for stock, or	2 cloves garlic, minced
3 cups (75 cl.) clam juice	salt and pepper
2 carrots, peeled	1 egg yolk, beaten
2 leeks, white part only	parsley
1 onion	

Filet fish and cut into 1¼-in. (3-cm.) cubes. Make 3 cups (75 cl.) fish stock from the fish bones, onion and parsley.

Make a julienne of the vegetables and cook in 1 tablespoon of butter and 2 tablespoons water over a low fire.

Put the pieces of fish into 6 individual casseroles (4-5 in., 10–12 cm. diameter, 2–2½ in., 5–6 cm. depth. Add the julienne of vegetables.

In a saucepan, combine the 3 cups fish stock or clam juice and 3 cups cream, and reduce by half. Season with salt, pepper and the garlic. Pour this reduction over the fish and vegetables.

Cut the puff pastry into six 4-in. (10 cm.) or larger rounds to fit top of casseroles. Paint the top lip of the casseroles with egg yolk, and seal pastry on the casserole. Brush tops of pastry with remaining egg yolk and bake in 400°F (200°C) oven for 15 to 20 minutes. It is done when top is puffed and golden. Serve immediately.

Serves 6.

FROZEN SOUFFLÉ MARIE BRIZARD, WITH KIWI COULIS
Soufflé glacé Marie Brizard au coulis de kiwi et basilic

Sweet tart pastry (pâte sablé - see Appendix C)

Soufflé:
½ cup (100 g.) sugar	6 egg whites
1 cup (25 cl.) cream	2 tablespoons (30 g.) sugar
3 oz. (8 cl.) Marie Brizzard liquor	salt

Kiwi Coulis:
2 kiwi, peeled, coarsely chopped	3½ tablespoons (40 g.) sugar
4 basil leaves	1 tablespoon lemon juice

Garnish:
2 kiwi fruit	8 basil leaves
8 raspberries	

Make the pastry tart dough and refrigerator for 1 hour. Remove and roll to 1/8 in. (3 mm.) thickness and cut dough to fit 8 individual tart molds. Bake 15 minutes at 350°F (180°C). Remove from oven and cool on rack.

Combine the 100 g. sugar, cream and Marie Brizard. Beat 8 to 10 minutes in a mixer until they form a firm cream.

Combine the egg whites and a pinch of salt and beat until stiff. At the end, slowly add the 2 tablespoons (30 g.) sugar and beat about 5 minutes until the sugar is dissolved and meringue is glossy.

Fold the cream mixture into the meringue delicately, and fill individual pastry molds. Place in the freezer until firm.

Place ingredients for the kiwi coulis in a blender and purée. Pass this mixture through a sieve and set aside.

To assemble, cut each kiwi into 4 slices. Have 8 raspberries and 8 basil leaves handy. Make a round of coulis on each plate. Pose a slice of kiwi topped with a raspberry on the coulis. Toward the top of the plate, place the unmolded soufflés and decorate with a basil leaf

Serve immediately with a glass of Beaume de Venise or other sweet dessert wine.

Serves 8.

★ ★ ★ ★ LE MOULIN D'HAUTERIVE, Chaublanc 71350 Saint-Gervais-en-Vallière. Tel: 85 91 55 56   Fax: 85 91 89 65.
PROPRIETORS: Michel & Christiane Moille.
ROOMS: 11, plus 11 suites, all with TV, direct telephone, bath, WC, mini-bar.
PRICES: Rooms: 530–650 F ($106–130); suites: 650–850 F ($130–170); ½-pension: 580–730 F ($116–146). Breakfast: 70 F ($14). Menus: 160–400 F ($32–80). Credit cards: AE, DC, EC, MC, Visa.
AMENITIES: Bar, lounge, tennis court, heated pool, sauna, solarium, Jacuzzi, exercise room, tennis, billiards, ping-pong, Minitel, photocopier, laundry, Dining in one of two dining rooms, on terrace, or on islet in Dheune River. Private parking, heliport. Swimming, tennis, fishing: at mill. Golf: 7 km. Riding: 15 km.
ASSOCIATIONS: Moulin Étape; Châteaux et Hôtels Indépendant.
MARKET DAYS: Beaune: Sat; Chagny: Thu, Sun; Chalon-sur-Saône: Tue, Wed, Fri, Sun; Dijon: Tue, Fri–Sun; Gevrey Chambertin: Tue; Meursault: Fri; Nuits-St-Georges: Fri.
DIRECTIONS: From Beaune 9 km. SE on D970 to St-Loup-de-la-Salle; D183 E 6 km. to Chaublanc; follow signs to the mill.
OPEN: Mar 1–Nov 30; Restaurant closed: Sun dinner; Mon (except Jul–Aug).

27. HOSTELLERIE DU VAL SUZON
Val-Suzon, Côte-d'Or, Burgundy

The Hostellerie du Val Suzon combines the best of the old and the
new, in a 2.5-acre park filled with flowers, trees, rivulets, trout
ponds and exotic-bird aviaries. The inn comprises two buildings:
the original 18th-century grain mill, later a coaching inn, which sits
by route N71, and a modern annex, called "Chalet de la Fontaine
aux Geais," in the far right-hand corner of the park.

Several comfortable bedrooms with antique beams and flowery
prints share the rustic mill building with the bar, salon, and two
dining rooms, all of simple, homey charm. In the salon you will meet
your gracious hostess Chantal Perreau.

The chalet also has a pleasant salon, and its ten rooms are more
spacious and more modern—each has a full bath, minibar and
television—but they lack some of the charm of the mill.

FOOD & WINE

In winter a cozy fireplace accompanies your dining. In other seasons, you can dine on a terrace outside the mill, and admire the park. In any season you will enjoy the food and wine. The old and the new come together again in chef Yves Perreau's kitchen, classic cuisine with modern accents. Three of his favorites: *Gâteau d'escargots et pommes de terre au beurre de persil* (snails in a parsley butter sauce, layered with thin potato cakes—see recipe); *Rosace de volaille de Bresse aux morilles et foie gras* (chicken breast stuffed with morel mushrooms and foie gras, served with corn fritters—see recipe); and *Crème caramelisée aux baies de cassis* (caramelized fresh currant soufflé). All delicious.

Perreau's wine cellar is diversified, if naturally heavy in Burgundies. He serves an excellent aligoté from the Domaine Robert Arnoux in Vosne-Romanée, whom he considers one of the best wine growers in the region.

SIGHTS & SUCH

Some guests never leave the park, some leave only to walk off some calories in the surrounding woods. However, there's cycling and swimming nearby, and golf only 20 minutes away. Dijon, 16 kilometers to the southeast, is a major tourist sight and the Côte-d'Or with its fabulous wineries is a must (see Chapters 25 and 26, and Michelin's green guide *Burgundy*).

POTATO PANCAKES STUFFED WITH SNAILS
SERVED WITH PARSLEY BUTTER
Gâteau d'escargots et pommes de terre au beurre de persil

6 dozen snails	5 oz. (150 g.) Italian parsley
1 lb. (500 g.) potatoes	3 oz. (9 cl.) dry white wine
3 oz. (90 g.) shallots, minced	2 cups (50 cl.) chicken stock
2 oz. (60 g.) garlic, minced	5 oz. (150 g.) cold butter

Place the garlic and shallots in the stock for ½ hour to blend. In a frying pan over low heat, sauté the snails in 2 tablespoons butter. Deglaze the pan with the white wine and reduce by half. Add the stock and reduce a little. Add the chopped parsley. Off the heat, gradually add the butter, cut in pieces, to enrich the sauce. Keep warm.

Peel the potatoes and slice into thin rounds. Make them into 12 overlapping circles *(rosaces)* and sauté in oil until light brown. Drain them on paper towels.

To serve, divide half of the snails equally on each of 6 warmed plates. Top each plate with a rosace of potatoes. Add the rest of the snails then top with the second potato rosace. Serve very warm.

Serves 6.

CHICKEN BREAST STUFFED WITH MORELS AND FOIE GRAS
Rosace de volaille de Bresse aux morilles et foie gras

6 chicken breasts (halves)
5 oz. (150 g.) fresh or 1 oz. (30 g.) dried morel mushrooms
¼ lb. (120 g.) foie gras de canard, cut in sticks
4 cups (1 liter) thick cream
4 cups (1 l.) chicken stock
Corn fritters
2 cups (250 g.) uncooked corn (fresh or frozen)
2 eggs
6 tablespoons flour

Cut a deep pocket in each chicken breast. Season with salt and pepper. Thoroughly wash the morel mushrooms. Stuff the chicken breasts with the mushrooms and the foie gras. Close the breasts and make into a roll. Wrap in buttered aluminum foil and poach in the chicken stock 7 to 8 minutes depending on the size. If using dried mushrooms, soak the mushrooms in warm water for 30 minutes, then remove and wash in cold fresh water several times. Save the first soaking water and use as part of the liquid in the sauce.

When the chicken is cooked, remove and keep warm. Add cream and mushroom water, if any, to the chicken stock and reduce by half.

For the corn fritters, combine and purée the corn, egg, flour and a pinch of salt in a blender or food processor. Cook the fritters in a frying pan with a little oil. Make the fritters about 2 inches in diameter. Drain on absorbent paper and keep warm in the oven until serving time.

To serve, cover the bottom of each warmed plate with sauce. Unwrap the chicken rolls and cut into ½-inch (1 cm.) slices. Arrange slices in a circle on the top of the sauce. Place 2 or 3 fritters in the center.

Serves 6.

★★★ HOSTELLERIE DU-VAL SUZON, 21121 Côte-d'Or. Tel: 80 35 60 15.
   Fax: 80 35 61 36.
PROPRIETORS: Chantal & Ives Perreau.
ROOMS: 16, plus 1 suite: 7 in mill, 10 in annex. All rooms with direct telephone,
   16 with bath or shower and WC; 10 with TV and minibar (the annex is on the
   property).
PRICES: Rooms: 370–520 F ($74–104); suite: 650–850 F ($130–170); ½-pension:
   455–500 F ($91–100). Breakfast: 52 F ($11). Menus: 128–400 F ($26–80), children
   85 F ($17). Credit cards: AE, DC, EC, MC, Visa.
AMENITIES: Bar, lounge, terrace, 2 dining rooms, 2.5-acre park, pond, river, aviary,
   parking. Swimming, tennis, riding, golf, boating: 15 km.
ASSOCIATIONS: Jeunes Restauranteurs d'Europe.
MARKET DAYS: Dijon: Tue, Fri, Sat.
DIRECTIONS: From Dijon 15 km. NW on N71.
OPEN: Dec 16–Nov 14; Restaurant closed: Tue lunch and Wed (Oct–Jun).

28. LE MOULIN DU LANDION
Dolancourt (Bar-sur-Aube), Aube, Champagne-Ardennes

The Moulin du Landion is an unusual inn in the heart of the Champagne country. The ancient mill consisted of buildings on either side of the Landion River, connected by a bridge. A century later, the restaurant was constructed around the mill and on the bridge—you can sit in the rustic dining room above the water, and count the turns of the 18-foot wheel.

This inn is a simple, homey place. The 16 bedrooms are of modest size, but adequate. All are modern, with bath or shower and WC, telephone, television, minibar, and balconies with a view of the park and/or river. The 1.5-acre park *à l'anglaise* has lawn, flowers, and trees, heated pool, and a dining terrace along the edge of the mill-race. And the food is much better than you expect at a "simple, homey place."

FOOD & WINE

Chef Paul Bajolle enjoys inventing new dishes, and doing things right. All breads, jams, and foie gras are made on the premises, and most of the fish he serves come from the Landion River. Here's a five-course menu for which Bajolle shared with us the recipes, two of which we present below: *Asperges à l'emulsion de fines herbes* (asparagus served with an emulsion of olive oil, puréed carrots, and herbs—an unusual, and unusually tasty dish); *Filets de truite à la vapeur, crème au Champagne* (trout filets served with a sauce of fish stock, cream, and Champagne—not unusual, since chefs in the Champagne area put Champagne in everything); *Filets d'agneau à l'ail doux* (lamb filets served with roasted garlic); *Plateau de fromages*, which included the local creamy Chaource and the pungent Burgundian Époisse; and for dessert, *Gratin de poires en sabayon au Grand Marnier* (zabaglione of pears with Grand Marnier).

SIGHTS & SUCH

At the mill: swim in the heated pool, catch trout in the river, or relax in the garden. Only 600 meters away is a 40-acre leisure park. Tennis at two kilometers, riding at 11, and golf at 20. Ten kilometers to the west is a Regional Park—a large wood containing two lakes: Lac du Temple and Lac d'Orient. The latter offers beaches, bathing, sailing, motor-boating, lake fishing, and windsurfing. You can picnic in or take walks through the surrounding forest.

The mill lies roughly midway between the cities of Troyes and Chaumont, near the small southern Champagne vineyards, and near de Gaulle's home at Colombey-les-Deux-Églises. See Chapter 29 for information about Troyes. And see Michelin's green guide *Champagne/Ardennes* for suggested tourist itineraries.

STEAMED TROUT FILETS WITH CHAMPAGNE CREAM SAUCE
Filet de truite à la vapeur, crème au Champagne

4 trout ½ lb. each (250 g.)	pinch of thyme
1 onion, chopped	3 tablespoons (45 g.) butter
1 clove garlic, cut in two	½ bottle Champagne
½ carrot, minced	or white wine
3 branches parsley	2 cups (½ liter) cream
salt and pepper	juice of half a lemon

Filet the trout and set them aside in the refrigerator.

In a sauce pan, put the bones of the trout, the onion, garlic, carrot, parsley, thyme and 1 tablespoon butter. Let this cook without browning, for 5 minutes. Add the Champagne, bring to a boil and reduce by half. Add the cream. Bring to a boil again and reduce by half again.

Pass the sauce through a fine sieve or strainer into a clean sauce pan. Add salt and pepper to taste.

Steam the trout filets (about 5 minutes). Pose them on plates along with small boiled potatoes.

To the sauce, add 2 tablespoons butter cut in small pieces and the juice of half a lemon. Serve on the filets of trout.

Serves 4.

ZABAGLIONE OF PEARS WITH GRAND MARNIER
Gratin de poires en sabayon au Grand Marnier

4 pears	4 tablespoons cold water
4 egg yolks	4 strawberries
4 tablespoons powdered sugar	mint
8 tablespoons Grand Marnier	

Assemble in a saucepan the egg yolks, sugar, Grand Marnier and water. Whisk well to blend. Put saucepan on a low fire and whisk without stopping until the zabaglione becomes nearly white and thickened.

Peel the pears. Cut in half and remove the seeds. Slice the pears lengthwise into thin slices.

Pour the zabaglione on a round plate or 4 individual plates. On top of this, place the slices of pear, leaving space in the center. Sprinkle powdered sugar over all the surface and pass in a very hot oven or broiler to brown the top.

To serve, place a strawberry and mint leaf in the center for each person. Serve very warm.

Serves 4.

★ ★ ★ LE MOULIN DU LANDION, Dolancourt 10200 Bar-sur-Aube.
  Tel: 25 27 92 17 Fax: 25 27 94 44.
PROPRIETORS: M. and Mme Paul Bajolle.
ROOMS: 16, all with color TV, direct telephone, mini-bar, balcony or terrace, bath
  or shower, WC.
PRICES: Rooms: 310–365 F ($62–73); ½-pension: 350 F ($70). Breakfast: 42 F ($8).
  Menus: 100–315 F ($20–63). Credit cards: AE, DC, EC, MC, Visa.
AMENITIES: Bar, lounge, garden, large park, terrace at edge of Landion River,
  heated pool. Dining overlooking mill wheel and millrace: inside, or on terrace.
  Fishing, on premises. Parking. Tennis: 2 km. Golf: 20 km. Boating and sailing:
  10 km. Riding: 11 km. Leisure park: 0.6 km. Ask Mme Bajolle about visiting
  champagne vineyards.
ASSOCIATIONS: Moulin Étape.
MARKET DAYS: Troyes: Sat, Sun.
DIRECTIONS: From Paris, 155 km. E on D19 (or A5) to Troyes. Continue 44 km.
  on N19 to Dolancourt; follow signs to Bar-sur-Aube and mill.
OPEN: Feb 21–Dec 19.

29. AUBERGE DE LA SCIERIE
La Vove, Aix-en-Othe, Aube, Champagne

Originally a tanning mill, then a sawmill, the ivy-covered Auberge de la Scierie has sat placidly in this shady park for over 300 years. The well-maintained park, five shaded acres crossed by the meandering Nosle River, is lovely for roaming.

The newish bedrooms overlook a heated swimming pool, and a children's play yard. All rooms are well-equipped, some furnished with antiques, others in a modern style. The old mill building also mixes the ancient with the modern. The salon, with library and fireplace, is ancient. So too is one of two dining rooms: rustic, with hand-hewn beams, fire places, and antiques. But the other dining room is modern—octagonal at one end, airy with large, full windows viewing the park. An outside dining terrace increases your options.

FOOD & WINE

Chef Duguet prepares traditional cuisine with original touches, specializing in fish dishes. Three of his specialties, which could compose a delightful meal: *Filet de sole au Champagne; Magret de canard aux oreillon de pêches* (duck breast with peaches); and *Crêpe de l'Auberge.* All well-made, and delicious. Another menu, less common and no less delicious: *Loup de mer au fenouil* (sea bass cooked with fennel); *Rognons de veau à ma façon* (veal kidneys in a cream sauce— see recipe); and *Chaud-froid d'ananas* (caramelized pineapple served with vanilla ice cream). Duguet recommends a cold Bandol rosé with the fish; a red burgundy, such as a Nuit Saint Georges, with the main course; and of course a glass of champagne with the dessert.

Since the inn is in Champagne and near Burgundy, the cellar naturally favors these wines, and is unusual in including good, lesser-known selections from western Burgundy, such as a Pinot de Coteaux de Saint-Bris.

The Auberge de la Scierie is well worth a stop.

SIGHTS & SUCH

Activities at or near the inn: fishing in the river; swimming in the heated pool; tennis at one kilometer, riding at five. For golf you must drive south 30 kilometers to Chaource (the city made famous by its cheese). At the same distance east, Troyes offers an old town with half-timbered houses, the Basilica of Saint-Urbain, the 13th- to 17th-century Saint-Pierre-et-Saint-Paul Cathedral, and many museums. The House of Tools and Craftsmen's Library celebrates manual artistry, the Archaeology and Fine Arts Museums have fine collections, and the Modern Art Museum is outstanding.

For visits to the lakes and woods east of Troyes—beaches, bathing, wind-surfing, walks in deep forest—see Chapter 28.

VEAL KIDNEYS BOURGUIGNON
Rognons de veau à ma façon

Here's another recipe made by feel. Use amounts that seem right for the number of people being served. You can't go wrong.

veal kidneys	red wine
onions	bouquet garni
flour	crème fraîche or whipping cream

Trim the kidneys of fat, etc. and sauté them until they're well browned.

Slice the onions and sauté them in a large frying pan. Place the kidneys on top of the onions and sprinkle with flour. Cook over a low heat for a few minutes.

Pour red wine over the kidneys and onions. Add the bouquet garni, cover and cook for 30 minutes.

Add cream, rectify the seasonings and spoon over the kidneys. See, it was easy!

★ ★ ★ AUBERGE DE LA SCIERIE, La Vove 10160 Aix-en-Othe. Tel: 25 46 71 26 Fax: 25 46 65 69.
PROPRIETORS: M. and Mme Duguet.
ROOMS: 15, all with color TV, direct telephone, bath or shower, WC.
PRICES: Rooms: 380 F ($76); ½-pension: 390 F ($78). Breakfast: 40 F ($8). Menus: 125–230 F ($25–46), children 60 F ($12). Credit cards: AE, DC, EC, MC, Visa.
AMENITIES: Bar, lounge, garden, terrace, 5-acre park, Nosle River, heated pool. Dining inside, or on terrace. Fishing: in river. Parking, heliport. Tennis: 1 km. Riding: 5 km. Golf: 30 km.
ASSOCIATIONS: Moulin Étape; Chaîne des Rôtisseurs; Logis de France.
MARKET DAYS: Aix-en-Othe: Sat.
DIRECTIONS: From Paris, N19 E 113 km. to Nogent-sur-Seine; D54/D374 S 38 km. to Aix-en-Othe; follow signs to the mill.
OPEN: Mar 1–Jan 31; Restaurant closed: Mon dinner, Tue (Oct 1– to Apr 1).

30. AUBERGE DU MOULIN DE MOMBREUX
Lumbres, Pas-de-Calais, Picardy

Your smiling hostess is Danielle Gaudry, your chef is her husband
Jean-Marc. They describe their inn as "A peaceful atmosphere,
troubled only by the rippling water and the song of the wind."
Surrounded by trees in a flowery park, the inn spans the Bléquin
River. The rustic 18th-century mill building has kept its huge gears
intact in the salon-bar, which is cozy with a corner fireplace. The
elegant restaurant occupies the second floor. Outside are the 15-
foot wheel sitting by the sluice and its waterfall, and a waterside
terrace for apéritifs—in good weather, you can order drinks and
pastries all afternoon long.

On the opposite bank stands the modern annex, with 24
bedrooms, lounge, another bar, and a large breakfast room. Rooms
are spacious, and furnished with flair. The ground-floor rooms are
just a few feet from the water.

FOOD & WINE

In the restaurant on the second floor, tables display fine china, silver, crystal, and a large wooden pepper mill. Walls are cream colored, relieved by a panel of a medieval garden scene in autumn colors, and drapes pick up the panel colors. M. Claude Pacot supervises perfect service. An ideal place to enjoy the artistry of Jean-Marc Gaudry. Only a few of the diners have a nice window view, but that doesn't matter—you come for the food.

Gaudry worked under Raymond Oliver, then under Louis Outhier. He learned his lessons well. He's a Maître Cuisinier de France, and member of the Académie Culinaire de France. His forte is inventive classic cuisine, specializing in fish and game. He goes to market each morning to select the best available products for the day's meals.

As an example of his inventiveness, consider this combination of ingredients: cauliflower, cream, bouillon, mussels, nutmeg, and salmon eggs. With these ingredients, he makes a delicious soup: *Crème de chou-fleur de l'Audomarois* (see recipe). Those who realize that an eel is just a slender fish—no more, no less—will enjoy Gaudry's *Anguille au vert* (eel prepared with numerous green vegetables and herbs). Other dishes to note: *Salade tiède de homard aux artichauts* (warm lobster salad with artichokes); and *Suprême de volaille fermières de Licques aux girolles et ravioles d'herbes* (breast of free-range chicken from Licques, with herb raviolis and girolle mushrooms).

SIGHTS & SUCH

You can swim, play tennis, or golf within one kilometer, but the Gaudrys recommend seeing the natural beauty of the green Audomarois countryside: Nearby are "the Clairmarais and Tournehem forests, the Romeläere Lake, the valleys of the Aa and Blequin Rivers (trout fishing), the Saint-Omer marshes, which can be visited by boat, and the beauty of the nature reserve of Nord-Pas-de-Calais."

See the Michelin green guide *Flandres/Artois/Picardie*.

CREAMED CAULIFLOWER SOUP WITH MUSSELS
Crème de chou-fleur de l'Audomarois

1 large cauliflower	1 lb. (500 g.) mussels
2 cups (50 cl.) chicken stock	3 oz. (9 cl.) white wine
salt, white pepper	chervil
grated nutmeg	chopped onions
1 cup (25 cl.) crème fraîche	parsley
or whipping cream	1½ oz. (40 g.) salmon eggs

Blanch the cauliflower in salted water for 4 to 5 minutes. Drain cauliflower and cut into florettes. Heat the stock to a simmer. Cook the cauliflower in the stock, adding salt, pepper and nutmeg. When the cauliflower is cooked, purée in a blender or food processor and add the crème fraîche. Bring to a light boil. Rectify the seasonings and pass the soup through a fine sieve.

Put the mussels into a large saucepan, add a little white wine, chopped onions and parsley. Cook, shaking the pan frequently until the mussels open. Remove the mussels from their shells and keep warm.

To serve, fill the soup bowls with soup, add the mussels, salmon eggs and chervil but do not stir. Serve hot or cold. If cold, thin the soup with a little more liquid—cream or milk.   Serves 6.

★ ★ ★ ★ LE MOULIN DE MOMBREUX, Route de Byenghem, 62330 Lumbres.
   Tel: 21 39 62 44. Fax: 21 39 13 13.
PROPRIETORS: Jean-Marc & Danielle Gaudry.
ROOMS: 24, all with bath or shower, WC, direct telephone, TV.
PRICES: Rooms: 500–700 F ($100–140). Breakfast: 59 F ($12). Menus: 200–530 F
   ($40–106), wine included. Credit cards: AE, CB, DC, EC, MC, Visa.
AMENITIES: Bar, lounge, garden, terrace, 5.5-acre park, Bléquin River, water fall.
   Dining inside, or on terrace. Parking. Tennis, riding nearby. Golf, beach and
   water sports 40 km.
ASSOCIATIONS: Moulin Étape.
MARKET DAYS: Boulogne-sur-Mer: Wed, Sat; Calais: Sun.
DIRECTIONS: From Boulogne-sur-Mer 40 km. E on N42 towards Lumbres, then
   S on D205; follow signs to the mill.
OPEN: Dec 30–Dec 19.

31. AUBERGE DU VIEUX MOULIN
Pesmes-Aubigny, Haute Saône, Franche-Comté

At the doorway to Burgundy, in the wooded valley of the Saône, stands a modest inn with gourmet restaurant, run by a dynamic mother-daughter duo: Louise and Elisabeth Mirbey, descendants of the original millers.

The mill has been in the Mirbey family since its construction more than 200 years ago. First a grain mill, later a saw mill, it ceased working in 1967, when the French government diverted the Résie River. There may or may not have been a good reason for the government to do this, but in any event we can be grateful to them: Louise Mirbey promptly converted it to an inn (which she was able to do since she had lived in the Jura with her grandmother, who ran a restaurant there).

Today, Louise and Elisabeth share the running of the inn: Elisabeth as chef and manager, Louise as wine-buyer and sommelier. Elisabeth is also founder and president of *L'Association des Dames Cuisinières de France* (The Women Chefs of France), which now includes women winemakers *(Les Dames Vigneronnes):* a total of 34 last time I looked (Not to be confused with *Les Femmes Cuisinières,* another organization with similar aims).

Their purpose is to promote the role of women in the male-dominated world of French cuisine. In fact, Elisabeth and two other women were the first *cuisinières* to prepare a meal at the Elysée Palace, when President Mitterand entertained Françoise Sagan.

The bedrooms at the mill are *very* modest. All have television, some have showers and WC. They have entrances from the outside of the mill. The dining room is *not* modest—it is elegant-rustic with open-beam ceiling, and filled with antiques: an exceptional breakfront, gilt-rimmed mirrors, bric-a-brac, sparkling crystal and silverware.

FOOD & WINE

For the most part, the food consists of regional specialties, following the seasons. On our last visit, Nona and I enjoyed this luncheon menu: *La Salade gourmande, filets d'oie fumé, pruneau à l'Armagnac* (salad with strips of goose breast, and prunes marinated in Armagnac); *Le Lapereau aux morilles* (saddle of rabbit with morel mushrooms in a cream sauce—see recipe). Following the tray of local cheeses, we enjoyed *Le Fondant au chocolat et sa crème vanillée* (chocolate fondant with vanilla cream sauce).

Other Mirbey specialties of Burgundy and Franche-Comté: *Escargots de Bourgogne en cassolette* (Burgundy snails cooked with bacon, served in ramekins—see recipe); and *Les Écrivisse au vin jaune* (crayfish in a sauce made with cream and vin jaune from the Jura).

SIGHTS & SUCH

You can fish at the inn and roam through the forest. And the mill is nicely situated for sight-seeing. Elizabeth Mirbey says "We're at the gates of Burgundy, in the Valley of the Saône": fewer than 50 kilometers from three-star Dijon, two-star Beaune and Besançon, and the Burgundy wine route. See *Sights & Such* in Chapters 25 to 27, and Michelin green guides *Burgundy* and *Jura/Franche-Comté*.

CASSEROLE OF BURGUNDY SNAILS
Escargots de Bourgogne en Cassolette

2 dozen snails
½ lb. (225 g.) mushrooms,
    quartered
4 slices thick sliced bacon
1 cup (100 g.) onion,
    chopped

6 oz. (20 cl.) crème fraîche
    or thick cream
3 oz. (10 cl.) white wine
3 oz. (90 g.) butter
salt and pepper
Chopped Italian parsley

Sauté separately the mushrooms and onions in 2 tablespoons butter. Set aside.

Over high heat, sauté the bacon cut in thin strips. Drain on paper towels.

In a large saucepan, melt 4 tablespoons butter. When the butter is melted, add the snails and then the onions, mushrooms and bacon. Add the cream, salt and pepper and let this reduce gently to a desired consistency.

Serve in small casseroles or bowls. Sprinkle with parsley.

Serves 4.

RABBIT WITH MOREL MUSHROOMS
Mitonnade de Lapereau aux Morilles

4 rabbit legs
1½ oz. (45 g.) dried morel
    mushrooms
2 carrots
2 onions
½ fennel bulb
4 cups (1 l.) rabbit, veal, or chicken stock

2 cups (½ l.) white wine
4 cups (1 l.) thick cream
3 shallots
butter, oil
salt, pepper, nutmeg
flour

In preparation, put the morel to soak in warm water for 30 minutes. Remove the morel, saving the soaking liquid (strain through cheesecloth and set aside.) Wash the morel in several changes of water to remove any sand.

Peel the carrots and slice in rounds.
Peel and quarter the onions
Chop the fennel in medium pieces.
Peel and finely chop the shallots.

In a large saucepan, melt 2 tablespoons butter and 2 tablespoons oil. Add the carrots, onions and fennel. Cook the vegetables until they begin to color, stirring frequently.

In a small saucepan, melt 2 tablespoons butter. Add the shallots and cook gently until they are transparent. Add the morels and mix. Season with salt, pepper and grated nutmeg. Add half the wine and half the cream and let cook several minutes.

Put 2 tablespoons oil in a frying pan and brown the rabbit legs on all sides. Sprinkle flour over the browned rabbit and stir. Remove the meat to a plate and pour off any fat in the frying pan. Deglaze the pan with the rest of the wine. Pour this wine into the saucepan containing the carrots, onions and fennel. Add salt and pepper and the rest of the cream. Mix gently. Place the rabbit on top of the vegetables and cover with the rabbit or veal stock and mushroom soaking liquid. Have enough liquid to just cover the meat. Cover the saucepan and cook about 1 hour.

To serve, place the rabbit legs on four warmed plates. Garnish the plate with the morel mushrooms. Strain the juice from the rabbit into the mushroom cream mixture. Rectify the seasoning and spoon over the rabbit. The plates can be decorated with a few branches of chervil or parsley.

Serves 4.

★★ AUBERGE DU VIEUX MOULIN, 70140 Pesmes-Aubigny. Tel: 84 31 61 61. Fax: 84 31 62 38. (★★★ Restaurant).
PROPRIETORS/HOSTESSES/CHEFS: Louise and Elisabeth Mirbey.
ROOMS: 7, all with TV, some with shower, WC.
PRICES: Rooms: 330-350 F ($66-70). Breakfast: 45 F ($9). Menus: 100-350 F ($20-70). Credit cards: AE, DC, EC, Visa.
AMENITIES: Bar, lounge, covered terrace. Dining inside, or on terrace. Fishing on the premises. Parking. Hiking. Tennis, riding: 5 km; boating: 10 km; swimming: 15 km, golf: 30 km.
ASSOCIATIONS: Moulin Étape; Châteaux et Hôtels Indépendants; Association des Femmes Cuisinières; Hôtels Relais Saint Pierre.
MARKET DAYS: Dole: Tue, Thu, Sat; Besançon: Mon-Sat.
DIRECTIONS: From Dijon, N5 SE 32 km. to Auxonne, D20/D112 NE 16 km. to Pesmes, 7 km N on D475/D280 to Aubigny; follow signs to the mill.
OPEN: All year—but reservations essential out-of-season.

32. LE MOULIN DE LA MÈRE MICHELLE
Les Planches, Arbois, Franche-Comté

The Cuisance River roars past the stone walls of this mill, dropping down a 30-foot cascade into a deep trout-filled pool that borders the mill and its terrace. Nearby are the springs that create the river, at the dead end of the Reculée des Planches (a deep valley with vertical sides—"the end of the world"). The mill was constructed as a walnut-oil mill in 1830, serving later as a paper mill, still later as a hydroelectric station—and in 1979, a hotel-restaurant.

Jean-Claude Delavenne and his wife Rachelle took great care in the restoration, and furnished the inn with lavish use of antiques. The mill itself provides ten guest rooms, two of which (rooms 5 and 10) are luxurious, with open beams, canopied beds, modern baths, minibar, etc. The others are more modest, but comfortable. A separate building, of the same age as the mill, has 12 additional rooms.

The rustic dining rooms have tile floors, Roman arches, open beams, Louis XIII furnishings and decor. A waterside dining terrace overlooks the cascade and pond.

FOOD & WINE

Delavenne specializes in regional dishes, using fresh local products served with local wines. A typical menu: *Émincé de truites marinée au citron* (trout filets marinated in lemon juice with mint); *Poularde de Bresse aux morilles et vin jaune* (Bresse chicken cooked in wine, with morel mushrooms, and a sauce made with vin jaune—the unusual wine of the Jura); and *Gâteau au noix et chocolat* (individual nut tarts made with honey, and served with chocolate-Crème de Menthe—see recipe). Other specialties: *Pochouse de truite au Savignin* (Stew of trout and Savignin wine); *Foie gras chaud aux pommes* (Foie gras served warm, with apples).

Delavanne has a good collection of wines from the Jura and Franche-Comté—wines which are not well-known, but deserve to be: Vin Jaune, Vin de Paille, and Savignin. The most unusual of the local wines is the vin jaune. Sweetish, it has some of the character of an amontillado, and is better as an apéritif than with a meal. It comes by its sherry character naturally: the yeast, which can live in highly alcoholic wines, arrived from Spain with 16th century yeast, and vintners have always used old casks, with some old wine and yeast remaining.

SIGHTS & SUCH

The swimming pool is surrounded by a terrace with umbrella tables and chaises longues. The tennis court is well-maintained, and expensive (40 francs). Fishing is available to guests (20 francs per day), and there's a wealth of sightseeing nearby. In Arbois, visit the wine museum and the home of Louis Pasteur. The Grotte des Planches (cavern) is worth a stop, and there are numerous cascades, lakes, and other scenic sights. See Chapter 33, and the Michelin green guide *Jura/Franche-Comté*.

WALNUT TART WITH CHOCOLATE SAUCE
Gâteau au noix et chocolat

Sweet tart pastry
   (See Appendix C)
Honey caramel sauce
3 tablespoons butter
½ cup (12 cl.) honey

½ cup (12 cl.) cream
2 cups (225 g.) walnuts,
   chopped
chocolate sauce
Crème de Menthe

Make the tart pastry and chill dough for one hour in the refrigerator. Remove and place on floured surface and roll to 1/8-inch thickness. Cut 8 rounds to fit individual tart molds.

To make the caramel sauce, combine the butter and honey and bring to a boil. Continue boiling until the foaming syrup begins to change to a darker brown. Add cream and cook for a few minutes. Add walnuts.

Fill the pastry lined molds with the caramel walnut mixture and bake 30 minutes at 350°F (180°C). Remove from the oven and cool on a rack.

To serve, place tarts on dessert plates and spoon chocolate sauce flavored with Creme de Menthe over or around it. Decorate with a leaf or two of mint.

Serves 8.

★★★ LE MOULIN DE LA MÈRE MICHELLE, Les Planches 39600 Arbois. Tel: 84 66 01 87, 84 37 14 44. Fax: 84 37 49 69.
PROPRIETORS: Rachelle & Jean-Claude Delavenne.
ROOMS: 22, all with bath, WC, direct telephone, TV, minibar.
PRICES: Rooms: 380–680 F ($76–136); ½-pension (required in season): 450–580 F ($90–116). Breakfast: 55 F ($11). Menus: 135–400 F ($27–80), Credit cards: CB, MC, Visa.
AMENITIES: Bar, lounge, garden, terrace, pond, river, waterfall, wood, tennis court 40 F ($8) per day, fishing 20 F ($4) per day, heated pool, archery, ping pong. Dining inside, or on terrace. Walks/trails from mill. Parking, garage. Boating, sailing, canoeing: 20 km. Riding: 7 km. Golf: 30 km.
ASSOCIATIONS: Moulin Étape; Châteaux et Hôtels Indépendants.
MARKET DAYS: Arbois: Tue; Poligny: Mon, Fri; Lons-le-Saunier: Thu, Sat.
DIRECTIONS: From Dijon, N5 SE 85 km. to Poligny, N83 N 10 km. to Arbois, D107 to Mesnay, D247; follow signs to the mill.
OPEN: Feb 1–Dec 31; Restaurant closed: lunch (out of season).

33. HOSTELLERIE DU MOULIN DES TRUITES BLEUES
St-Laurent-en-Grandvaux, Jura

As we motored up N5 towards Switzerland, winding through a
beech and pine forest, we rounded a curve to see the stone walls of
the "Mill of the Blue Trout" rising out of the river. It filled the
ravine, except for a 50-foot waterfall along one side: Camelot,
rising out of a misty moor. Only 40 miles from Geneva, it was far
from civilization, yet obviously civilized. And ancient.

A portion of the walls remains from a Roman garrison of the
second century. Before that? The site may have had a role in the
conquering of Gaul. Some archaeologists now believe that Caesar's
defeat of Vercingétorix at "Alesia" in 52 B.C. took place at a Gallic
fortress within seven miles of the Moulin des Truites Bleues.

When refurbishing the mill in 1964, owner Robert Levavasseur
wanted to keep the inn in harmony with its surroundings, and with
its history. He discovered that the newer parts of the building date

from the 11th and 17th centuries. In the 16th, a Spanish fort occupied the site. The mill itself operated from the middle ages until the 19th century. At various times it belonged to Burgundy, France, Austria, and Spain. This gave the owner a lot of latitude—almost anything would do, so long as it was old, and compatible.

He furnished the public rooms with antiques, mostly from the 18th and 19th centuries. Perhaps the most-attractive room is the bar. Each ceiling square, between heavy crossed beams, contains concentric squares of different colors: brick red, cream with hand-painted flowers, blue-green, and then burgundy centers with a horseshoe inscribed. Cream-colored panels, with hand-painted flowers to match the ceiling squares, cover the walls. Above the panels, a wooden rack displays antique faience, vases, a large ceramic coq. The table cloths and upholstered chairs pick up the red in the ceiling. Antique lamps and other artifacts abound.

Lacy metal work separates the piano platform from the rest of the bar, and a close look shows the metal to be horseshoes, welded together in different patterns. Horseshoes also form candle holders. (Who had the horse mania remains a mystery. Perhaps Caesar?)

In the dining room stands a legacy from the Spanish: a huge stone fireplace. Open on all four sides, it separates the room into smaller dining areas, and sets the rustic tone. Round, white-cloaked tables, comfortably spaced, have four carved wooden chairs with leather backs and fabric-covered cushions. Antique plates hang on the massive open beams. The dining room is the favorite both of Levavasseur and his co-director, Mme Denise Pérenet.

Pérenet also loves the sumptuous guest rooms, recently redecorated. "Monsieur Levavasseur designed the decoration," she said proudly. "He has a flair to combine the antique and the modern." Ceilings are white. White and ochre trim provides accents to burgundy walls, carpets, drapes and coverlets. Some rooms have French doors opening onto balconies, with white wrought-iron chairs. All have modern bathrooms, half have color television. "Some of our guests don't want television," Pérenet explained. "That's one of the things they're escaping."

The rooms differ substantially. Rooms 4, 7, 8, and 16 are the most luxurious, and have the choice views; some small rooms are pleasant, and cost much less. But avoid those that overlook highway N5—when the windows are open, the road noise rushes in. Several rooms, or suites, are rented *en permanence,* and are not available to transient guests.

FOOD & WINE

At the Moulin des Truites Bleues you would expect to find blue trout, and you do. The rivers, lakes, and menu are full of trout. The staff catch them on the property, and prepare them in several ways, including grilled, pan-fried, poached, and variously stuffed. A favorite of the young chef, Thierry Volatier, is *Filets de truite Lacuzon*, a tasty combination of trout, herbs, ham, Paris and morel mushrooms, wine, cream, and potatoes (see recipe).

Volatier is a master of Franc-Comtoise cuisine. He offers many dishes, all traditional or classic, created with regional ingredients and recipes. A typical tourist menu: *Petite gelée de pintade à l'Arbois et son coulis de tomate pimenté* (cold guinea fowl in gelatin, with spicy tomato sauce); *Magret de canard au miel* (duck breast with honey, one of Volatier's few concessions to nouvelle cuisine); cheeses; and a selection of desserts.

The gastronomic menu adds one course and 100 francs or so, and offers more latitude to the talented chef. A third, less-expensive menu is available on week days. Specialties well worth remembering (and making): *Poulet de Bresse aux morilles et vin jaune.* This combines the best of chickens, the best of wild mushrooms, and a simple but voluptuous sauce—see recipe. And for dessert, a dish of strawberries, strawberry liqueur, almonds, and more cream *(Gratin de fraises).*

In season, Volatier has a hunter's menu. This includes *Gigue de chevreuil grand veneur* (saddle of venison), and *Faisan à la Souvarov* (pheasant stuffed with foie gras and truffles, then braised with Madeira and more truffles).

The cellar provides a selection of regional wines, recommended over the few good, higher-priced Burgundies and Bordeaux.

If you wish to picnic, start your shopping at Michel Rebouillat's at La Savine, one kilometer east of Saint-Laurent-en-Grandvaux, and six kilometers from the mill. He sells the best of the region's *charcuterie,* including smoked trout and ham, and sausages. From there, retreat to St-Laurent for bread, wine, and pastries.

SIGHTS & SUCH

This is an all-year inn, with attractive activities in each season. Without leaving the property, you can wander along a half-mile of the rapid river, on foot or on skis (useful exercise before setting down to a generous meal). The nearest village, five kilometers to the east on N5, is Saint-Laurent-en-Grandvaux. This delights only those fond of zinc and galvanized iron. Metal not only covers the roofs, but also the walls of many of the buildings. Even the church has armor plate.

Farther afield, but within ten minute's drive, you can swim, boat, ride, and play tennis. You can fish in the mill's Lemme River, in several other rivers, and in the lakes (full of pike and perch, as well as trout). The mill staff recommends using a barbless hook, so as not to injure the fish, and returning them to the water. While walking along the Lemme, I came across a German fisherman, and watched while he landed a nice trout, carefully removed the hook, and gently placed the fish back in the river. I asked why one would go to the trouble of catching a fish, only to return it. He looked at me in disdain, and I think he said that "Anyone who could ask such a question couldn't understand the answer."

Within half an hour's drive you find several waterfalls, lakes, gorges, picturesque hamlets, and striking views. Most impressive are the Cascades of Hérisson: multiple waterfalls and cascades that drop more than 900 feet in three kilometers. From the hamlet of Bonlieu (13 kilometers west on N78), take the forest road that starts at the side of the Poutre restaurant, drive north two kilometers, and park your car near the Forge waterfall. The trail to the west leads to four other falls. Two, l'Éventail and the Grand Saut, each fall more than 200 feet. As a bonus, visit the little cave "Grotte Lacuzon." (See the Michelin green guide *Jura, Franche-Comté.*)

Back in Bonlieu, which has fewer residents (150) than visitors, try the restaurant Poutre, one star Michelin, with menus ranging from inexpensive to costly.

If it's winter, you can cross-country ski locally, or drive to Les Rousses and downhill ski. Les Rousses offers instruction in both types of skiing. If less ambitious, make a snowman, or sit comfortably in the mill looking out on the beautiful snowscape.

A caveat: on our last visit, we noted that the inn had become a bit shabby, and that it was no longer listed in Michelin's *France.* The food remained very good, and we were assured that plans were in place to freshen up the building. Let us know your impressions.

FILETS OF TROUT LACUZON
Filets de truites Lacuzon

4 trout
1 carrot
1 onion
1 leek
bouquet garni (parsley,
   thyme, bay leaf)
1 shallot, minced
1 quart (1 liter) white wine
2 cups (50 cl.) whipping cream

¼ lb. (100 g.) raw ham
   (prosciutto will do)
½ lb. (250 g.) mushrooms,
   cooked in water
8 large morel mushrooms
1 lb. (500 g.) potatoes
fleurons (puff pastry tidbits)
2 lemons

Cut the filets from the trout and set aside in the refrigerator. Make a fish stock using the head and bones of the trout, the carrot, onion, leek, bouquet garnie and white wine. Let it cook for 1 hour.

For the sauce, take half this fish stock, add the chopped shallot and reduce by half. Add the cream and reduce further until you have desired consistency. Add the ham, cut in thin slices, the cooked mushrooms and the morels. Check the seasonings.

Poach the trout filets in the rest of the fish stock.

To serve, place the trout on warmed plates. Coat with the sauce and decorate with the fleuron and lemon halves. Also add steamed potatoes.

Serves 4.

BRESSE CHICKEN WITH MORELS AND JURA YELLOW WINE
Poulet de Bresse aux morilles et vin jaune

1 chicken (best available)
¼ lb (100 g.) morel mushrooms
   or 1 oz. (28 g.) dried morels
2 oz. (50 g.) butter
3 oz. (9 cl.) Cognac or brandy

¼ cup (5 cl.) Madeira
2 cups (5 dl.) vin jaune
   or dry white wine
1 quart (1 liter) cream

Wash the mushrooms in several changes of water (they can be gritty). If using dried mushrooms, soak them in warm water for 30 minutes and then wash in several changes of fresh water.

Cut the chicken into serving pieces. Brown the pieces in butter along with the mushrooms.

Flame the chicken and mushrooms with the Cognac and Madeira. Add the wine and cook until the chicken is tender. When finished, add the cream and reduce sauce to a good consistency.

Serves 6.

★★★ HOSTELLERIE DU MOULIN DES TRUITES BLEUES, 39150 Saint-Laurent-en-Grandvaux. Tel: 84 60 83 03, 84 60 83 09. Fax: 84 60 87 23.

PROPRIETORS: Robert Levavasseur and Denise Pérenet. CHEF: Thierry Volatier.

ROOMS: 20, 10 with TV, 10 without, all with bath, WC.

PRICES: Rooms: 450–725 F ($90–145). ½-pension: 610–650 F ($122–130). Breakfast: 60 F ($12). Menus: 140–380 F ($28–76). Credit cards: AE, DC, Visa.

AMENITIES: Bar, lounge, dining room, garden. Fishing: in Lemme River by inn; in numerous other nearby rivers and lakes. Boating: 6 km. Tennis, swimming, riding: 4 km. Skiing: Cross-country locally; downhill near Les Rousses, 19 km east on N5. Golf: 25 km.

ASSOCIATIONS: Moulin Étape; Châteaux et Hôtels Indépendants.

MARKET DAYS: Champagnole: Sat; Lons-le-Saunier: Thu, Sat; St-Claude: Thu, Sat.

DIRECTIONS: From Dijon, 150 km. SE on N5 to St-Laurent-en-Grandvaux. From Geneva, N1 North to Nyon exit, left through Côte de Nyon, N5 to St-Laurent. From Lyon, N73 NE to Lons-le-Saunier, N78 E to St-Laurent. Mill is on N5, 4 km N of St-Laurent.

OPEN: All year.

34–43. ADDITIONAL NORTHEAST FAVORITES

34. AU MOULIN DE FLAGY
Flagy, Seine-et-Marne, Île-de-France

This 13th-century flour mill, with half-timbered building, was a gift from Saint Louis to his mother, Blanche of Castille. It sits at the edge of a medieval village, and reeks of age. The comfortable rooms (named after grains) are reached by a stairway that would have been perfect in the middle ages, but if you're over five-foot tall, you have to duck. The bar is nice, with mill mechanisms outside its window. Dine by candlelight in a room overlooking river and garden, and with a walk-in fireplace.

★★★ AU MOULIN, 77940 Flagy. Tel: (1) 60 96 67 89 Fax: (1) 60 96 69 51.
PROPRIETORS: M. et Mme Scheidecker. CHEF: Régis Durand.
ROOMS: 10, all with, direct telephone, bath or shower and WC; 3 with TV.
PRICES: Rooms: 240–500 F ($48–100). ½-pension (Min. 4 days): 350–438 F ($70–88). Breakfast: 45 F ($9). Menus: 170–220 F ($34–44), children 75 F ($15). Credit cards: AE, CB, DC, EC, MC, Visa.
AMENITIES: Bar, lounge, terrace, garden, Orvanne River, fishing, woods. Parking. Tennis, riding nearby.
MARKET DAYS: Fontainebleau: Tue, Fri, Sun.
DIRECTIONS: From Paris, 88 km. SE on A6, Fontainebleau exit; N6 to Moret-sur-Loing; D218 to Villecerf; D22 to Flagy.
OPEN: Jan 20–Sep 17; Sep 30–Dec 16; Restaurant closed: Sun dinner; Mon.

35. LE MOULIN DE POINCY

Meaux-Poincy, Seine-et-Marne, Île-de-France

Armel Abit serves inventive and well-prepared food on the rose-garden terrace. Willow trees lead down to the river. The mill has Poincy's oldest building (abode of the monks of the Abbey of Meaux), and its newest cuisine. (Restaurant only.)

★★★ LE MOULIN DE POINCY, Rue du Moulin, 77470 Poincy-Meaux.
   Tel.: (1) 60 23 06 80. Fax: (1) 60 23 12 56.
CHEF: Armel Abit.
PRICES: Menus: 160–450 F, including wine ($32–90). Credit cards: AE, CB, EC,
   MC, Visa.
AMENITIES: Bar, lounge, terrace, parking. Dining inside, or on terrace.
DIRECTIONS: From Paris, W on N34/D5, 54 km. to Meaux. Poincy is 2 km. NE
   of Meaux.
CLOSED: Tue dinner, Wed.

36. LE VIEUX MOULIN

Autun, Saône-et-Loire, Burgundy

In the heart of Burgundy, in a 2000-year-old Roman town, this ancient mill most recently operated as a forge and saw mill. In 1958 it became an inn—a pleasant place to stop, and even more pleasant to dine. Try this lovely dessert.

RASPBERRY SOUFFLÉ
Soufflé aux framboises

1½ lbs. (700 g.) raspberries   3 oz. (2 glasses) Grand Marnier
1 tablespoon powdered sugar   sugar
8 egg whites

Marinate ½ lb. (225 g.) of raspberries in the powdered sugar and Grand Marnier.

Put the remaining raspberries in a blender and purée. Pour into a saucepan, add sugar to taste and cook until thickened.

Beat the egg whites until firm. Gently fold in the boiling raspberry purée. Add two thirds of the marinated raspberries and pour into a buttered souffle mold. Place the remaining raspberries on top the souffle and bake 10 minutes in a 375°F (190°C) oven. Serve immediately.   Serves 4.

★★★ LE VIEUX MOULIN, Porte-d'Arroux 71400 Autun. Tel: 85 52 10 90. Fax: 85 86 32 15.
PROPRIETORS: M. & Mme Tarel.
ROOMS: 16, all with direct telephone, TV; most with bath, WC.
PRICES: Rooms: 240–350 F ($48–70). Breakfast: 45 F ($9). Menus: 90–250 F ($18–50). Credit cards: AE, EC, MC, Visa.
WINES: Rully, Givry, Santenay, Chassagne-Montrachet, Mercury, Saint-Véran, Montagny.
AMENITIES: Bar, lounge, garden, Arroux River, pond, woods. Leisure park with swimming, tennis, golf, riding: 2 km. Fishing by mill. Parking.
ASSOCIATIONS: Moulin Étape; Restauranteurs de Métier; Les Cuisiniers et Hôteliers de Métier.
MARKET DAYS: Autun: Wed, Fri.
DIRECTIONS: In Autun: Porte Arroux - Route de Saulieu by Lucenay-l'Eveque - D 980 ; follow signs to the mill.
OPEN: Mar 1–Dec 31; Restaurant closed: Sun Dinner and Mon (out of season).

37. LE MOULIN DES TEMPLIERS
Avallon, Yonne, Burgundy

This is the only mill in the book which does not have a restaurant. However, fine restaurants are nearby in Avallon, and at L'Espérance and the Moulin des Ruats (see Chapters 23, 24), and this little hotel is too nice to miss—a modest gem on the Cousin River with friendly welcome and gentle comfort. The small rooms are wildly decorated, the atmosphere exquisite. The bountiful breakfasts are best taken in the garden on the river bank.

★★ LE MOULIN DES TEMPLIERS, Pontaubert 89200 Avallon. (Vallée du Cousin) Tel: 86 34 10 80.
PROPRIETOR: Mme Hilmoine.
ROOMS: 14, all with bath or shower, telephone; 11 with WC.
PRICES: Rooms: 250–350 F ($50–70). Breakfast: 36 F ($7). No credit cards.
AMENITIES: Bar, lounge, terrace on Cousin River, woods. Parking. Tennis, riding, golf nearby. Breakfast inside, or on terrace.
MARKET DAYS: Avallon: Thu, Sat.
DIRECTIONS: In Vallée du Cousin, 4 km. SW of Avallon, towards Vézelay.
OPEN: Mar 16–Oct 31.

38. LE MOULIN DE LA COUDRE
Venoy, Yonne, Burgundy

A charming mill-inn just east of Auxerre. Try the Cuisse de canard à l'Irancy (duck cooked in Irancy, a local red wine), or Jambon braisé au Chablis (ham braised in Chablis). Cellar has many first-growth Chablis. (Restaurant only; one toque GaultMillau.)

★★ LE MOULIN DE LA COUDRE. 89290 Venoy. Tel: 86 40 23 79.
Fax: 86 40 23 55.
PRICES: Menus: 105 F (week days), 138–360 F ($21, 28–72). Children: 60 F ($12).
Credit cards: CB, EC, MC, Visa.
MARKET DAYS: Chablis: Sun; Noyers: Wed; Auxerre: Tue, Fri, Sat.
DIRECTIONS: At Venoy, 7 km. E of Auxerre. Take Auxerre–Sud exit from A6.
OPEN: All year except Jan. Closed Sun.

39. LE MOULIN DE MARTOREY

Saint-Rémy/Chalon-sur-Saône, Saône-et-Loire, Burgundy

Beautiful, rustic mill on the Saône River. Jean-Pierre Gillot, a former student of Troisgros, creates amazing, creative dishes that have earned him a Michelin star and three GaultMillau toques. His wife is hostess, directs the service, and manages the cellar with passion and skill. (Restaurant only.)

★★★   MOULIN DE MARTOREY, *Saint-Rémy 71100 Chalon-sur-Saône.*
Tel: 85 48 12 98. Fax: 85 48 73 67.
OWNER/CHEF: Jean-Pierre Gillot. HOSTESS: Pierrette Gillot.
SPECIALTIES: *Mignon de Lotte au jus d'oseille et thé de legumes* (monkfish with sauce of sorrel and vegetable tea); *Poulet de Bresse en trois preparations* (triple preparation of Bresse chicken).
WINES: 1992 Rully Pucelle (Jacqueson); 1990 Mercurey Clos des Parraults (Juillot).
PRICES: Menus: 175–390 F ($38–78). Credit cards: AE, CB, DC, EC, MC, Visa.
DIRECTIONS: A6 to Chalons South exit (Eastern Burgundy); towards Le Creusot.
OPEN: Jan 1–Aug 10, Aug 11–Dec 31; Restaurant Closed: Sun dinner, Mon.

40. LE MOULIN DE BOURGCHÂTEAU
Louhans, Saône-et-Loire, Franche-Comté

This inn is in the middle of Louhans—known for its monthly Bresse chicken market. On a natural pool in the La Seille River, it seems to be in the countryside. Many of the old mill gears and shafts are in place, as decorations. Gonzalès' Bressane specialties have earned him a *GaultMillau* toque (see recipe).

PERCH FILET WITH RED-WINE SAUCE
Filet de sandre au pinot noir

1 lb (400 g) filet of perch	4 tablespoons veal stock
2 shallots	6 tablespoons (80 g.) butter
7 oz. (20 cl.) dry red wine	salt and pepper.

Finely chop the shallots and add to the wine in a sauce pan. Reduce to three-fourths. Add the veal stock and cook over a low fire for 5 minutes. Add the butter to the sauce to thicken and enrich.

Cut perch into 4 portions. Season with salt and pepper. In a frying pan, melt some butter, sauté fish over low fire for 8 minutes.

Cover the serving plate with the wine sauce, and top with the perch. Accompany with turnips cooked in butter.   Serves 4.

★★ LE MOULIN DE BOURGCHÂTEAU, 71500 Louhans. Tel: 85 75 37 12. Fax: 85 75 45 11.
PROPRIETORS: Patrick & Marie-Christine Gonzalès. CHEF: Patrick Gonzalès.
ROOMS: 18, all with bath, WC, direct telephone, TV.
SPECIALTIES: *Filet de sandre au pinot noir* (Perch filet with red-wine sauce—see recipe); *Poulet de Bresse sauté au vinaigre* (Bresse chicken sautéed with vinegar).
WINES: Côte Chalonnaise: Rully, Givry, Mercurey.
PRICES: Rooms: 220–300 F ($44–60). Breakfast: 45 F ($9). Menus: 100–150 F ($20–30). Credit cards: AE, CB, EC, MC, Visa.
AMENITIES: Bar, lounge, La Seille River, parking. Tennis, riding nearby.
ASSOCIATIONS: Moulin Étape.
MARKET DAYS: Louhans: 1st Mon of month.
DIRECTIONS: A6 to Chalons-sur-Saône Sud exit, then 38 km. SE on D978 to Louhans.
OPEN: Jan 21–Dec 19; Restaurant closed Sun (Oct–Easter); Mon lunch.

41. AUBERGE DU MOULIN DE LACHAT

Enfonvelles,Haute Marne, Champagne-Ardennes

In a little village in the middle of a forest, this inn is unusual in that the proprietor-chef—a former sports professional—also offers tennis and riding lessons, and exercize equipment. You can easily use up any extra calories you may find in his delicious duck breast with wild fruits.

★★ AUBERGE DU MOULIN DE LACHAT, Enfonvelles 52400 Bourbonne-les-Bains. Tel: 25 90 09 54. Fax: 25 90 21 82.
PROPRIETOR/CHEF: Christian Arends.
ROOMS: 13, some with bath or shower, WC, direct telephone, TV, minibar.
PRICES: Rooms: 250–410 F ($50–82); ½-pension: 360 F ($72). Full pension: 430 F ($86); Breakfast: 44 F ($9). Menus: 98–180 F ($20–36). Credit cards: AE, CB, Visa.
SPECIALTIES: *Filet de perche à la crème d'échalottes* (perch filet with creamed shallots); *Magret de canard aux fruits des bois* (duck breast with fruit from the woods), or *Aiguillette de poulet sauce moutard* (chicken with mustard).
AMENITIES: Bar, lounge, garden, terrace, Apance River, wood, tennis court, heated pool. Dining inside, or on terrace. Fishing, swimming, tennis, riding, punting on premises (Arends gives tennis and riding lessons). Sauna and fitness room. Parking. Heliport, private airfield on premises. Golf: 40 km.
ASSOCIATIONS: Moulin Étape, Logis de France, Maison de la France.
MARKET DAYS: Bourbonne-les-Bains: Tue, Wed.
DIRECTIONS: From Paris, 200 km. E on A5 to Montigny-le-Roi exit, E 26 km. on D417 to Fresne-sur-Apance, D5 S 1 km. to D170, left to Enfonvelle; follow signs to the mill.
OPEN: Apr 1–Nov 12.

42. LA RUBANERIE

La Claquette-Rothau-Schirmeck, Bas-Rhin, Alsace

Originally a forge (a *claquette*), this mill more recently made ribbons. Now it furnishes electric power for the inn. A five-acre park, with the Bruche river—a nice setting in Alsace-Lorraine. Mme Spach organizes hikes in the Vosges Mountains. The dining room specializes in Alsatian delights and local wines.

★★ LA RUBANERIE, 67570 La Claquette-Schirmeck. Tel: 88 97 01 95.
    Fax: 88 47 17 34.
PROPRIETORS: M. & Mme Spach and daughter.
ROOMS: 16, all with bath or shower, WC, direct telephone, cable TV.
PRICES: Rooms: 280–440 F ($56–88); ½-pension: from 310 F ($61). Breakfast: 42 F
    ($8). Menus: 140–260 F ($28–52). Credit cards: AE, CB, DC, Visa.
AMENITIES: Bar, lounge, terrace, 5-acre park, river, woods. Heated swimming pool,
    sauna. Parking. Tennis, riding nearby.
ASSOCIATIONS: Moulin Étape.
MARKET DAYS: Strasbourg: Tue, Fri, Sat; Obernai: Thu; Molsheim: Mon;
    Schirmeck: Wed.
DIRECTIONS: From Strasbourg 48 km W on A352/N420 to Schirmeck, then S
    2 km. to mill.
OPEN: All year; Restaurant closed: Sun (except dinner for residents).

43. LE MOULIN DU PRIEURÉ

Bonnevaux-le-Prieuré, Doubs, Franche-Comté

Rustic, well-equipped rooms and a classic cuisine worth a
GaultMillau toque. All in a serene valley by the Jura Mountains.

★★★ LE MOULIN DU PRIEURÉ, 25620 Bonnevaux-le-Prieuré.
    Tel: 81 59 21 47. Fax: 81 59 28 79.
PROPRIETORS: Renée & Marc Gatez. CHEF: Marc Gatez.
ROOMS: 8, all with bath or shower, WC, telephone, TV, mini-bar, coffee maker.
PRICES: Rooms: 550–700 F ($110–140). Breakfast: 30 F ($6). Menus: 200–350 F
    ($40–70). Credit cards: AE, DC, EC, MC, Visa.
AMENITIES: Bar, lounge, garden, terrace, Brème River, wood. Fishing on premises.
    Parking. Tennis, riding, canoeing/kayaking: 6 km. Golf: 8 km.
ASSOCIATIONS: Moulin Étape; Châteaux et Hôtels Indépendants.
MARKET DAYS: Besançon: Mon-Sat.
DIRECTIONS: From Besançon, S on N7/D67 20 km; left on D280; follow signs to
    the mill.
OPEN: Mar 11–Nov 10. Restaurant closed: Tue; Wed lunch.

III. SOUTHEAST FRANCE

Southeast France: the Massif-Central/Auvergne, the Rhône/Alps, Provence/Côte-d'Azur/Riviera, and Languedoc–Rousillon.

MASSIF-CENTRAL/AUVERGNE: A vast highland filling the middle of southern France, the Massif Central is composed of ancient mountains, extinct volcanoes, high plains, deep gorges, hundreds of lakes, and many rivers. The Loire, Dordogne, Allier, Sioule, Cère, and numerous smaller rivers start here—the waters of which were called at one time "The White Oil," because of the many hydroelectric plants.

One of the poorest regions in France, the Auvergne is almost entirely rural. Only the capital, Clermont-Ferrand, has any sort of urban lifestyle, and even it feels like a village. The people are rigidly conservative, and deeply religious. Being long cut off from the mainstream of French life has left them tough, self-reliant and resistant to change. An illustration of this is that the Auvergnats still use the imperfect subjunctive in their speech, which disappeared from mainstream French speech over half a century ago. Thus the people have a history, tradition and a culture of their own.

The area makes a popular vacation spot for Parisians—some seeking complete change, others wishing to go back to their roots. Which may explain why Auvernaise cuisine is all the rage in Paris. This cuisine involves cheese, pork products, beans, lentils, cabbage, and wild produce: chestnuts, blueberries, and mushrooms. But the best is the cheese: Cantal, a hard cheese resembling cheddar; fine blues like the Fourme d'Ambert and Bleu d'Auvergne; creamy Saint Nectaire; a score or more of goat cheeses; and Tomme Aligot, the fresh curds used in making Cantal, which is used in an excellent recipe with mashed potatoes and garlic, called *Aligot*. The best-known wine is Saint-Pourçain, a white from the Allier.

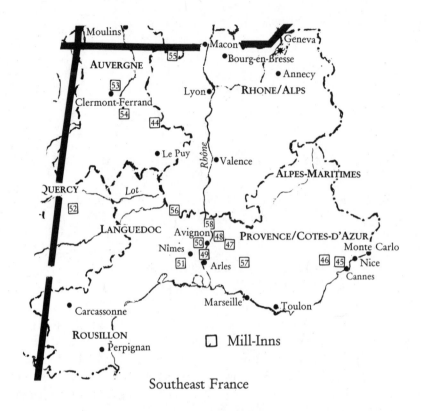

Southeast France

RHÔNE/ALPS: Lyons is considered by many to be the gastro-nomic capital of France. One measure of this is the quality of the restaurants in Lyons and vicinity. They carry a total of 61 Gault-Millau toques, even after GaultMillau's 1996 "house cleaning."

Another measure is the quality of the open-air markets. Browse through Lyons' Marché du Quai Saint Antoine, by the river (Tuesday to Sunday), where local farmers sell their produce. Charcuterie, and cheesemakers from the Rhône, the Savoie, and the Dauphiné sell cheeses unknown to most Americans: Beaufort, a Savoie cheese similar to Gruyère; Arômes à la Gêne—generic name for several cheeses from the Lyons area—coated with *gêne* (or *marc*, the dry grape skins following the second pressing). These include Rigotte de Condrieu, Pélardon, and Saint-Marcellin, the latter from the Isère; and Beaufort d'été, a cheese made from "summer milk" (June to early October, when the cows graze in flowery mountain meadows).

The wines of the Rhône Valley can be exceptional—full, dry, rich, and fruity. The best are the Hermitage and Côte Rotie, Crozes-

Hermitages, Saint Joseph, and Cornas—made from 80 to 100 percent Syrah. The cellar master at Chapoutier told me that he keeps his Hermitages in barrel for four years before bottling—the wines are not to be drunk early. White wines from the Viognier grape (Chateau Grillet and Condrieu) are soft, rich, full-bodied, with a fine bouquet.

PROVENCE/CÔTE-D'AZUR/LANGUEDOC: Moving down the Rhône Valley, somewhere between Montélimar and Orange you find the sun warmer, the sky bluer, the countryside more arid, and you know you are in Provence. Over 2100 years ago, Greek settlers on the Mediterranean Coast asked Rome to help them ward off local tribesmen. Rome complied, then took over the Greek settlements, turning what are now Provence, the Côte-d'Azur, and Languedoc into a prosperous Roman province (hence the name Provence). There remain numerous Roman theaters, arenas, temples, and aqueducts—preserved in surprisingly good state by the good weather.

The warm sun, brilliant light, and colors attracted many painters, including Van Gogh, Cezanne, and Picasso. They also attracted many tourists, and recently many foreign settlers eager to find the idyllic life described by Peter Mayle[12,13]. And a crucial facet of this idyll is the food.

The most important elements in the food of the Midi are olive oil and garlic. Next are the local herbs: basil, rosemary, wild thyme, fennel. Essential vegetables are tomatoes, zucchini squash, eggplant, artichokes, and peppers. There are many kinds of river and ocean fish and shellfish. Meats include pré-salé lamb, kid, pork, and game: *lièvre* (hare), *lapin* (rabbit), and *sanglier* and *marcassin* (wild boar—large and small). From northern Languedoc comes Roquefort, the king of the blue cheeses, made from ewe's milk and aged in underground rock caves near the village of Roquefort-sur-Soulzon.

Specialties: The most-famous dish is *Bouillabaisse,* a rich fish-and-shellfish stew; *Aioli,* (garlic mayonnaise to put into the Bouillabaisse); *Aïgo sau,* (a bouillabaisse variant without saffron); and *Tapenade,* a paste of olives and anchovies served on toast, and used in cooking.

The Southern Rhône produces several well-known wines: Lirac, Gigondas, Châteauneuf-du-Pape, and Côtes du Rhône Villages. Some are fruity and light, others full-bodied and more powerful. Provence, Languedoc, and Rousillon produce large amounts of wine, most of it ordinary, but some excellent. Tavel is the best-known and most-expensive rosé. To my palette, Bandol rosé is as good. Bandol whites are also nice. An exciting white wine is the Beaumes-de-Venise, a rich, sweet wine similar to Sauternes, great with foie gras, or dessert.

44. HÔTEL MISTOU

Pontempeyrat, Haute-Loire, Auvergne

This 18th-century water mill sits in a park on the banks of the Ance River, a trout stream in the heart of the Haute-Loire forests. A little stream, or race, tumbles in a cascade under the building. Again, the mill seems far from civilization: Le Puy is 40 kilometers to the south, and Lyon 60 to the northeast. It couldn't be more tranquil. Nor more friendly—Jacqueline and Bernard Roux are ideal hosts.

The mill had the unusual function of operating a cooling system to conserve eggs. In 1875 it became one of the first mill-inns, and at present it operates a turbine to provide electricity for the inn, garden, and weir. The 24 bedrooms—some in a chalet-style annex—are newly redecorated and comfortable. The two dining rooms are elegant, with antique sideboards, light pastel drapes, open beam ceilings, and polished wooden floors. Many of the tables have views of the river.

FOOD & WINE

Bernard Roux specializes in fish and game (in season). For example, this menu: *Potée de truite a l'Auvergnate et Saint-Pourcain blanc* (trout baked in white wine with vegetables); *Chartreuse de faisan au chou* (cabbage stuffed with pheasant, mushrooms, and foie gras, served with raisin sauce—see recipe); and *Parfait aux cacahuettes et sauce au café* (peanut butter parfait with coffee-flavored *crème anglaise*—see recipe).

Some other specialties (these recommended by GaultMillau[27]): *Noix de coquilles Saint-Jacques au chou et cinq épices* (scallops with cabbage and five spices); and *Le filet de boeuf aux huîtres et jus de pleurotes* (beef filet with oysters and juice of oyster mushrooms). Roux well-deserves his toque.

He has an excellent cellar from which to choose, including lesser-known Auvergne wines such as the Saint-Pourçain.

SIGHTS & SUCH

Relax in the garden, stroll along the river, walk through the woods, and play tennis at nearby Ussom-en-Foret. For the myriad tourist sights, see Michelin's green guide *Auvergne*.

CABBAGE STUFFED WITH PHEASANT, MUSHROOMS, FOIE GRAS
Chartreuse de faisan au chou

1 pheasant	Herbes de provence (thyme,
1 head Chinese cabbage	summer savory, rosemary,
1 onion, sliced	bay leaf)
¼ lb. (100 g.) foie gras	salt and pepper
4 carrots	8 tablespoons (100 g.) butter
½ lb. (225 g.) cèpes	1 lb. (500 g.) bacon
(boletus mushrooms)	

Sauce:

4 oz. (120 g.) golden raisins	4 oz. (120 g.) butter
2 cups (½ l.) white wine	2 tablespoons (40 g.) tomato
2 tablespoons caramel	paste
2 shallots	½ bunch chives
2 tablespoons (20 g.) corn starch	

Soak the raisins in water for 5 hours. Drain and set aside.
Debone the pheasant and cut the meat in rather thick pieces. Heat a frying pan very hot, add a little oil, and sear the meat—but don't cook it. Set aside.
Clean the mushrooms and cut in slices. In a clean frying pan, melt 2 tablespoons butter and sauté the mushrooms. Set aside.

In the same pan, melt 2 tablespoons butter and sauté the onion slices until they are lightly golden.

Remove the center vein on the cabbage leaves. Cook the leaves in boiling water for 8 minutes. Drain well.

Steam separately the carrots cut in one-eighth inch (5-mm.) slices and the bacon cut in one-eighth inch (5-mm.) slices.

Butter generously a large stainless steel platter and cover the bottom with ¼ of the cabbage leaves. Add in layers the following ingredients, in this order:

2. slices of carrot
3. slices of onion
4. salt and pepper
5. ¼ of cabbage leaves
6. pheasant
7. salt and pepper
8. herbes de provence

9. bacon pieces
10. ¼ of cabbage leaves
11. mushrooms
12. foie gras, cut in cubes
13. ¼ of cabbage leaves
14. pieces of butter

Press loaf together so it will hold its shape. Cover the dish with aluminum foil and cook in the oven 30 minutes at 450°F (230°C).

In the meantime, make the caramel. In a small saucepan, heat ¼ cup (50 g.) sugar and 2 tablespoons water. Bring to a boil and cook until medium brown in color. Immediately add 2 tablespoons more of water and stir until the caramel is smooth.

To make the sauce, chop the shallots and sauté in a frying pan. Add the tomato paste and the caramel. Let this cook about 2 minutes. Add the white wine and bring to a boil. Thicken the sauce with the corn starch dissolved in a little water. Bring to a boil again and add the 8 oz. (100 g.) of butter (cut in pieces and added slowly). Add the raisins and chives.

To serve, cut the pheasant loaf in slices and place a slice on each warmed plate. Surround with the sauce.

Serves 6.

PEANUT BUTTER PARFAIT
WITH COFFEE-FLAVORED CRÈME ANGLAISE
Parfait aux cacahuettes et sauce au café

½ lb. (250 g.) smooth   8 egg yolks
   peanut butter   1½ cups (375 g.) whipping cream
½ cup (12 cl.) milk   Crème Anglaise (Appendix C.)
3 tablespoons instant espresso coffee
1 cup (25 cl.) sugar syrup (1½ cups sugar to 1 cup water
   or 300 g. sugar to 25 cl. water)

Warm milk to about 80°F (30°C) and whisk in the peanut butter. Set aside.

Bring sugar syrup to boil.

Put egg yolks in a bowl and whisk well. Beat in the boiling syrup and continue beating until cool.

Add the peanut butter mixture to the eggs. Whip the cream and fold it in.

Pour this parfait into a mold or loaf pan and put in freezer for at least 24 hours.

Make a crème anglaise. While sauce is still hot, add 3 tablespoons of instant expresso coffee. Cool.

To serve, remove parfait from freezer and let sit a few minutes to soften slightly. Unmold and cut into slices. Serve with coffee sauce. Decorate with mint leaves.   Serves 8.

★★ HÔTEL MISTOU, 43500 Craponne-Pontempeyrat. Tel: 77 50 62 46. Fax: 77 50 66 70.
PROPRIETORS: Jacqueline & Bernard Roux. Chef: Bernard Roux.
ROOMS: 24, all with bath, WC, direct telephone, TV.
PRICES: Rooms: 300–460 F ($60–92); ½-pension: 360–470 F ($66–94) Breakfast: 45 F ($9). Menus: 120–295 F ($24–59), Children: 70 F ($14). Credit cards: AE, DC, EC, MC, Visa.
AMENITIES: Bar, lounge, terrace. Trout river, fishing, woods, hiking, parking. Tennis nearby.
ASSOCIATIONS: Moulin Étape, Relais du Silence, Logis de France.
DIRECTIONS: From Lyon: S and W on A7/A47/A72 to Andrezieux exit; D498 SW 47 km. to Pontempeyrat; 1 km. SE to mill. From Le Puy, NW then N on N102/D906/D1/D493, 45 km. to Pontempeyrat.
OPEN: Easter–Oct 31; Restaurant closed: Lunch except Jul, Aug, and weekends.

45. LE MOULIN DE MOUGINS
Mougins, Alpes-Maritimes, Côte d'Azur

One of the best-known mill-inns in France—with one of France's 20 best restaurants—is the Moulin de Mougins, near the village of Mougins in the Maritime Alps. Only a few minutes from Cannes, with its film festival and jet setters, and less than an hour from Nice and the other French Riviera pleasure spots, the mill acquired a patina of international glamour, and it has attracted hordes of appreciative visitors to sample its food and sing its praises.

The mill dates from the sixteenth century, and produced olive oil until 1960. (This is one of three mills in this collection that were propelled not by water, but by oxen or mules—a *"moulin à sang,"* rather than a *"moulin à eau."*) Converted to an inn in the early sixties, it was purchased by Roger Vergé a few years later, while he still worked under Vidal at "Le Club" in Cavalière, on the Riviera.

The inn is like a two-story cottage with massive stone walls. Outside terraces have rattan chairs and white awnings, and of course dining tables. Dining tables also sit in the garden, which presents not only colorful flowers, but vegetables and herbs for Vergé's kitchen.

Inside, you find a snug sitting area, with a welcoming fire on cool days. The rooms and suites are decorated with exquisite taste, and filled with beautiful antiques. Guests can remote-control their room air conditioning. The marble bathrooms are well-equipped. But don't become enamored by the lovely bedrooms and suites—you don't *have* to be a head of state or a famous cinema or sports personality to get a room, but it would certainly help. As Gault-Millau[28] says "The three rooms and two small suites are delightful and much cheaper than a grand hotel, but harder to obtain than a place in Paradise." When you have trouble getting a room, go to another hotel in Mougins, and come to the Moulin for lunch or dinner. (See Michelin's red guide *France*[32].)

Each lounge and dining room has one or more original pieces of art. Paintings by Cesar and Muhl, and sculptures by Armand. The most dramatic and impressive is at the entrance lobby to the dining rooms: six violins (or violas) in brass and wood, some split, clustered together (Armand). The dining rooms are modest in size, a total of about forty settings, but with terrace and garden service added, the mill can serve many more.

FOOD & WINE

Relais & Châteaux[35] said (correctly) that "In the moulin of happiness, Roger Vergé cultivates the love of great cuisine like one of the fine arts; with passion." From the mid-seventies, the mill carried three Michelin stars, indicating that a meal there is "worth a journey." From 1987 it also carried four GaultMillau toques. Michelin reduced the stars to two, and GaultMillau reduced the toques to three. What happened?

For several years, Vergé has been a man of competition and marketing. An audacious and insatiable entrepreneur, he creates a bistro here, a restaurant there, a cooking school. He prepares culinary products to sell all over the world. He writes books. He's become the master of a little empire. He travels all over world to lecture, teach, and cook—to East Africa, the Caribbean, Disney's Epcot Center, New York, San Francisco . . . In short, he may spend less time than before in his kitchen at the Moulin de Mougins. However, Nona and I have recently enjoyed perfect lunches and dinners at Vergé's Moulin. We think that it is still "worth a journey."

Vergé's tables sport fine china, silver, crystal, and flowers The service is impeccable. The menu varies with the season. Here are some dishes for which Vergé graciously provided us the recipes: an unusual, delicious (and expensive) *Poupeton de fleur de courgettes aux truffes*[39] (Stuffed zucchini flowers with truffles); a hearty filet of beef with currants *(Filet de boeuf aux raisins à la Mathurini*[40]*)*. Meals usually start with a luscious *amuse-bouche*, include a tray of well-finished cheeses after the main course, and end with complementary *Gourmandises* served with the coffee.

The wine list includes a good selection of wines from the south of France, plus fine Burgundies. Try the regional wines—some aren't available in the U.S., and most offer good value.

SIGHTS & SUCH

The ancient, medieval village of Mougins, population 13,000, prides itself as being a "City of Art and Gastronomy," and also as a *Ville Sportive*. Picasso and Picabia both lived and painted here, and local artists' works can be seen in several galleries. Also worth a visit: the Museum of Photography, and the Automobile Museum

Visiting is pleasant and convenient: with its ancient houses and narrow streets, Mougins has solved the traffic problem plaguing most cities in France. Cars are not allowed. Free municipal parking lots are less than a kilometer from town.

Mougins bases its Ville Sportive label on a large group of clubs and associations that share municipal facilities. There are three tennis clubs, four gymnastic clubs, and at least one each for swimming, golf, riding, cycling, roller skating, handball, karate, judo, and boule (or pétanque). For information on any of the clubs—address, telephone number, schedule, and provision for visitors—call the Syndicat d'Initiative, telephone 93 75 87 67, or write them at rue Jean-Charles Mallet, 06250 Mougins.

Villeneuve-Loubet, sixteen kilometers toward Nice, boasts a museum uniquely French: the Musée de l'Art Culinaire. This will interest any food lover. It is set up in the house where, on October 28, 1846, Auguste Escoffier was born. Called "The king of chefs, and the chef of kings," Escoffier, at the age of 26, prepared menus for the son of Queen Victoria, the future Edward VII. Ten years later, Escoffier began an association with the hotelier Ritz, becoming chef of the Grand Hotel in Monte Carlo, then chef of the Savoy in London, at the new Ritz Hotel in Paris, and finally at the new Carlton in London. The French President decorated him with the Legion of Honor. (Yet through all of this, Mme Escoffier never quite adjusted to her husband's profession, which she considered to be little more than that of a servant.)

If you are interested in attending Vergé's cooking school, you may choose between two "campuses": one in Mougins at Vergé's second mill, the Restaurant l'Amandier (Tel. 93 75 35 70), and the other in Nice, at the Hôtel Beau Rivages (93 75 35 70). Courses are one week; two-hour classes are also available.

For the many other sights of the Riviera, see the Michelin green guide *Côte d'Azur*.

STUFFED ZUCCHINI FLOWERS WITH TRUFFLES

Les Fleurs de courgettes aux truffes

1 lb. (500 g.) fresh mushrooms	6 small black truffles (about
Juice of one lemon	½ oz. each) canned or fresh
1 shallot	6 zucchini flowers
8 oz. plus 1 tablespoon (225 g.)	with zucchini attached
unsalted butter	1 lb. (500 g.) fresh spinach
2½ oz. crème fraîche	Fresh ground pepper, salt
or heavy cream	sprigs of chervil (optional)
2 egg yolks	

Trim stems of the mushrooms and wipe clean of any dirt. Place mushrooms in food processor and finely chop without puréeing. Put them in a bowl and sprinkle with lemon juice to prevent discoloring.

Peel the shallot and chop finely.

Melt 1 tablespoon butter in a medium skillet. Add the shallot and sauté over medium heat until the butter begins to sizzle. Add the mushrooms, season with salt, and cook for 3 to 5 minutes.

Drain the mushrooms saving the juice. Place the mushrooms in a large saucepan and cook over high heat until all the moisture has evaporated. Combine the crème fraîche and egg yolks in a small mixing bowl and whisk until blended. Whisk this mixture into the mushrooms and cook over high heat for about 2 minutes. Adjust the seasoning, if necessary. Place the mushrooms on a plate and let cool.

Drain the truffles in a sieve set over the saucepan containing the mushroom juice.

Gently pat any moisture from the petals of the zucchini flowers (don't wash). Gently open out the petals of each blossom and fill the center of each with ½ tablespoon of the mushroom mixture. Nestle a truffle in the center of each blossom and carefully close the petals up around the truffle and stuffing. Place the flowers on the top of a couscousière or in a bamboo steamer. Cover with aluminum foil.

Remove stems from the spinach, wash leaves thoroughly, drain.

Place the saucepan containing the mushroom and truffle juice over medium heat and let simmer and reduce until only 3 tablespoons remain.

Cut the remaining butter into small pieces and add it, a little at a time, whisking over high heat after each addition until the butter is thoroughly incorporated. Season with salt and pepper and remove from the heat.

About 20 minutes before serving, fill the bottom of the couscousière with water and place the top part with the squash blossoms over the water. If you're steaming the flowers in a bamboo steamer, fill the wok with a little water and place the steamer over it. Place over high heat and steam for about 15 minutes. The flowers will be perfectly cooked when a knife can be inserted easily into the zucchini.

While the flowers steam, reheat the sauce if necessary.

To serve, spread the spinach leaves over 6 warmed serving plates. Place a zucchini blossom on each plate. Season with salt and pepper and spoon a little sauce over each. Sprinkle each portion with chervil, if using, and serve.   Serves 6.

FILET OF BEEF WITH CURRANTS MATHURINI
Filet de boeuf aux raisins à la Mathurini

2 slices (6–7 oz. or 200 g. each) beef filet or contre-filet
4 tablespoons currants
1 tablespoon coarsely crushed black pepper
4 tablespoons (50 g.) butter
3 tablespoons (5 cl.) Cognac or Armagnac
3 tablespoons (5 cl.) beef stock
salt and crushed pepper

Bring 2 cups water to a boil and add currants. Boil 5 minutes, then drain and refresh under cold water. Set aside.

Salt beef on both sides and roll in crushed pepper, pressing it well into meat with the flat of your hand.

Heat a little butter in a small frying pan and cook meat 2 to 3 minutes on each side, over moderately high heat (cooking time should be adjusted to thickness of meat and desired doneness). When cooked, remove from pan and keep warm.

Pour off butter from pan. Add currants and Armagnac or Cognac away from heat so that liquid will loosen browned bits in pan. Reduce over low heat, add stock and simmer for 2 minutes. Gradually add remaining butter to finish the sauce.

To serve, arrange steaks on 2 hot plates. Pour the sauce over.

Serves 2.

★ ★ ★ ★ LE MOULIN DE MOUGINS, 424 Chemin du Moulin, Quartier Notre-Dame-de-Vie, 06250 Mougins. Tel: 93.75.78.24. Fax: 93.90.18.55.

PROPRIETORS: Denise & Roger Vergé. CHEF: Roger Vergé. DIRECTOR: Denise Roger.

ROOMS: 3, plus 2 suites, all with bath or shower, WC, direct telephone, TV, air conditioning, garden view.

PRICES: Rooms: 800–900 F ($160–180); suites: 1300 F ($260. Breakfast: 75 F ($15). Menus: Lunch: 295 F, incl. wine ($60); Dinner: 585–700 F ($117–140). Credit cards: AE, CB, DC, EC, MC, Visa.

AMENITIES: Bar, lounge, terrace. Parking, heliport. Tennis 1 km; swimming 2 km; riding 4 km; golf 2 km. Beach and water sports 30 km. Dining inside, or on terrace.

ASSOCIATIONS: Relais & Châteaux; Traditions & Qualité; Maîtres Cusiniers de France.

MARKET DAYS: Mougins: Tue–Sun; Grasse: Tue–Sat; Vallauris: Wed, Sun.

DIRECTIONS: From Cannes, N on N285 to Mougins. Mill is 2 km. S of town, on Chemin du Moulin, near Ave Notre Dame de Vie.

OPEN: Mar 10–Feb 4; Restaurant closed: Thu noon; Mon (except Jul 15–Aug 31).

46. LE MOULIN DE LA CAMANDOULE
Fayence, Var, Provence

Here's the quintessential mill-inn. On arrival you pass under a stone Roman aqueduct into a different time. You walk past an old stone well and large trough full of fish to a wide terrace. Here's a friendly house dog with a squeaky toy, just begging you to play. You look out over a cherry orchard and well-clipped grass to a river. As usual with mills, this is a friendly and fun inn. No need to hush your voice or tip-toe around—a relaxed and comfortable sort of place.

The inn is neatly described in an invitation to participants of the Cannes Film (or other) Festival. Entitled "A Festival Sanctuary," it reads in part: "In just half an hour you can be whisked away from the festival frenzy and enjoy peace and tranquility in the idyllic surroundings of the *arrière pays*.

"Just 33 kilometers from Cannes, below the hilltop village of Fayence, is situated the *Moulin de la Camandoule*, an ancient water mill converted into a comfortable three-star hotel and restaurant of a unique kind. Lovingly preserved, the original 19th-century milling machinery—the presses and the wheels—and the Roman aqueduct that used to bring water to the mill, have all been kept in their proper place (so much so that it would only take a fortnight to get the mill working again). Such is the historical interest generated by the mill (it dates from the 15th century) that it attracts visitors . . . who see it as much a museum as a hotel/restaurant.

"Included in the 12-acre estate are several terraces, an old cherry orchard, a river (La Camandre), and a near-Olympic-sized swimming pool, around which are served light lunches of fresh seafood and barbecued meat. And there is also, of course, an extensive bar. . . .

"Each room is different and individual, but all share a view of the estate, Fayence, and the surrounding hills. All have private bathrooms, direct-dial telephones, and television, and are centrally heated for the cooler winter nights. . . .

"Whether just for one evening, or for the duration of the festival, the *Moulin de la Camandoule* is the perfect place to escape the pressures and stresses of the festival . . . ."

Shirley and Wolf Rilla (a British/German couple) bought the inn in 1986, and have made improvements since. Personal touches, such as family paintings, books, and bric-a-brac, add to the delightful atmosphere. And the charming Shirley Rilla and Restaurant Manager Jean-Brice Raybaud, are very welcoming.

FOOD & WINE

Chef Philippe Choisy joined the mill in 1994. He was 27 years old, and had studied under Roger Vergé (Chapter 45). According to Shirley Rilla, he has raised the high standard of food even higher—and his predecessor, chef Oliver Rispoli, had already earned a toque from GaultMillau. Choisy offers two menus, both of which concentrate on Provençal flavors. The menu of the season, only 180 francs, offers a choice of four first courses, four main courses, a tray of local cheeses, and three desserts.

The "Menu au Moulin" has seven courses, including foie gras, lobster, and rack of lamb. One course is a refreshing *Granite de sauge et marc de Provence*, the Provençal equivalent to the Normandy *trou Normand*, with marc replacing Calvados. They serve a glass of Port wine with the cheese course, a Roquefort. The dessert is raspberry mousse and fresh cheese, with a Cointreau sauce. At 260 francs, this menu must be considered a bargain.

Specialties of Chef Choisy include a new treatment of asparagus: *Pointes d'asperges vertes au sabayon de roquette;* and *Filet de boeuf à la purée d'olives noir croustillant de pommes de terre* (beef filet with an olive purée, and crusty potato rosettes—see recipe).

The *Grill de la Piscine*, or swimming-pool grill, has its own menu at 95 francs—three courses with lots of choices—and an extensive à la carte menu.

SIGHTS & SUCH

The hill-top village of Fayence is delightful to explore, especially the old quarter. See Michelin's green guide *Côte-d'Azur*. (From April through October demi-pension is obligatory, and from June through September the minimum stay is three days.)

BEEF FILET WITH OLIVE PURÉE
AND CRUSTY POTATO ROSETTES
*Filet de boeuf à la purée d'olives noir,
croustillant de pommes de terre*

4 slices filet mignon	2 tablespoons tapenade
5½ oz. (150 g.) each	4 large potatoes
2 cups (½ liter) port	olive oil
2 cups (½ liter) red wine	4 slices white bread
4 cups (1 liter) veal	salt and pepper
or chicken stock	

Sauce: reduce red wine over medium heat to half volume. Add port and reduce again by half. Add stock and gently simmer for 1½ hours. To finish sauce, stir in the tapenade and season to taste.

Croustillant of potatoes: peel and cut each potato in thin rounds. Make an overlapping circle with the potato slices (rosace). Cook in a frying pan with olive oil until crisp. Drain on a paper towel and keep warm. Repeat this three more times.

Sauté the filets of beef to desired doneness.

To assemble, put the potato circles in the oven to renew crispness. Put the meat on four rounds of white bread cut to the size of each piece of meat. Place on warmed plates. Pour the sauce over the steaks and place the potato circles on top. Serve immediately.

Serves 4.

★ ★ ★ LE MOULIN DE LA CAMANDOULE, Chémin Notre-Dame-des-Cypres, 83440 Fayence. Tel.: 9487 06 00 22. Fax: 98 06 18 00.
PROPRIETORS: Wolf and Shirley Rilla. CHEF: Philippe Choisy. RESTAURANT MANAGER: Jean-Brice Raybaud.
ROOMS: 10, plus 2 suites, all with bath, WC, direct telephone, TV.
PRICES: Rooms: 295–635 F ($59–127); suites: 635–675 F ($127–135); ½-pension (Obligatory from Mar 16 to Oct 31): 445–565 F ($89–113). Breakfast: 50 F ($10). Menus: 180–270 F ($36–54). Credit cards: MC, Visa.
AMENITIES: Bar, lounge, swimming pool, poolside terrace and restaurant, open-air bar, private 33-acre park. Parking. Dining inside, or on terrace. Fishing in river at inn. Tennis: 2 km.
ASSOCIATIONS: Moulin Étape.
MARKET DAYS: Fayence: Tue, Thu, Sat.
DIRECTIONS: Cannes 12 km. W on A6 to D37, 8 km. N to D562, 8 km. on D562/D19 to Fayence; follow signs to the mill.
OPEN: Dec 23–Nov 1; Restaurant closed: Tue lunch.

47. DOMAINE LE MOULIN BLANC
Gordes, Vaucluse, Provence

Forget the world. Retreat to this beautiful, well-restored, serene old mill. The setting, in the heart of historic Provence and the Lubéron, is lovely. On one side, green meadows and farmlands, and startlingly green hills, changing to blue and violet in the distance. On the other side, protection by rocky, forested cliffs. The peace and tranquility are immediately felt. The inn is gracious and luxurious, without pretense, the staff is friendly, the seven acres of grounds—with gardens, cypress and pine trees, lawns, swimming pool and tennis court—are well-tended.

Inside, the mill is cool, quiet, and elegant. The bedrooms are nicely furnished, some with four-poster beds. (Request a room overlooking the garden, rather than the road.) A vaulted area houses the lounge and one of the dining rooms. A pretty courtyard is ideal for summer dining.

FOOD & WINE

Chef Anthony Baud recently came from the two-toque Château du Chèvre d'Or in Eze, so his cuisine is bound to be good—perhaps he can increase the Moulin Blanc's GaultMillau toques from one to two. However, we have not visited the inn since his arrival, and know little about his repertoire. You must judge the cuisine for yourself—and please let us know your impressions.

SIGHTS & SUCH

When (and if) you tire of the amenities of the mill, visit Gordes. Its houses rise in tiers above the valley, on the edge of the Vaucluse Plateau. Visit the château, and the Sénanque Abbey. Drive to the Fontaine-de-Vaucluse, the source of the Sorgue River, and a three-star sight (see Michelin's green guide *Provence*).

★ ★ ★ ★ DOMAINE LE MOULIN BLANC, Chemin du Moulin, Les Beaumettes 84220 Gordes. Tel: 90 72 34 50. Fax: 90 72 25 41.

PROPRIETOR: Mireille Diez. CHEF: Anthony Baud.

ROOMS: 17, plus 1 suite, all with bath or shower, WC, direct telephone, TV, minibar. Five rooms have private terraces.

PRICES: Rooms: 620–950 F ($124–190); suite: 925–1180 F ($185–236); ½-pension: 510–665 F ($102–133). Breakfast: 65 F ($13). Menus: 160–350 F ($32–70). Credit cards: AE, DC, EC, MC, Visa.

AMENITIES: Bar, lounge, terrace, 5-acre park, river, tennis court, swimming pool, parking. Riding and golf nearby. Dining inside, or on terrace.

ASSOCIATIONS: Châteaux et Hôtels Indépendants.

MARKET DAYS: Gordes: Tue; Cavaillon: Mon; Carpentras: Fri; Avignon: Tue–Sun.

DIRECTIONS: From Avignon: 35 km. on D22/N100, towards Apt.

OPEN: All year.

48. HOSTELLERIE DU MOULIN DE LA ROQUE
Althen-des-Paluds, Vaucluse, Provence

If you can't wangle an invitation from Peter Mayle,[12,13] the next best place from which to discover Provence is the Moulin de la Roque—at the foot of Mount Ventoux, just ten minutes from Avignon and from Châteauneuf-du-Pape. It's only 20 minutes from the fabulous Fountain of Vaucluse, the source of the Sorgue River, which powered the important Moulin de la Roque for 250 years. The millrace still flows under the building, part of which dates from the 17th century.

Once you arrive at the Moulin de Roques, however, you may decide to spend most of your time there, and miss some of the sights. The mill is a tranquil retreat, elegant and engaging. Rooms are spacious, modern and luxurious, yet cozy Provençal. Eighteen rooms have a water view. The park is large, with tennis court, swimming pool, flowered lawns, and woods for strolling. Under the plantain trees, you can enjoy fresh-air exercise with various equipment. On the hall table lie English- and French-language newspapers for guests who wish to know what's going on in the world.

FOOD & WINE

The dining room is large, bathed in light, and softly decorated in beige: wall paper, tile floor, tablecloths, and chairs. The chefs change frequently, and the present chef, Philippe Chaléon, changes his menus frequently, according to the season and the availability of fresh items in Avignon or Carpentras.

A typical 220 F menu might start with a choice of *Huîtres de Marennes, vinaigre d'echalotes* (fresh Atlantic oysters with shallot vinegar), or *Salade homardine, vinaigrette d'agrume* (lobster salad with fresh citrus vinaigrette). The main course might be a choice between *Fricassée de langoustines et Saint-Jacques au curry de legumes* (sautéed prawns and scallops, served with curried vegetables and a cream sauce—see recipe), or *Pot au feu de poularde en croûte* (individual bowls of stuffed chicken breasts on vegetables, covered with puff pastry). This could be followed by an exceptional selection of cheeses, then pears with an almond sauce *(Gratin de poires au sabayon d'amandes).*

SIGHTS & SUCH

Provence offers many worthwhile sights—16 identified by Michelin as "worth the journey" (see the Michelin green guide *Provence*, available in English). For delightful insight into Provençal character and customs, we recommend Peter Mayle's *A Year in Provence*[12] and *Toujours Provence*[13].

SAUTÉED PRAWNS AND SCALLOPS,
SERVED WITH CURRIED VEGETABLES AND A CREAM SAUCE
Fricassée de langoustines et Saint-Jacques au curry de legumes

16 langoustine or large shrimp	8 tablespoons (100 g.) butter
16 large scallops	½ cup (10 cl.) white wine
½ lb. (250 g.) carrots	½ cup (10 cl.) cream
1 leek	1¼ cup (30 cl.) fish stock
3 stalks celery	curry powder
2 apples	salt and pepper

Cut the carrots, leeks and celery in fine juilienne. Cook them in a little of the fish stock until they are barely tender. Drain the vegetables saving the cooking liquid. Keep the vegetables warm.

Peel and cut the apples in two. Slice the apple halves in a fan shape. Place the fans in a buttered frying pan and let caramelize in a hot oven.

In a sauce pan, place the white wine, fish stock, and vegetable stock. Reduce this by half over a medium heat. Add the cream and curry powder (according to taste) and reduce by a quarter. Off the heat, gradually add the butter, cut in small pieces.

Season the langoustine and scallops with salt and pepper and sauté the seafood rapidly in a very hot frying pan.

To serve, place the vegetables in the center of the serving plates. Cover this with a apple fan. Place the seafood around this and add the sauce.

Serves 4.

★ ★ ★ ★ HOSTELLERIE DU MOULIN DE LA ROQUE, 84210 Althen-des-Paluds. Tel: 90 62 14 62. Fax: 90 62 18 50. (U.S. Agent: G in Appendix B.)

DIRECTOR: Philippe Chaléon.

ROOMS: 25, plus 2 suites, all with bath or shower, WC, direct telephone, TV, radio, mini-bar. 3 rooms have private terraces.

PRICES: Rooms: 500–1200 F ($100–240); suites: 800–1200 F ($160–240); ½-pension: 400–750 F ($80–150). Breakfast: 80 F ($16). Menus: 220–400 F ($44–80) Credit cards: AE, DC, EC, MC, Visa.

AMENITIES: Bar, lounge, garden, terrace, park, wood, fishing in canal (which passes under mill), tennis court, swimming pool, exercise equipment under trees, ping-pong, pétanque. Parking. Golf: 16 km.

ASSOCIATIONS: Moulin Étape.

MARKET DAYS: Avignon: Tue–Sun; Carpentras: Fri.

DIRECTIONS: From Avignon 17 km. NE on D942 to D89, left 0.6 km, left again to mill.

OPEN: May 15–Oct 31.

49. LA RÉGALIDO
Fontvielle, Bouche-du-Rhône, Provence

We were first attracted to La Régalido by Richard de Combray in a travel piece: "Fourteen perfect guest rooms, the best food in Provence, and a welcome that outwarms a blazing hearth," he wrote. "It's as though you had made a mistake and arrived at someone's meticulously tended home and the owner ushered you inside, thinking that you were some long-lost friend."[21]

Nona and I experienced La Régalido's welcome, and wondered how Jean-Pierre Michel could tend to his fabled kitchen and still find time to greet guests so warmly. We were also charmed by the inn—an old stone building wrapped in ivy and capped with Roman tiles, with a large, luscious garden running its full length.

This garden is Mijeanne Michel's domaine, as is the decor of the mill, which she planned with professional flair. The charming sitting room has comfortable couches and chairs grouped before a walk-in fireplace, where a log fire is lit on chilly days. Paintings and old copper adorn the walls. The bedrooms are individually decorated—no two alike. All have luxurious bathrooms; some have a terrace with a view of the picturesque old village.

The vaulted dining room, with tapestry-covered chairs and round, elegantly set tables looks out on the dining terrace and garden Here meals are served during the summer, shaded by fig and olive trees, and brightened by mimosa and roses.

It's delightful, and yet it is *not* a water mill. Jean-Pierre made this very clear to us:

"Our inn is in effect an ancient olive oil mill, of which the mill stones were turned by donkeys. It is therefore not a *moulin à eau* (water mill), nor a *moulin à vent* (windmill), like the famous mill of Fontvielle called 'moulin de Daudet,' where the celebrated poet-author wrote his famous *Lettres de Mon Moulin*. However, in one of his novels, Alphonse Daudet speaks of the 'moulin Mitifiot,' the true name of the mill where our inn is situated. Now, after the transformations, there remains only the vaulted room, our present dining room, where the presses and millstones used to be."

Never mind. When you also consider the food, it's as nice as any water mill. The only drawback is that, as a member of Relais & Châteaux, the prices are rather steep.

FOOD & WINE

Michel prepares traditional cuisine with Provençal accents (olives, olive oil, local herbs, garlic, and seafood). That he does it very well is attested by a Michelin star and a GaultMillau toque. Some typical seafood dishes: *Mousseline de loup au beurre blanc à anis* (sea bass mousseline with anis-flavored beurre blanc); *Gratin de moules de Bouzigues aux épinards* (gratinée of spinach and Bouzigues mussels. Another delicious dish substitutes snails for mussels in this recipe); *Aïgo sau* (Provençal fish soup that Michel calls "Light bouillabaisse"). Main courses, delicious but simple include a longtime Michel favorite: *Tranche de gigot au gousses d'ail confits* (leg of lamb strewn with garlic).

For dessert, Michel recommended *Glace miel – romarin* (An ice cream made with honey and rosemary—see recipe); and *Fougasse* (a sweet, orange-flavored yeast bread, a specialty of the region).

Local wines (Coteaux de Baux, Châteauneuf du Pape, and other Provençal vineyards) feature prominently on the wine list and offer good value. The list also offers fine Burgundy and Bordeaux, at higher prices. As usual, we recommend the local vineyards.

SIGHTS & SUCH

The Moulin de Daudet, referred to by Michel, sits just outside of town, a sort of museum which merits a visit. And within a radius of 50 kilometers are five sights which Michelin rates three-star (merits a journey): Les Baux-de-Provence, the Roman Arles and Nîmes, Avignon, and the Pont-du-Gard. Two stars (worth a detour) include the Camargue, with flamingos, horses, and cowboys. See the Michelin green tourist guide *Provence*.

HONEY–ROSEMARY ICE CREAM
Glace miel–romarin

It is rather unusual to be served ice cream flavored with herbs. Here is an ice cream with the illusive flavor of rosemary.

10 egg yolks	6 sprigs rosemary
¼ cup (50 g.) sugar	8 oz. (250 g.) honey
1 quart (1 liter) milk	

Beat the egg yolks and sugar until they become light and creamy.

Bring the milk to a boil. Add the rosemary and steep or infuse for 15 minutes. Strain, add the milk to the egg-sugar mixture and cook until this coats the spoon.

Cool mixture and freeze in ice cream maker.

Serve decorated with small spring of rosemary.   Serves 6.

★★★★ La RÉGALIDO, rue Frédéric Mistral, 13990 Fontvieille Tel: 90 54 60 22. Fax: 90 54 64 29.

PROPRIETORS: Jean-Pierre and Mijeanne Michel. CHEF: Jean-Pierre Michel.

ROOMS: 15, including some suites, all with bath, WC, direct telephone, TV.

PRICES: Rooms: 650–1400 F ($130–280); ½-pension: 850–1100 F ($170–220). Breakfast: 90 F ($18). Menus: 160 F ($32–lunch, wine incl.), 300–390 F ($60–78), children 130 F ($26). Credit cards: AE, CB, DC, EC, MC, Visa.

AMENITIES: Bar, lounge, garden, terrace, parking. Dining inside, or on terrace. Swimming: 1 km. Tennis: 1 km. Golf: 8 km.

ASSOCIATIONS: Relais & Châteaux.

MARKET DAYS: Fontvieille: Mon, Fri; Arles: Wed, Sat.

DIRECTIONS: In center of village, 9 km. NE of Arles.

OPEN: Feb 1–Dec 31; Restaurant closed: Tue lunch (except Jul–Sep); Mon.

50. LE VIEUX MOULIN
Remoulin, Gard, Languedoc

From the shaded terraces that flank the old mill, the Pont du Gard seems near enough to touch, though it's 200 yards away—a majestic, two-tier aqueduct striding 960 feet across the Gardon River and its canyon. From the dining room—through an arched window that matches the Roman arches in the aqueduct—the bridge seems closer still. Also through the arched windows in some of the bedrooms, and from the private beach below the inn, you see the imposing, 2,000-year-old stone structure. At night it's illuminated, looking like a Hollywood set. It dominates and shelters the old flour mill, in a restful way.

Two of the rooms look out to the Pont du Gard; others view the terrace, the shaded parking area, or the Gardon River. All are furnished in a comfortable Provençal style.

FOOD & WINE

The large dining room has deep ceiling beams, a checkerboard floor of gray and brick tiles, and mullioned windows. Cream-colored walls display pictures. Shelves and cupboard display antique bric-a-brac and copper items: molds, bowls, and bed warmers. A bar sits opposite the arched window. Tables, round or square, are covered in pale yellow and served by ladder-backed, wicker-seat chairs. A comfortable room in which to enjoy a traditional cuisine made and served with local wines.

During our first dinner—I don't know whether it was in honor of our visit—the music system quietly played Tommy Dorsey tunes. We started our dinner with the famous melon of Cavaillon: *Petit melon de Cavaillon rafraîchi au Beaume de Venise, copeau de bacon et menthe fraîche* (Melon with Beaume de Venise, Slivers of Smoked Ham, and Fresh Mint). Cavaillon melon is the super cantaloupe that Alexandre Dumas loved so much, that he donated to the library at Cavaillon some 190 books, including all of his own works, in exchange for a lifetime supply of the melon. Director Raymond Aparis sent us the recipe for this dish and several others, two of which we include below.

Another pleasant starter course: *Courgette fleur farci de la mousse de truite du Gardon, beurre de cerfeuil* (zucchini blossoms stuffed with trout mousse, with chervil butter). A delightful main course is the *Tian de filet d'agneau au confit de legumes Provençaux, jus des garrigues* (Gratin of Lamb Filet with Preserved Provençal Vegetables). And for dessert: *Tarte Tatin de pêches de Provence, sorbet et coulis à la framboise* (Provençal Peach Tart, with Raspberry Sorbet and Sauce).

The cellar specializes in regional wines, such as the Coteaux du Pont du Gard.

SIGHTS & SUCH

The most-important sight is, of course, the Pont du Gard. There's a one-way auto bridge at the lower level of the aqueduct, and you can step from the bridge to the Pont over an 18-inch chasm that's a bit unnerving. The braver souls can climb and walk along the top level of the Pont. Or, you can sit at an umbrella table in the mill's terrace with an apéritif and watch other tourists brave the heights.

Sights in the area are many: the cities of Avignon, Nîmes, Arles, and Usès; the Camargue, the Baux, the Alpilles, and numerous other choice points. See Michelin's green tourist guide *Provence*.

MELON WITH BEAUME DE VENISE, SLIVERS OF SMOKED HAM, AND FRESH MINT
Petit melon de Cavaillon rafraîchi au Beaume de Venise
copeau de bacon et menthe fraîche

The petits melons of Cavaillon are a great favorite with the French. Although they look like small cantaloupe, they are sweeter and with more perfume. A ripe canteloupe can be used instead but the results aren't quite the same. The Beaume de Venise is a sweet, fragrant wine from Provence. A muscat wine can be substituted.

However you get there, this is a refreshing first course in the summertime.

6 small melons	3 oz. (8 cl) Beaume de Venise
6 oz. (180 g.) prosciutto	Fresh mint leaves

Cut off the top of the melons and remove the seeds. With a melon baller, remove the flesh from inside the melon. Pour the wine over the balls. Refill the shells, placing pieces of prosciutto between the melon balls. Decorate with mint leaves. Place in refrigerator and keep cold until time to serve.   Serves 6.

GRATIN OF LAMB FILET WITH PRESERVED PROVENÇAL VEGETABLES
Tian de filet d'agneau au confit
de legumes Provençaux, jus des garrigues

1½ lbs.(600 g.) lamb filet	4 cloves garlic
1½ lbs (600 g.) zucchini	fresh basil
¾ lb. (300 g.) eggplant	branch of thyme
3 tomatoes	½ cup (12 cl.) veal stock
¼ cup (6 cl.) white wine	2 tablespoons butter

Salt and pepper the lamb filets and sauté in a hot frying pan along with the garlic and branch of thyme. When the meat is cooked rare, remove to a plate deep enough to collect the juice or blood from the cooked meat.

Peel the eggplant and cut in rounds 2 inches (5 cm.) thick. Sauté in olive oil and season with salt and pepper. Do the same with the zucchini.

Peel, halve, and seed the tomatoes. Mash the half tomato with your hands.

Place six 4-in. (10-cm.) pastry rings or 6 small casseroles on a baking sheet. Layer the eggplant, the zucchini and then the thinly sliced basil leaves in the molds. Top with a crushed tomato half. Cut the lamb into thin slices and make a circle of meat on top of the filled molds. Heat in a medium oven 375°F (190°C) for 5 minutes.

In the meantime, reduce the veal stock by a fourth. Add the juice from the lamb and the butter. Keep warm.

To serve, unmold each tian on a warmed plate and pour the sauce around it.

Serves 6.

★★★ LE VIEUX MOULIN, Vers-Pont-du-Gard, 30210 Remoulins. Tel: 66 37 14 35. Fax: 66 37 26 48.

DIRECTOR: Raymond Aparis. CHEF: Roger Cuinier.

ROOMS: 18, all rooms with direct telephone; 11 with bath or shower and WC; 5 with bath or shower, with a WC on the same floor; 2 with WC. Two have a view of the Pont, others of the terrace, parking area, or Gardon River.

PRICES: Rooms: 150–495 F ($30–99); ½-pension: 295–468 F ($59–94). Breakfast: 60 F ($12). Menus: 125–185 F ($25–37). Credit cards: AE, DC, EC, MC, Visa.

AMENITIES: Bar, TV salon, lounge, garden, terrace, park, Gardon River. Dining inside, or on terrace, both with view of pont and river. Private beach with fishing, swimming, canoeing. Tennis, golf, riding, nearby. Parking.

ASSOCIATIONS: Moulin Étape; Châteaux et Hôtels Indépendants.

MARKET DAYS: Avignon: Tue to Fri, Sun; Nîmes: Tue, Fri.

DIRECTIONS: From Avignon, N100 W 22 km. to Remoulins; W on D981 3 km; left toward Pont du Gard.

OPEN: Mar 15–Nov 1; Restaurant closed: Mon.

51. AUBERGE DU PONT ROMAIN
Sommières, Gard, Languedoc-Rousillon

There's not another water-mill inn like it. From the outside, the Auberge du Pont Romain looks like a large factory building, complete with factory chimney. Perhaps that's because it *was* a factory. In the mid-19th century, the mill manufactured carpets. Then, in 1876, silkworms were raised in part of the immense premises. This led to hosiery manufacture and dyeing. Later, it became a distillery. The austere façade has most of its windows plastered over. This resulted from the traditional disinclination to pay taxes, and the fact that the government computed the tax based upon the number of openings in the building.

But step inside, to the flowered courtyard, to the garden—trees, flowers, pool, terraces—to the shady park from which you can contemplate the Roman bridge, and you're in another world.

The Roman bridge dates from Emperor Tiberius' reign. It was completed in the year one! You can see it from some garden-side rooms (e.g. room eight), and if the huge and comfortable rooms lack a garden view, they probably have a view of the medieval city.

The public rooms include a bar and lounge, and three dining rooms with comfortable cane chairs, tables set with fine china, silver, crystal, and flowers, and large windows opening onto the garden. There is also an exposition of carpet samples from the original factory. (The inn won a 1991 competition as "The hotel best preserving the national heritage.")

FOOD & WINE

Chef Michel produces an elaborate, inventive cuisine. One of his favorite dishes is *Filets de sole en feuillantine sauce Lawrence Durrell* (stuffed filet of sole in puff pastry, with Lawrence Durrell sauce). While awaiting the arrival of the English writer for dinner one evening, the chef was skimming through Durrell's *Smile of the Tao*. Suddenly, he took some leeks, and cut them into fine slices like the Taoist philosopher, and proceeded to create the new sauce, which he dedicated to his inspirer (see recipe). Another favorite is *Foie gras de canard mi-cuit de la maison* (lightly cooked duck liver, also available for off-sale purchase). He is proud of his dessert cart, which includes a delicious coconut and honey tart called *Soleîado*.

Other spécialités: *Ris de veau au vin de cerise* (veal sweetbreads in cherry sauce); *Escargots au Roquefort* (snails with Roquefort cheese sauce); and *Terrine de canard aux myrtilles* (terrine of duck and blueberries).

Wines to note: Costière du Gard, Domaine de l'Amarine (dry white); Coteaux du Languedoc, Brugière (red); and Muscat de Lunel, Clos Bellevue (dessert).

SIGHTS & SUCH

There is much to do in the inn's park: swim, fish, canoe, exercise. Sightseeing nearby: the village; the Pont du Gard (See Chapter 50); Nîmes, the Camargue, the sea, and the Cévennes (see Michelin's green guide *Provence*).

STUFFED FILET OF SOLE IN PUFF PASTRY
SAUCE LAWRENCE DURRELL
Filets de sole en feuillantine sauce Lawrence Durrell

Sauce:

3 oz. (9 cl.) white wine	½ leek, mostly white
3 oz. (9 cl.) muscat wine	2 stalks celery
1½ cups (350 g.) crème fraîche	2 oz. (60 g.) mushrooms
or whipping cream	parsley
3 tablespoons olive oil	1 small carrot
½ bunch watercress	½ teaspoon cinnamon
1 large shallot	

Chop the vegetables fine and sweat them in a large frying pan with the olive oil. Add the white wine and muscat and reduce by half. Add the cream, season with salt and cinnamon and purée in a blender or food processor. Bring to a boil and set aside.

Sole:

1 lb. (500 g.) filet of sole	3 stalks celery
1 package puff pastry	½ teaspoon mustard seeds
1 egg yolk	1 bunch spinach, washed
1 small carrot	½ cup (12 cl.) cream
1 shallot	salt, pepper, cumin and ginger
½ bunch watercress	2 cups (50 cl.) white wine

Cut the filet of sole into 8 pieces. Set aside.

Chop all the vegetables fine, place in a frying pan and sweat in the olive oil. Add the mustard seed and 2 cups white wine. Reduce until almost dry. Add the cream. Season with salt, pepper, cumin and ginger. Cool and place in the refrigerator.

Cut the puff pastry into eight 4-inch (10-cm.) rounds. Place a piece of sole on each of 4 rounds of pastry. Top each with the vegetable stuffing and then another piece of sole on top. Place the four other rounds of pastry on top, sealing the edges with beaten egg yolk. Paint the tops of the pastry with the rest of the egg yolk. Bake 20 to 25 minutes in a 425°F (330°C) oven

Cook the spinach in 1 tablespoon butter. Make a bed of spinach on each plate and serve the stuffed pastry on the spinach.

Serves 4.

★★★ L'AUBERGE DU PONT ROMAIN, 2 rue Emile-Jamais, 30250 Sommière.
Tel: 66 80 00 58. Fax: 66 80 31 52.
PROPRIETORS: Monique & Bernard Michel. CHEF: Bernard Michel.
ROOMS: 19, all with bath or shower, direct telephone, air cond.; 16 with WC.
PRICES: Rooms: 265–450 F ($53–90); ½-pension: 325–420 F ($65–84). Breakfast:
45 F ($9). Menus: 155–225 F ($31–45). Credit cards: AE, CB, DC, Visa.
AMENITIES: Bar, lounge, terrace, garden, Vidourle River. Parking. Fishing,
swimming pool, table tennis, canoeing, aqua-gym, sauna. Bicycle rental. Tennis
1 km. Golf, riding: 8 km.
ASSOCIATIONS: Châteaux et Hôtels Indépendants.
MARKET DAYS: Sommières: Sat; Nîmes: Mon, Fri: Montpellier: Tue–Sat.
DIRECTIONS: From Nîmes, 28 km. SW on D40 to Sommières.
OPEN: Mar 15–Oct 31, Dec 12–jan 14. Restaurant closed: Wed (exc. Jun 15–Sep 15).

52. LE MOULIN D'ALEXANDRE
Sainte-Eulalie d'Olt, Aveyron, Languedoc

You probably have not heard of Sainte-Eulalie d'Olt, on the Lot River (the Lot used to be the Olt). Annie Candoré—and Nathalie Mouriès[35]—describe it as "one of the most beautiful medieval villages of France." And the Moulin d'Alexandre sits right in the middle of it. This 320-year-old water mill—really two mills—is named after the present owners, M. and Mme Alexandre, who purchased and refurbished it in 1980. The result is a modest, but pleasant and comfortable hotel and restaurant.

The smallish guest rooms have television, direct telephone, bath or shower, and wc. The mill wheel turns (not too noisily), and other machinery is in a usable state—machinery is a "passion" of your host.

The terrace is good sized, with umbrella tables to ward off the Midi sun. The dining room has stone arches in the Roman style, open beamed ceilings, tiled floors, antique tables and chairs, and typical French flowered wall paper—a pleasant room in which to enjoy Alexandre's offerings.

FOOD & WINE

The menu includes several regional specialties: *Confit de canard aux cèpes* (Duck confit with boletus mushrooms); *Cassoulet maison*— whether you like cassoulet in the Toulousain or the Castelnaudry style, you'll like Alexandre's; and for dessert, *Mille feuilles aux fraises avec son coulis* (Napoleon with strawberries and strawberry coulis—see recipe).

Other specialties: *Salade aux deux truites* (salad with both fresh and smoked trout); and *Terrine de foie gras maison.* He also makes a *Pâté de marcassin* (a terrine of young wild boar); and duck in various guises—galantine, magret smoked or with green peppercorns, and confit with cèpes. The menu contains roughly 30 items.

Among the regional wines in Alexandre's cellar: Marcillac Rouge, and Galliac Perlé Blanc—both "Cuvée du Patron."

SIGHTS & SUCH

Sainte-Eulalie d'Olt is in a little green valley, surrounded by hills wooded with oaks and chestnuts—a village of 310 inhabitants, clustered around the 15th-century Château de Curières de Castelnau. The church is a fine work of Roman and Gothic art. And walking the old, flower-bordered streets is a delight.

You are in the center of wondrous things. To the west you have the lovely Lot Valley, and the Gorges du Lot. To the southeast, the three-star Gorges du Tarn—a smaller, greener Grand Canyon. Throughout the area, you find interesting caves, rivers and rocky ridges. See Michelin's *Gorges du Tarn/Cévennes/Bas Languedoc.*

NAPOLEON WITH STRAWBERRIES AND STRAWBERRY COULIS
Milles feuilles aux fraises avec son coulis

1 pkg. (500 g.) puff pastry	2½ cups strawberries
3 oz. (90 g.) sugar	2 cups (50 cl.) crème fraîche
crème pâtissière*	or thick whipping cream
	powdered sugar

Roll each sheet of puff pastry to the size 10 by 12 in. (25 by 30 cm.) Cut 12 discs, 4 in. (10 cm.) in diameter. Sprinkle with sugar and prick top with a fork. Bake at 400°F (200°C) until lightly

browned.
Make a crème pâtissière* and cool. Set aside.
Cut 1 cup of strawberries into halves or quarters.
Whip the cream and 1/3 cup (90 g.) sugar until stiff
Purée the remaining strawberries, adding sugar to taste.
To assemble, place one disc on each plate. Top with the crème
pâtissière. Add another disc. Top this with the strawberries and the
whipped cream. Top with the last disc and sprinkle with powdered
sugar. Surround the pastry with the strawberry coulis.

Serves 6.

* *See Appendix C.*

★★ LE MOULIN D'ALEXANDRE, Sainte-Eulalie d'Olt, 12130 Saint-Geniez-d'Olt. Tel: 65 47 45 85.
PROPRIETORS: M. & Mme Alexandre. CHEF: M. Alexandre
ROOMS: 9, all with bath or shower and WC, direct telephone, TV, air cond., mini-bar, safe.
PRICES: Rooms: 230–280 F ($46–56); ½-pension: 210–260 F ($41–52). Breakfast: 40 F ($8). Menus: 85–130 F ($17–26). Credit cards: None.
AMENITIES: Bar, lounge, garden, terrace, river, punts. Parking. Tennis: in the village. Swimming, bicycles, riding: 2.5 km. Golf: 25 km.
ASSOCIATIONS: Moulin Étape.
MARKET DAYS: Laissac: Tue.
DIRECTIONS: From Toulouse N88, NE 177 km. to Rodez; then D988 NE and E 42 km. to Sainte-Eulalie d'Olt. The mill is in the center of the village.
OPEN: All year; Restaurant closed: Sun dinner (Nov 1–Easter).

53–58. ADDITIONAL SOUTHEAST FAVORITES

53. MOULIN DE VILLEROZE
Riom, Puy-de-Dôme, Auvergne

Juvigny's polished and inventive cuisine gets better every year, and
GaultMillau has awarded him a toque. Well worth the short detour
from Clermont-Ferrand. (Restaurant only.)

★★ MOULIN DE VILLEROZE, 144 Route de Marrsat, 63200 Riom.
   Tel: 73 38 58 23. Fax: 73 38 01 84.
CHEF: Dominique Juvigny.
PRICES: Menus: 145–320 F ($29–64). Credit cards: AE, DC, EC, MC, Visa.
AMENITIES: Bar, lounge, terrace on the edge of the Ambène River. Dining inside,
   or on terrace.
DIRECTIONS: From Clermont-Ferrand, 9 km. N on N9 to Riom; 2.5 km. SW on
   D83.
OPEN: Sep 1–Aug 15; Restaurant closed: Sun dinner, Mon.

54. AUBERGE DU MOULIN DE CIVADOUX
Sauxillanges, Puy-de-Dôme, Auvergne

A very nice restaurant in a very modest, very welcoming family inn. They raise their own trout, and prepare them well. Wines of Boudes and Saint-Pourçain.

★ AUBERGE DU MOULIN DE CIVADOUX, Route de Saint-Genès-Tourette, 63490 Saint-Quentin-sur-Sauxillanges. Tel: 73 96 81 94.
PROPRIETORS: M. & Mme Domarle. CHEF: Mlle Béatrice Domarle.
ROOMS: 3, plus 4 individual chalets, all with WC, some with bath or shower.
PRICES: ½-pension 175–225 F ($35–45); Menus: 59–175 F ($12–35). Credit cards: AE, EC, MC, Visa.
AMENITIES: Bar, lounge, terrace, pond. Trout and salmon fishing. Riding. Tennis 2 km. Parking.
DIRECTIONS: From Clermont-Ferrand, A75 S to Issoire, then W 15 km. to Sauxillanges.
OPEN: Feb 10–Jan 11. Restaurant closed: Mon, except Jul–Aug.

---

55. AUBERGE DU MOULIN DE RONGEFER
Charlieu, Loire, Rhône-Alps

Chef Alain Barret prepares imaginative and delicious fare, served in a charming, comfortable rustic dining room, or on the flowered terrace. (One toque. Restaurant only.)

★★★ AUBERGE DU MOULIN DE RONGEFER, Saint-Nizier-sous-Charlieu 42190 Charlieu. Tel: 77 60 01 57.
CHEF: Alain Barret.
PRICES: Menus: 95 F ($19–week days & Sat lunch); 160–310 F ($32–62). Credit cards: CB, Visa.
AMENITIES: Bar, terrace. Parking. Dining inside, or on terrace.
DIRECTIONS: From Lyon, 84 km. NW on N7 to Roanne, then 15 km. N on D482 to Pouilly, right 1 km. on D4 to St-Nizier.
OPEN: Mar 1–Jul 31, Aug 21–Jan 31. Restaurant closed: Sun & Tue dinner; Wed.

56. LA GUARIBOTE
Le Gua-Joyeuse, Ardèche, Rhône-Alps

Located in a chestnut grove, in a beautiful valley on the edge of the Beaume River. Part of the mill dates from the 13th century. Fine, innovative cuisine using local products.

★★ LA GUARIBOTE, Le Gua, Route de Valgorge, 07260 Joyeuse. Tel: 75 39 44 09 Fax: 75 39 55 89.
PROPRIETOR: M. Hervé Garnier.
ROOMS: 12, in modern wooden chalets on the grounds. Rooms with bath or shower, WC, and private terraces or balconies.
PRICES: Rooms: 260–290 F ($52–58). ½-pension: 300 F ($60). Breakfast: 40 F ($8). Menus: 112–295 F ($23–59), children: 65 F ($13). Credit cards: AE, DC, EC, MC, Visa.
AMENITIES: Bar, lounge, terrace, Beaume River (swimming from pebbled beach), woods, hiking, fishing. M. Garnier, a pilot, can take you on an aerial tour of the region. Parking.
DIRECTIONS: From Lyon, 135 km. S on A7 to N104. W on N104/D104 70 km. to Joyeuse, 12 km. N on D203 to Le Gua.
OPEN: Easter–Sep 30.

57. LE MOULIN DE LOURMARIN
Lourmarin, Vaucluse, Provence

The village, the olive-oil mill, the reception, all are exquisite. And the restaurant has earned two GaultMillau toques. Rooms are a bit pricey, but worth it. An unusual and tasty recipe follows.

SAUTÉED RED MULLET WITH BRAISED CHINESE CABBAGE, ANCHOVY, AND ZEST OF ORANGE
Rouget de roche poêlé au lard gras étuvé de choux chinois léger jus à l'anchois et écorces d'oranges

6 filets of fish (rock fish,   2 oranges
    red snapper)   1 tablespoon cream
6 leaves of Chinese cabbage   3½ oz. (10 cl.) fish stock

| 12 slices thin sliced bacon | 20 anchovy filets, finely chopped |
| 7 tablespoons (75 g.) butter | salt, pepper, sugar, olive oil |

To prepare the fish, lard each filet with a slice of bacon running the length of the fish. Hold in place with wooden toothpicks. Save the rest of the bacon to use with the cabbage.

Prepare the cabbage leaves by washing them and cutting them in small cubes. Cut the bacon in small cubes also.

Remove the zest from the oranges, cutting in fine julienne. Juice the oranges and set the juice aside.

In a large frying pan, sauté the cabbage and the bacon together. When cooked, deglaze the pan with a drop or two of olive oil and half the orange juice. Set aside.

In the same pan, add a little olive oil and sauté the fish. Cook one side only, over high heat, bacon side down. Remove when the bacon is crisp and fish is half cooked.

In the same pan, heat the anchovy. Add the rest of the orange juice, the fish stock and cream. Let this reduce. Enrich the stock by adding the butter, cut in small pieces. Do this over very low heat, adding pieces of butter slowly to form a emulsion. Correct the seasoning and add a little more orange juice if needed.

To serve, make a bed of cabbage and bacon on the warmed plates. Top this with the fish (removing tooth picks first). Decorate the edge of the plate with the orange zest. Spoon sauce over the fish.

Serves 6.

★★★★ LE MOULIN DE LOURMARIN, Rue du Temple, 84160 Lourmarin. Tel 90 68 06 69. Fax: 90 68 31 76.

PROPRIETORS: M. & Mme Claude Loubet. CHEF: Edouard Loubet-Croix.

ROOMS: 20, plus 2 suites, all with bath or shower, WC, direct telephone, TV, mini-bar, air conditioning.

PRICES: Rooms: 750–1900 F ($150–380); suites: 1600–2600 F ($320–520); ½-pension: 800–950 F ($160–190). Breakfast: 85 F ($17). Menus: 180–320 F ($36–64). Credit cards: AE, CB, DC, EC, MC, Visa.

AMENITIES: Bar, lounge, garden, terrace, sauna, parking. Dining inside, or on terrace. Swimming: 2 km. Tennis: 1 km. Golf: 18 km. Riding: 4 km.

MARKET DAYS: Lourmarin: Fri; Bonnieux: Fri; Lambesc: Fri; Aix-en-Provence: every day but Wed.

DIRECTIONS: From Marseille or Aix-en-Provence, take A51 N to Pertuis exit. From Pertuis, 12 km. W on D973 to Cadenet, then 4.5 km. N on D943 to Lourmarin.

OPEN: Feb 15–Jan 1. Restaurant closed: Tue (except Jul–Aug).

58. HOSTELLERIE DU VIEUX CHÂTEAU
Sérignan-du-Comtat, Vaucluse, Provence

The millrace still runs under the restaurant of this peaceful inn. Try their *lotte* (monkfish) with raspberry vinegar, and their duck breast with cassis. (The inn dates from 1991, and the government is still in the process of classifying it—the three stars are our best guess as to the outcome.)

★ ★ ★ HOSTELLERIE DU VIEUX CHÂTEAU, Route de Sainte-Cécile, 84830 Sérignan-du-Comtat. Tel: 90 70 05 58. Fax: 90 70 05 62.
PROPRIETORS: M. & Mme Jean-Pierre Truchot.
ROOMS: 7, all with bath, WC, direct telephone, TV.
PRICES: Rooms: 400–800 F ($80–160); ½-pension: 380–580 F ($76–116). Breakfast: 45 F ($9). Menus: 145–350 F ($29–70), children 60 F ($12). Credit cards: AE, CB, EC, MC, Visa.
AMENITIES: Bar, lounge, terrace, park, Béal River, pond, woods. Swimming pool. Tennis, riding, golf nearby. Parking.
ASSOCIATIONS: Moulin Étape.
MARKET DAYS: Orange: Thu; Bollène: Mon.
DIRECTIONS: From Orange, 7 km. N on A7.
OPEN: Dec 31–Dec 18; Restaurant closed: Sun dinner, Mon (out of season).

IV. SOUTHWEST FRANCE

The Southwest (as defined here) is bounded by the Charente and the Limousin on the North, the Pyrénées on the South, the Atlantic Ocean on the west, and the western edge of the Massif Central/Tarn/Languedoc on the East. Thus the area includes the Périgord; the prehistoric caves of the Dordogne; three great rivers: the Dordogne, the Garonne, and the Lot; the Gironde, formed by the confluence of the first two rivers, and hence Bordeaux and the wine country; Gascony, home of Dumas' d'Artagnan; and finally, the French portion of the Basque region.

THE DORDOGNE (LIMOUSIN/PÉRIGORD/QUERCY): This area is distinguished by rolling hills and sheer cliffs ascending from beautiful meadows or valleys—the cliffs often capped by a castle or hamlet. The region includes prehistoric caves, with well-preserved wall paintings, numerous villages rated officially among *Les Plus Beaux Villages de France,* of which there are fewer than 100 in the whole country, and, of course, the Dordogne and Lot rivers.

Limoges is the capital of Limousin, a large, sprawling city famous for porcelain and enamel ware. It is still attractive in its old quarter, with numerous interesting houses, and, on the rue de la Boucherie, a tiny square and chapel dedicated to Saint Aurélien, patron saint of the butchers.

Leaving Limoges, continue south through the unspoiled green countryside. You quickly reach the mysterious region of Black Périgord, home of the black truffle and *foie gras d'oie* or *canard* (fatted liver of goose or duck). When the foie gras is "harvested," the rest of the goose, and the legs of the duck, are preserved in their own fat, making *confits.* The fileted breast of the duck is sold separately as *magret de canard.*

Excellent wine is made in the lower Dordogne, near Bergerac. On the left bank of the Lot River, west of Cahors they make a deep red wine from the Malbec grape (the "black wine of Cahors").

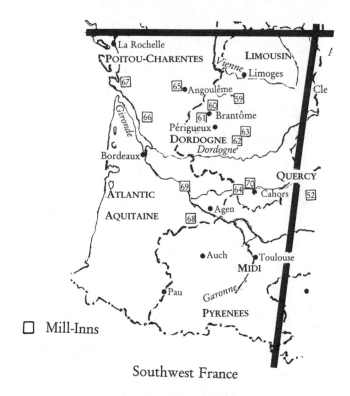

Southwest France

☐ Mill-Inns

Wine is made on the Côtes-de-Fronton, just north of Toulouse. As we keep saying, although grands crus may be available, it is worthwhile to try the local wines, often very enjoyable, and little-known in the United States.

THE ATLANTIC (CHARENTES, GIRONDE, LANDES/GASCONY, PYRÉNÉES-MARITIMES): The Charente has several interesting cities with a lot of history: La Rochelle, with a fascinating harbor; Saintes and Angoulème, with ancient walls and old towns; Royan, with sand beaches and mussel growers. Perhaps the most-interesting, with respect to food and drink, is Cognac, where the best brandy in the world is made. The famous Cognac manufacturers clustered here welcome visitors for tasting and, they hope, purchasing.

The Gironde, the large estuary formed where the Dordogne and Garonne rivers meet, means Bordeaux and its fabulous wines. The region produces more than 400 million bottles annually, about half of the total French A.O.C. wine production. Many of the vineyards welcome visitors for tours and tasting (see the current issue of Michelin's green guide *Pyrénées/Aquitaine,* or any good book on French wines (cf. Bibliography). Bordeaux is much more than the center of a wine industry; it is the capital of Aquitaine, and well worth a visit, even if you don't drink wine. (See Michelin's guide.)

The food of the Bordeaux region, the cuisine Bordelaise, depends largely on fish from the Gironde (shad, salmon, eel, mussels), often served with a *sauce Bordelaise:* a red-wine sauce with shallots, a bit of Cognac, white pepper, thyme, nutmeg, and beef marrow.

The Landes de Gascogne, or Gascony, is famous, due to many novels by Dumas and others featuring poor young men, such as d'Artagnan, who could find no other way to fame or fortune than with their sword. Extending from the Gironde to the Pyrénées, the Côte d'Argent, or silver coast, used to be a region of sand dunes and marshes, and now is long stretches of sandy beaches, with numerous small lakes and forests of pine. The Côtes-de-Buzet, west of Agen, produces palatable wine and Armagnac, a brandy rivaling Cognac.

59. LE MOULIN DE LA GORCE
La Roche-l'Abeille, Haute-Vienne, Limousin

The Moulin de la Gorce is *really* special. First, there's the setting: around the end of a small lake, in a forest-ringed valley, with the lake fed by a rushing trout stream and furnished with ducks. Then there's the much-starred and -toqued restaurant. And finally, the friendly and happy Bertranet family.

Built in 1569, the Moulin de la Gorce ground grain until the 1970's. Jean Bertranet and his wife Annie converted it to a restaurant in 1979, extending it to a luxurious hotel three years later. Bertranet, an eminent Limoges *pâtissier-traiteur* (Pastry and delicatessen chef), wanted to expand his culinary horizons. By 1982, he had earned a Michelin star, and by 1985 had a second; he also has two GaultMillau toques. The Bertranet's daughter, Mme Brémont, and her husband Ives complete the family. The ladies work the office and dining rooms, the men the kitchen—Ives Brémont is sous-chef.

Bertranet restored the buildings beautifully, and chose to make some rooms rustic and ornate, others light and modern. For example, one of two dining rooms has light-colored walls and ceiling, dark blue carpeting, and modern tables, cloaked in white. Chairs have white fabric cushions and seat backs. Each table has candelabra with white candles, blue-and-white plates, and sparkling crystal. A beautiful, light, airy room.

The other dining room is the acme of elegant rusticity—open-beamed ceiling above stone walls, large stone fireplace, simulated-flagstone floor. Pink linen covers ten round and oval tables. The chairs are covered in linen, with flowers that pick up the pink. In one corner a wooden staircase leads to a balcony with more tables. Shelves display faience and stainless serving pieces, and more faience, small paintings, and tapestries decorate the walls. The inn sells the tapestries—reproductions of ancient works, primarily hunting scenes.

The nine bedrooms show a similar contrast. Some have white walls and ceiling, blue carpeting, white-covered beds, and a miscellany of antique tables and chairs—a pleasant example of sumptuous simplicity. Some bedrooms have open-beamed ceilings and antique canopied beds, the canopies in a flowered print, sitting on carpeting with a different flowered print. Chairs are covered with still another print. And on the walls, tapestries with colors that clash with all of the other prints. An incredible ensemble that only the French would have the courage to try. Walls of these ornate rooms are sometimes a solid color, sometimes still another pattern.

Guests can dine in either dining room or, weather permitting, on the lakeside terrace—it's especially nice to take breakfast or tea by the lake and watch the ducks and the fat carp. At tea, ask for the *tuiles amandes*, "almond tiles," which are large, lacy cookies shaped like roof tiles—delicious, and so thin that they can blow away in a light breeze. Altogether a most pleasant inn.

FOOD & WINE

Among the few regional Limousin specialties on Bertranet's menu: *Les oeufs brouillés aux truffes dans leur coque* (eggs scrambled with truffles); *Foie gras frais de canard, cuit en terrine au Moulin* (duck liver terrine), and *Lièvre à la Royale* (rabbit or hare "Royale"). This has two forms: hare stuffed with vegetables and liver, or pieces of rabbit with basil *(Les Noisettes de lapereau "façon Royale" au basilic)*. Another regional dish, and an excellent one, is *Le Médaillon de ris de veau à l'eminçé d'artichauts* (sweetbreads with artichokes). Finally, try the following dish, which is delicious but unusual in the United States: *Joues de porc mijotées aux senteurs de romarin* (cheeks of pork, stewed in red wine with rosemary—see recipe).

Bertranet always has an excellent selection of regional cheeses, and you can't go wrong with any of this *pâtissier's* desserts. We like particularly the *millefeuille craquant au chocolat* (Napoleon with chocolate).

The wine cellar is large and varied, with many wines offering good value. Included are an excellent Sancerre, and an exceptional Cahors. Gourmets from Limoges frequently make the journey to La Roche-l'Abeille for dinner, which goes to explain why Le Moulin de la Gorce has 80 place settings, with guest rooms for only for 18 or so.

SIGHTS & SUCH

Several battles during the Hundred Years War took place near La Roche-l'Abeille (which translates as the rock of the bees). In fact, on June 25, 1569, the same year the mill was built, a major battle took place near the road leading to the mill's lake. The Protestants—led by Coligny and accompanied by sixteen-year-old Henry of Navarre (the future King Henry IV)—routed the Catholics, with many casualties. At that time, bee culture was an important industry in the area, and legend says that the bees attacked the Catholic soldiers and put them to flight. It may be possible today to see descendants of those bees.

Those not interested in bees can fish in the lake or the stream (the chef may prepare the catch). Walks through the countryside are pleasant. Limoges is only 30 kilometers to the north, on the Vienne River. There's an important château, a large museum, and enamel and porcelain factories, (see the Michelin green guide *Berry/Limousin*).

At Arnac-Pompadour, 35 kilometers south and east of the mill, sits the château of Madame de Pompadour (a gift from Louis XV—it gave her title, although she never lived there). A prominent national stud farm occupies the château and its stables. Only 12 kilometers away (south on D704) is Saint-Yrieix-la-Perche, a pleasant market town which boasts an excellent porcelain museum. Limoges owes its fame as a porcelain center to Saint-Yrieix. It was here that deposits of pure white clay were discovered in the 18th century—clay as fine as that of China. Also at Saint-Yrieix is the Collégiale du Moûtier, dating from the 11th century, with a mixture of Roman and gothic art.

A 37-km excursion leaves Saint-Yrieix to the NW on D901, to the tiny village of Le Chalard, with an 11th-century church and lovely views over the Limousin countryside. Then on to Ladignac-le-Long, which boasts a Roman church with octagonal bell tower. Take D11 south to Jumilhac-le-Grand, which has an imposing 13th-century château, containing interesting furnishings and sculptures. Highways D78/D18/D704 return you to La Roche-l'Abeille and the Moulin de la Gorce in time for an apéritif and a *tuile* by the lake.

CHEEKS OF PORK, STEWED IN RED WINE WITH ROSEMARY
Joues de porc mijotées aux senteurs de romarin

Here's a different dish. Only a great chef could come up with such a tasty use of this small, almost unknown piece of meat. Try it—you'll like it.

30 pork cheeks (2 lbs.—1 kg.)	3 qts. (3 l.) meat stock
1 qt. (1 l.) red wine	rosemary, thyme, bay leaf

Garniture:

2 carrots, diced	½ onion, diced
1 leek, thinly sliced	

Trim the pork cheeks of fat. Brown the meat in a large, lightly greased frying pan. When nicely colored, remove the meat and add the garniture. Sauté over low heat until the vegetables soften. Add the wine and deglaze the pan. Bring to a boil and reduce. Return the pork cheeks, and add the rosemary, thyme, bay leaf and meat stock. Cook gently until meat is very tender (1 to 1½ hours). Remove the meat to a dish and keep warm. Reduce the liquid by half. Strain, forcing some of the vegetables through the strainer to thicken the sauce. Return the meat to the sauce, heat, and season with salt and pepper.

Serves 6.

★★★ LE MOULIN DE LA GORCE, La Roche-l'Abeille 87800 Nexon. Tel: 55 00 70 86. Fax: 55 00 76 57.

PROPRIETORS: Jean & Annie Bertranet. CHEF: Jean Bertranet.

ROOMS: 9, plus 1 suite, all with bath or shower and WC, direct telephone, TV.

PRICES: Rooms: 480–900 F ($96–180); suite: 1300 F ($260); ½-pension: 800–1100 F ($160–220). Breakfast: 75 F ($15). Menus: 180–480 F ($36–96). Credit cards: AE, CB, DC, EC, MC, Visa.

AMENITIES: Bar, lounge, terrace, large pond, woods. Fishing in pond. Tennis 1 km, swimming 8 km, golf 30 km. Dining inside, or on terrace. Parking.

ASSOCIATIONS: Relais & Châteaux.

DIRECTIONS: From Paris, S on N20 to Limoges, then D704/D17 to La Roche-l'Abeille; follow signs to the mill.

OPEN: Feb 10–Jan 1; Restaurant closed: Sun dinner, Mon (Sep 20–Apr 15).

60. LE MOULIN DU ROC

Champagnac-de-Belair, Dordogne, Aquitaine

And now, the "Mill of the Rock," one of our very favorites. On arriving, you walk through a bright, busy garden to a vine-covered stone building. To the left of the garden, a flower-bordered terrace hugs the river's edge, shaded by bamboo and graced with fanciful wrought-iron gazebos with fin-de-siècle tables and chairs. From the terrace, a wooden bridge arches across the stream to lawns with chaises longues inviting you to relax and enjoy the beauty of the water, flowers, and trees. The village church steeple peeks over the trees behind the mill. Romantic and captivating, it's the sort of place where you expect to find Gigi gazing into Gaston's eyes, over a *thé citron*.

The owners, Lucien and Solange Gardillou, have a gentle, belle-epoch courtesy and charm, in keeping with the surroundings. Solange is an attractive blond with a shy smile. Her dashing husband is more out-going, and has a touch of gray at the temples. The 16th-century walnut-oil mill (this is walnut country) sits on the bank of the Dronne River, near the hamlet of Champagnac-de-Belair, six kilometers northeast of Brantôme. The Gardillous restored the mill almost by themselves, with little help from architects, decorators, plumbers, or other craftsmen. They preserved many of the original weathered beams, and kept much of the working machinery to decorate the small lounges and dining rooms. In one lounge, perfect for an apéritif or after-dinner coffee, half of the space is taken up by huge millstones, shafts and gears. You put your apéritif on a glass-top "table" with lustrous mill parts underneath.

Throughout the inn furniture is heavy, carved, and antique. Paintings, flower arrangements, and interesting bric-a-brac—gathered in forays throughout Europe—cover most surfaces, including those in the bedrooms. Wherever you look there is something to please the eye or pique your curiosity.

On entering the mill, you first see the concierge's desk and a large lobster aquarium. As you follow the maid to your room, you pass through a lounge and sitting area decorated as described. From the windows—cut through two-foot thick stone walls—you can see the river, edged with brilliant gardens, and more gazebos. Solange named the most pleasant room we've had, one to which we like to return, "L'Églantine," after a rose. A second-floor suite, it includes a small sitting room, large bedroom, modern bath, and private balcony under the eaves. All of the furnishings and decorations are antique, from the large walnut writing desk to the silk-covered chairs. Colors are rich rusts and reds. The television and mini-bar hide inside a lavishly veneered cabinet.

To reach the suite you climb a circular iron staircase too narrow for luggage (the luggage arrives through a walk-in closet, with a door opening onto the upper road). On the balcony, you may be greeted by fresh flowers and a complimentary bottle of chilled wine.

The balcony gives a delicious sense of privacy. It's furnished with a chaise longue, table and chairs—a nice spot to sit with tea or wine and savor the view. Punts bob gently in the flower-bordered brook. An occasional guest strolls along the banks, or over the wooden bridge towards the lawns, tennis court, and enclosed pool. Except for the slowly turning mill wheel, there is no sound.

FOOD & WINE

The dining rooms exude elegant, quiet gentility, and at the same time, conviviality. The tables are set with rich linen, fine china and silver. In one dining room, the tables have glass tops that reveal beautifully sculptured butterflies underneath. Table lamps match the sculptured supports.

Solange Gardillou had little formal training for the kitchen, and became chef by accident. The former chef, an alcoholic, was abusive when he drank. After he attacked Mme Gardillou and was fired, she bravely donned a chef's hat. Her only training had been in her mother's kitchen—traditional, heavy Périgordine fare. She found that she was an inventive cook, adding lightness and grace to the traditional dishes, and, moreover, that she loved doing it. She soon earned Michelin stars and GaultMillau toques, and has become one of the foremost women chefs in France.

She also discovered a talent as a baker. The croissants and breads come from the mill's kitchens, and couldn't be better. Sample them at breakfast, served on a silver tray in your room, or on your balcony, or on the terrace.

Menus are moderate to expensive. The lower-priced menu has the same number of courses as the more-expensive, the main differences being that in the first three courses you have no choice, and the courses are more modest.

On our last visit, with the more-expensive menu we started with *Foie gras frais en terrine et sa salade à l'huile de noix* (fresh goose liver terrine and walnut-oil salad; this is not only walnut country—it's also foie gras country). Next came *les Filets de truite fourrés aux cèpes* (trout stuffed with boletus mushrooms). For the meat course, I enjoyed *Aiguillettes de canette à la marinade d'herbes fraîches* (duck breast served with an infusion of fresh herbs and wine—see recipe), and Nona had the *Roti d'agneau à l'ail doux* (roast lamb with fresh garlic), which she thought the best she'd ever eaten. *Le crottin de chèvre roti* (goat cheese melted on toast) was followed by a choice of desserts which included *Marquise au chocolat* (a sinful mixture of chocolate, butter, and eggs).

We drank wines from the Dordogne: a dry white Montravel with the trout, followed by a light red Pécharmant La Terrasse. The wine cellar, however, has an exceptional collection of Bordeaux— more than 20,000 bottles, with many priced near cost. They offer excellent value. Gardillou and his son François will help with the wine selection if asked, and during the evening Lucien will stop by your table to ask how you are enjoying the meal, and to chat for a few minutes. You feel he's especially pleased that you are here.

Both sons work in the mill: Alain with Solange in the kitchen, and François in charge of the cellar, and learning administration. The Moulin du Roc should be in good hands far into the future.

For other fine dining in the area, see Chapter 61, Hôtel le Moulin de l'Abbaye. Régis Bulot of l'Abbaye and Lucien Gardillou agree on how to succeed in the restaurant business:

> "Use the finest local ingredients, and treat each guest as an honored friend, whose pleasure and comfort are your only concerns."

SIGHTS & SUCH

With a heated pool, tennis court, and the other facilities mentioned, why not spend all of your time at the mill? Because the mill is in Périgord and the Dordogne, a fascinating part of France.

Years ago, the Moulin du Roc was one of ten water mills in an eight-mile stretch, each producing walnut oil. Only one operating mill remains: the 700-year-old mill of M. Marcel Debord, by the tiny village of Rochevideau, equidistant from Champagnac-de-Belair and Brantôme. Mme Gardillou comes here to buy the oil for her fabulous salads. We decided to visit the mill and get a liter for ourselves. The Debord family welcomes visitors, pleased with a chance to explain their process and to lament the passing of the water mills.

"You can only have so many restaurants and inns," said Marcel Debord. "The rest of the mills just rust, and decay, and die."

Their process for extracting oil from the walnuts is ancient and simple: whack each nut with a wooden mallet, remove the shells, grind the nutmeats, heat them over a wood fire, then press out the oil. The mill does the grinding and pressing. It takes 10 to 12 pounds of shelled walnuts for a liter of oil, and the cost to us was less than 10 dollars. They also make hazelnut oil. Directions: Rochevideau lies eight kilometers east of Brantôme on D78. Debord's is the closest farm west of the village, on the north side. You won't find a sign—just drive into the courtyard.

This is not only walnut and foie gras country, it's also truffle country. In Sorges, 23 kilometers southeast on D3 and D24, a small museum devotes itself to the black Périgord truffle, an essential element of french cuisine even at $600 per pound. The museum has an exhibit on the truffle, and can arrange walks through truffle farms (telephone 53.05.90.11 for an appointment).

For Brantôme, Bordeilles, and other nearby sights, see the next chapter. If your trip doesn't include a stop in Les Eyzies-de-Tayac or the Dordogne Valley, take a day's outing there—only an hour's drive. You'll find prehistoric caves, cliff dwellings, and several of the prettiest villages in France. See Chapters 62, 63, and Michelin's green guide *Dordogne/Périgord/Quercy*.

A word on parking: the courtyard runs out of room, and cars fill it to overflowing. If you arrive late, or must leave early, park on the upper road that runs behind the mill.

Here we feel comfy, at home, perfectly pampered—one of those places you hate to leave. When it's time to check out, we begin thinking about when we can come back. And so may you.

SLICES OF DUCK BREAST MARINATED IN FRESH HERBS
Aiguillettes de canette à la marinade d'herbes fraîches

4 duck breasts	1 branch tarragon
1 shallot, minced	3 branches chervil (or
4 oz. (12 cl.) white wine	1 teaspoon dried chervil)
4 teaspoons whole-grain	2 tablespoons balsamic vinegar
Meaux or Dijon mustard	2 tablespoons walnut oil

In a heavy frying pan, cook the duck breasts until they are rosée or still quite pink. Remove from the pan and keep warm.

Remove the fat from the frying pan and cook the shallots lightly. Deglaze the pan with the wine and reduce a little. Remove from the fire and add the mustard, herbs, vinegar and oil. Let infuse for a few minutes.

Slice the duck breasts in thin slices, place on serving plates and top with the mustard-oil vinaigrette.   Serves 4.

★★★★ HOSTELLERIE DU MOULIN DU ROC, 24530 Champagnac-de-Belair. Tel: 53 54 80 36. Fax: 53 54 21 31.
PROPRIETORS: Lucien & Solange Gardillou. CHEF: Solange Gardillou.
ROOMS: 10, plus 4 suites, all with bath or shower and WC, direct telephone, TV, mini-bar.
PRICES: Rooms: 400–600 F ($80–120); suites: 680 F ($136); ½-pension—required in high season: 600–700 F ($120–140). Breakfast: 55 F ($11). Menus: 200–280 F ($40–56). Credit cards: AE, CB, DC, EC, MC, Visa.
AMENITIES: Bar, lounges, large garden, terrace, tennis court, heated pool, heliport. Fishing by inn. Golf, boating: 20 km. Parking: in courtyard, or in back of mill.
MARKET DAY: Brantôme: Fri.
DIRECTIONS: From Périgueux, D939 N 24 km. to Brantôme, then D78/D83 NE 6 km to Champagnac.
OPEN: Feb 16–Nov 14, Dec 16–Jan 14; Restaurant closed: Tue; Wed lunch.

61. HÔTEL LE MOULIN DE L'ABBAYE
Brantôme, Dordogne, Périgord

Fifteen miles north of Périgueux, two branches of the Dronne River
form an island on which sits Brantôme, the "Venice of Périgord."
With its graceful Benedictine abbey, gray-stone houses, narrow streets,
and flower-bordered lawns, Brantôme is a little gem. There are few,
if any, more-captivating villages in France. A "must" visit, and an
excellent place to stop.

The two local inns that carry Michelin stars are former water
mills. You already met one of them in Chapter 60. The other, at the
edge of town on the right bank of the Dronne, is the Hôtel le
Moulin de l'Abbaye (Mill of the Abbey). From both dining room and
terrace, guests look across the broad lawn and tree-lined river, to an
odd right-angle bridge, the ancient abbey, and the old town.

In 1979, Régis and Katy Bulot bought the 15th-century mill, then
in ruins, and refurbished it beautifully.

There are 14 rooms and six suites, for a total of 20. Six rooms and two suites in the mill itself, and four rooms and two suites in each of two other buildings: the ancient home of the miller at the foot of the caves, overlooking the mill, and the ancient home of Abbot Pierre de Bourdielle ("Brantôme"), nearby. The rooms in the mill are small but luxurious. Some have old-to-antique furnishings, including four-poster beds; others are modern. All have modern bathrooms, telephones, and television. Since the mill wheel continues to turn, the three rooms closest to the action are soundproofed and airconditioned. Most rooms have a pleasant view of the river; others overlook the garden, mill, or village. Bulot named the rooms for classified Bordeaux châteaux (curiously including all of the *premier crus* except Lafite- and Mouton-Rothschild).

FOOD & WINE

For the first few years, the Bulots were hands-on hosts. Cathy managed the hotel and its eight comfortable rooms; Régis ran the kitchen and dining room. When Bulot opened the restaurant in 1980, his cuisine, traditional Perigordine with a hint of the nouvelle, was an immediate success. By 1983 he had earned two Michelin stars—almost unheard-of in that short a time. We understood why at our first meal, which included the famous Périgordine fresh foie gras; succulent chicken with truffle sauce; and for dessert, a tart plum-and-berry compote made with three liqueurs. We enjoyed a young "Black" wine from Cahors, and with the dessert, a sweet Monbazillac. In addition to local wines, the cellar provides a fair number of Burgundy and Bordeaux.

There followed a period where Bulot was busy with the family's other hotel properties. The Bulots are part of the busy Benoist family that owns several hotels, three of which, including the Moulin de l'Abbaye, belong to the Relais & Châteaux chain, of which Bulot is president. For eight years the chef was the young, talented Christian Ravinel, and I could easily write eight pages of reminiscence about Ravinel meals. However, he recently left, to be replaced by Guy Guénégo, a chef from Courchevel.

We haven't sampled Guénégo's version of Périgordine fare, but on the basis of recipes Bulot sent us, we are optimistic. We share here the recipe for *Biscuit aux amandes et aux fraises, sabayon au Monbazillac* (almond biscuit with strawberries and zabaglione). We eagerly look forward to our next visit.

The broad terrace overlooks the river and the town beyond.

Shaded in the daytime and illuminated in the evening, it's an idyllic place for an apéritif or meal. The softly-lit dining room is quietly elegant, with beamed ceiling, stone fireplace, and tiled floor. Round, lace-covered tables are set with sparkling crystal and silver. Stone-arched windows look out on the terrace, river, and garden. The service is quietly courteous and efficient.

SIGHTS & SUCH

Walk out the front door of the mill and turn right, and there's the Abbey to which the mill belonged, built by Charlemagne in 769. Its most famous abbot, Pierre de Bourdeilles, retired from war and gallantry in 1569. Using the pen name "Brantôme," he amused himself by writing spicy chronicles about the scandalous court of the day. His best-known work: *Vie des dames galantes* (Life of the Courtesan). He used the bell tower, with France's oldest bell, as his studio.

The tower is now a museum. Part of the Abbey serves as a town hall and school, and the chapel serves its normal religious functions. We attended Sunday mass, pleased to find that the young priest spoke slowly enough for the traveller with imperfect French.

Creeper-clad stone houses cluster along the bank of the river opposite the Abbey, with punts moored to their stoops, and beyond these houses lies the ancient village. Everyone seems relaxed, friendly, smiling. Even an unsuccessful fisherman. We saw the same man several times, standing in the river in hip boots, casting. Though we never saw him catch a thing, he always smiled and touched his hat.

On Friday morning the village comes alive, as farmers and merchants set up market stalls. Although we've never found a village market we didn't like, Brantôme rates highly—at least eight on a scale of ten. Especially interesting: local cheeses, such as the mild-flavored Echourgnac made in a nearby Trappist monastery, and live, fat trout that had evaded our fisherman.

Outside the mill, turning left instead of toward the Abbey leads to a narrow road flanked with cliff houses, *maisons Troglodytes,* on the right. They are really caverns cut deep into the hillside, with conventional façades. Little garden patches, one for each cave-house, lie between the road and the river. The only people about are apt to be a resident tending her garden, and an occasional fisherman.

Follow the Dronne ten kilometers south, to Bourdeilles. The old Château de Bourdeilles has sumptuous fifteenth and 16th-century furnishings and, from the tower, an excellent view of the village, river, and countryside. Opposite the château the seignorial Moulin de Bordeilles covers its own little island—not yet an inn, but ideal for one. It looks like a large houseboat moving upstream, and locals call it the "Bateau-Moulin." There are pleasant picnic spots by the river, and shops nearby for picnic supplies.

Also nearby are an operating walnut-oil mill that welcomes visitors, and a truffle museum and farm (descriptions in Chapter 60).

If your itinerary does not include a stop in Les Éyzies-de-Tayac, or the Dordogne and Vézere Valleys, consider a day's outing there—only 80 kilometers (50 Mi.) from Brantôme. Prehistoric caves, cliff dwellings, and some of the prettiest villages in France await you. For directions and details, see Chapter 62. Also, refer to the Michelin green guide *Dordogne/Périgord/Quercy* (available in English).

Return to the mill in time for an apéritif and dinner, and park in the cavern cut into the cliff across the road from the mill.

ALMOND BISCUIT WITH STRAWBERRIES AND ZABAGLIONE
Biscuit aux amandes et aux fraises, sabayon au Monbazillac

4 egg whites
½ cup plus 2 tablespoons
   (150 g.) powdered sugar
1¼ cups (150 g.) powdered
   almonds
½ lb. (250 g.) strawberries

3 oz. Monbazillac
   or other sweet white wine
3 egg yolks
¼ cup (50 g.) sugar
5 oz. (15 cl.) cream

Whip the egg whites until they are firm. Fold in the powdered sugar and then the powdered almonds. Spread evenly to a ½-in. (1 cm.) depth on a buttered cookie sheet. Bake about 20 minutes at 350°F (180°C). Let cool.

Cut the biscuit into four rounds of 4-in. (10-cm.) diameter. Sprinkle the rounds with 4 tablespoons Monbazillac.

Place the rounds on the center of each plate. Cut the strawberries into pieces and put a circle of berries on each round.

For the zabaglione, whip the egg yolks with the regular sugar and remaining Monbazillac in the top of a double broiler. Cook until it starts to thicken. Remove from the heat and continue beating until cool. Whip the cream and fold into the zabaglione.

Top the strawberry and biscuit rounds with the zabaglione sauce and brown under the broiler.   Serves 4.

★★★★ AUBERGE LE MOULIN DE L'ABBAYE, 1 route de Bourdeilles, 24310 Brantôme. Tel: 53 05 80 22. Fax: 53 05 75 27.

PROPRIETORS: Régis and Cathy Bulot. CHEF: Guy Guénégo.

ROOMS: 16, plus 4 suites, all with bath or shower, WC, direct telephone, TV.

PRICES: Rooms: 550–950 F ($140–250); suites: 1100–1400 F ($220–280); ½-pension: 800–900 F ($160–180). Breakfast: 70 F ($14). Menus: 220–450 F ($40–90). Credit cards: AE, DC, EC, MC, Visa.

AMENITIES: Bar, lounge, terrace, park, Dronne River, parking. Fishing in river, by inn. Tennis: 0.8 km. Golf, boating: 20 km.

ASSOCIATIONS: Relais & Châteaux.

MARKET DAYS: Brantôme: Fri; Périgueux: Wed, Sat.

DIRECTIONS: From Périgueux, D939 N 24 km.

OPEN: May 1–Oct 30. Restaurant closed Mon lunch.

62. LE MOULIN DE LA BEUNE
Les Eyzies-de-Tayac, Dordogne, Périgord

Les Eyzies-de-Tayac is the best base from which to visit the Dordogne and Vézere valleys, with their prehistoric caves and picturesque villages, and of all the hotels in Les Eyzies, we prefer the Moulin de la Beune. It's on the side of the Beune River, near the main road through Les Eyzies, but about 40 feet below it.

On arriving at the mill, it's hard to imagine that you're in one of the most-visited places in France. The Beune River runs quietly at your feet. The little garden, with several tables, is a haven of peace. The rooms are all excellent, and decorated with taste. Most have a view of the river. The rooms are in one mill, the restaurant in a second, a few feet away. Monsieur and Madame Soulié bought the inn in 1989, and operate it with the same care and attention to their guests as had Serge and Thérèse Duducourt for many years.

FOOD & WINE

The restaurant, called "Au Vieux Moulin," occupies a separate building, with rotating mill wheel visible from inside the dining room where a glass enclosure surrounds the rotating machinery.

A typical mid-priced menu started with an assortment of *Amuse-bouches*. Next came *Risotto aux truffes de Saint-Jean* (a tasty dish of rice and truffles); then an unusual—and unusually good—duck breast with apple-based sauce: *Magret de canard et son Milhas de pommes*; to cleanse the palate: a *Bouquet de salade et son fromage de chèvre* (Salad greens with goat cheese); finally a *Soufflé glacé aux noix* (ice cream with walnuts). With the duck, we enjoyed a Bergerac red. M. Soulié has a varied cellar, which includes several wines from the lower Dordogne, as well as Cahors.

SIGHTS & SUCH

Les Eyzies offers a swimming pool and tennis, but you won't have time for that. Prehistoric caves, with famous paintings, need your attention. A visit to the National Museum of Prehistory is in order. Numerous picturesque villages await you—Limeuil, Beynac-et-Cazenac, la Roque-Gageac, Domme, Sarlat. The Dordogne River Valley invites you to picnic or kayak. And numerous shops offer cans or jars of the Périgord food items: foie gras, truffles, patés, walnut oil . . . Consult Michelin's *Dordogne/Périgord/Quercy*.

★★ LE MOULIN DE LA BEUNE, and LE RESTAURANT AU VIEUX MOULIN, 24620 Les Eyzies de Tayac. Tel: 53 06 94 33 (hotel); 53 06 93 39 (restaurant). Fax: 53 06 98 06.
PROPRIETORS: Georges et Mme A. Soulié. CHEF: Georges Soulié.
ROOMS: 20, all with direct telephone; 14 with bath, 6 with shower, all with WC, and with views of one or other of the streams.
PRICES: Rooms: 260–350 F ($52–70); ½-pension: 320 F ($64); Breakfast: 40 F ($8). Menus: 99–280 F ($18–56), children 50 F ($10). Credit cards: CB, MC, Visa.
AMENITIES: Bar, lounge, terrace, park, two streams, parking. Tennis & swimming in the village. Golf, in Bugue. Canoes/kayaks: in the rivers.
MARKET DAYS: Les Eyzies de Tayac: Mon.
DIRECTIONS: by the side of the Beune River, near the main road through Les Eyzies, but about 40 feet below, so that you look down on it from the road.
OPEN: Hotel: Apr 1–Oct 31. Restaurant open Feb 16–Jan 2; closed Tue lunch.

63. LE MANOIR D'HAUTEGENTE
Terrason, Dordogne, Aquitaine

The Manoir d'Hautegente (colloquial for "high wheel") sits in a shady garden complete with stone walls, radiant flowers, and a bubbling stream. The owner-chef Mme Edith Hamelin, joined recently by her son Patrick and his young family, offers exceptional comfort, classic regional cuisine, and—often—friendship. Many guests become family friends, returning each year.

The mill was built in the 13th-century, and became a forge for the warrior monks of the Abbey of Saint-Amand-de-Coly. It turned for more than 700 years until it was destroyed in 1944. For three centuries, it was the property of the Hamelin family, who restored the forge after the war, later converting it into a family residence, then an inn. All that remains of the original mill are some ruins, the levee, and some millstones.

The vine-covered inn lies in a beautiful valley filled with graceful old oak and walnut trees. Ducks stroll along the stream bank in front of the manor. Inside, the lounges and rooms are tastefully decorated with family paintings and furniture. On cool evenings, a fire is lit in one of the lounges. All of the guest rooms are comfortable, but perhaps the most pleasant is *Liserone,* overlooking the river.

FOOD & WINE

Mme Hamelin prepares regional dishes, with a blend of the classic and the new. She frequently includes foie gras as an ingredient (she makes her own foie gras, which is available off-sale at the inn). One of her favorite dishes is a *Duo de langoustines au foie gras* (an inventive combination of crayfish and foie gras). Another is *Pigeon farci au foie gras et sa sauce aux truffes* (Pigeon stuffed with foie gras, served with a truffle sauce—how "Périgord" can you get?). She also loves sweetbreads, serving them with a sauce made from the semi-sweet white wine of the Dordogne (*Ris de veau au Monbazillac),* or in a shrimp dish (*Braisière de ris de veau au écrivisses*—see recipe).

Mme Hamelin has two seasonal menus, plus a small à la carte list. We like to order regional wines for the dinner, and afterward enjoy an Armagnac with the coffee.

SIGHTS & SUCH

You can stroll in the flowered park and wooded grounds, swim in the pool, fish in the river, or play tennis in nearby courts. But don't spend all of your time at these activities. In the Dordogne, as mentioned in Chapter 62, numerous prehistoric caves, picturesque villages, and lovely river valleys await you. See Michelin's green guide *Dordogne/Périgord/Quercy* (in English) or *Périgord/Berry/Limousin/Quercy.*

BRAISED SWEETBREADS WITH SHRIMP
Braisière de ris de veau au écrivisses

1¼ lbs. (600 g.) veal sweetbreads	½ cup (10 cl.) white wine
1½ lbs (800 g.) shrimp	½ cup (10 cl.) cognac
½ cup (10 cl.) veal stock	5 tablespoons butter
fresh herbs (chives, chervil, etc.)	

The night before, cover the sweetbreads with cold water and let soak overnight in the refrigerator.

The next day, drain the sweetbreads and then blanch them for 5 minutes. Cool and trim them of fat and membranes. Set aside.

Flame one-fourth of the shrimp with half of the cognac. Crush them in a mortar or food processor. Add the white wine and one-half cup (10 cl.) water. Put the shrimp in a saucepan, add salt and pepper and cook gently for 15 minutes. Pass the crushed shrimp through a strainer and reduce the liquid (shrimp stock). Add the veal stock and reduce further. Enrich the sauce by slowly adding 4 tablespoons of cold butter, cut in pieces. Rectify the seasonings.

Cut the sweetbreads in quarters and brown them gently in butter. Salt and pepper them.

Sauté the rest of the shrimp quickly in 1 tablespoon of butter. Flame with the remaining cognac. Salt and pepper.

Place the sweetbreads on 4 heated plates. Surround with the shrimp. Pour the sauce around the sweetbreads and shrimp and sprinkle with the fresh herbs.

Serves 4.

★★★ LE MANOIR D'HAUTEGENTE, Coly 24120 Terrasson. Tel: 53 51 68 03.
   Fax: 53 50 38 52.
PROPRIETORS: Edith Hamelin and son Patrick. CHEF: Edith Hamelin.
ROOMS: 12, all with bath or shower and WC, direct telephone, TV, mini-bar.
PRICES: Rooms: 500–950 F ($100–190); ½-pension: 480–730 F ($94–138). Breakfast:
   60 F ($11). Menus: 195–260 F ($39–52) Dinner only. Half-pension required in
   summer. Credit cards: CB, EC, MC, Visa.
AMENITIES: Bar, lounge, garden, river, fishing, heated swimming pool. Tennis 4
   km, riding 8 km, golf 20 km. Parking, garage.
ASSOCIATIONS: Moulin Étape; Châteaux et Hôtels Indépendants; Relais du
   Silence.
MARKET DAYS: Terrasson: Thu; Brive-la-Gaillarde: Tue, Thu, Sat; Sarlat-la-
   Canéda: Wed, Sat.
DIRECTIONS: From Brive-la-Gaillarde, 27 km. W to Lardin-St-Lazare, then SE 7
   km. on D704/D62 to Coly.
OPEN: Apr 1–Nov 11; Restaurant closed: Mon–Wed lunch.

64. LA SOURCE BLEUE
Touzac, Lot, Midi-Pyrénées

Three mills built here in the 14th-century, although at the edge of Lot River, were powered by a millpond fed by a blue spring. The spring (La Source Bleue), the river, the large park, and the giant bamboo forest, combine to lend a magical charm to the site.

Your hosts, Jean-Pierre and Siâm Bouyou are a charming and interesting couple. Mme Bouyou, of Welsh origin, formerly taught Yoga in the nearby village of Montaigu-Quercy. Although they employ a chef, the cuisine is overseen by Jean-Pierre.

The large, rustic bedrooms,arranged in the ruins of an old mill building, are a delight, as is the elegant, rustic dining room. Outside spreads a shady terrace, a wood of cedar and silver birch, and a bight in the river, with punts available.

FOOD & WINE

Each time we dined here, we found the food to be simple, well-prepared, and of fresh ingredients. The principal menu offers five courses with a choice among two or more items in each. A typical selection: for the first course a terrine of duck foie gras, a specialty of the house (see recipe). The second course may be another specialty: *Saumon cuit sur sa peau* (salmon cooked in its skin); for a main course, another specialty: *Filet de boeuf Maître d'Hôtel* (filet mignon). Next comes the cheese tray or a *Salade de chèvre chaud* (salad with warm goat cheese). Finally, a tray of luscious desserts.

With the terrine, we recommend a glass of Sauternes; with the fish, a glass of dry white Bergerac, and with the meat and cheese courses, a good Cahors red.

SIGHTS & SUCH

This inn was known to Colette, and to her friend, the actress Marguerite Moréno, who lived here a number of years. Even if you do not remember her, you may find the nearby Marguerite Moréno museum of interest.

There are many places to visit along or near the Lot River, between Saint-Cirq-Lapopie in the east (the "most-picturesque village in France"), and Villeneuve-sur-Lot in the west. Don't miss the grotto at Pech-Merle, the city of Cahors, and the village of Tournon-d'Agenais. Around Cahors, take the wine circuit. For more details, see Michelin's *Dordogne/Périgord/Quercy*.

DUCK FOIE GRAS TERRINE
La Terrine de foie gras de canard

2 lbs. (1 kg.) fresh duck foie gras (fatted duck liver)
salt and pepper
3 oz. (9 cl.) French Sauternes (or other sweet white wine)

Trim the liver, salt and pepper it, and let marinate in the Sauternes for 24 hours.

The next day, place the liver in a terrine set in a baking dish, and pour boiling water around the terrine. Bake for 35 minutes at 200°F (80°C). Take the terrine from the oven and remove the excess fat. Cool and then refrigerate until the next day.

Serve with a few springs of young lettuce dressed with a light vinaigrette, and thinly sliced white toast.

This is very good served with a chilled French Sauternes, or muscat wine.

★★★ LA SOURCE BLEUE, Moulin de Leygues, 46700 Touzac. Tel: 65 36 52 01. Fax: 65 24 65 69.

PROPRIETORS: Jean-Pierre & Siâm Bouyou.

ROOMS: 15, plus 2 suites, all with bath or shower and WC, direct telephone, 5 with TV. 3-day minimum stay in season.

PRICES: Rooms: 300 F ($60); suites: 455 F ($91); ½-pension: 300–435 F ($60–87). Breakfast: 35 F ($7). Menus: 140–220 F ($28–44). Credit cards: AE, CB, EC, MC, Visa.

AMENITIES: Bar, lounge, terrace, large park, Lot River, wood. fishing, boating. Heated swimming pool. Sauna and gym (100 F supplement). Tennis, riding nearby. Parking.

ASSOCIATIONS: Logis de France.

MARKET DAYS: Fumel: Thu; Villeneuve-sur-Lot: Sat; Cahors: Wed, Sat.

DIRECTIONS: From Cahors, 48 km. W on D911. At Touzac, cross Lot River. Follow signs to the mill.

OPEN: Apr 1–Dec 31; Restaurant closed: Wed lunch.

65. L'HOSTELLERIE DU MOULIN DU MAINE BRUN
LE MOULIN GOURMAND
Hiersac, Charente, Poitou-Charentes

Away from all noise, in the heart of the smiling Cognac countryside, this 16th-century, stone flour mill sits on the banks of a nice little river, the Nouère. Transformed into an elegant hotel, the mill offers fine accommodations, and even finer fare.

Until recently one of the Relais et Chateâux, the inn now belongs to the Relais du Silence family. Each bedroom has a balcony or private terrace, with quiet views of the river, and of the deer park. Bedrooms and public rooms are provided with Louis XVI or Empire furnishings. The bar and dining room are warm and inviting—elegant, but unpretentious. And don't miss lunching on the flagstone terrace at the edge of the river.

The mill's huge park includes wooded paths for walking, the animal park with deer and elk, and a vineyard which produces an unusual, white Cognac, used for long drinks with tonic or soda. It's easy to spend several days here.

FOOD & WINE

In 1996, Le Moulin Gourmand retained its two toques, even after GaultMillau's unprecedented "house cleaning," which saw many chefs losing one or more. But Bruno Nicollet has not rested on his laurels.

Several of his specialties involve foie gras, like the beef filet (*Filet de boeuf poêlé au jus de truffes et foie gras*), and the duck foie gras with old Cognac *(Foie gras de canard au vieux cognac)*. Another recipe involving Cognac: *La Matelote de lotte au pineau rouge* (monkfish stew with red Pineau de Charente—an apéritif made with Cognac and wine). Other specialties include a marvelous mouclade, roast lamb, and an assortment of desserts. Nicollet has a sizeable menu, and a cellar with a large selection of fine Bordeaux wines.

SIGHTS & SUCH

There is much to see and do at the inn and its 100 acres: the deer park the Nouère River, the wood, the pool, and the vineyard.

Stroll through the old walled city of Angoulême, with its ancient ramparts and interesting museums. Nearby one can visit two paper mills—Le Moulin de Fleurac on the Charente River, and Moulin du Verger—both still fabricating paper. And do not miss Cognac, where world-famous distilleries eagerly await your tasting of their product. (See Michelin's *Poitou/Vendée/Charentes*.)

★ ★ ★ ★ L'HOSTELLERIE DU MOULIN DU MAIN BRUN, RN 141 "La Vigerie"
   16290 Asnières-sur-Nouère. Tel: 45 90 83 00. Fax: 45 96 91 14. (Restaurant LE
   MOULIN GOURMAND)
PROPRIETORS: Irène Menager and family. CHEF: Bruno Nicollet.
ROOMS: 18, plus 2 suites, all with bath or shower and WC, antique furnishings, TV,
   direct telephone, private terrace.
PRICES: Rooms: 400–750 F ($80–150); suites: 1250 F ($250); ½-pension: 545–620 F
   ($109–124). Breakfast: 60 F ($12). Menus: 125–370 F ($25–74). Credit cards:
   AE, DC, EC, MC, Visa.
AMENITIES: Bar, lounge, garden, terrace, park, river, swimming pool, private zoo.
   Parking. Dining inside, or on terrace. Tennis 5 km, golf: 20 km.
ASSOCIATIONS: Relais du Silence.
MARKET DAYS: Angoulême: Tue–Sun; Jarnac: Tue–Sun; Cognac: Tue, Fri, Sat.
DIRECTIONS: From Paris, 470 km. on A10 to Saintes, 59 km. E on N141 to Hier-
   sac, then D14/D96 N 5 km to Asnière-sur-Nouère; follow signs to the mill.
OPEN: Jan 1–Oct 31; Restaurant closed: Sun dinner and Mon, Jan–Apr.

66. LE MOULIN DE MARCOUZE

Mosnac-sur-Seugne, Charente-Maritime, Poitou-Charentes

In May 1986, in a wood southwest of Cognac, Dominique Bouchet bought an abandoned 17th-century water mill, the Moulin de Marcouze. It had rusted and decayed for forty years since it ceased grinding in 1947, but Bouchet fell in love with it—he wanted it for a restaurant. This astonished everyone. For the past six years, Bouchet had been *Chef des Cuisines* of Paris' fabled three-star Tour d'Argent. By 1986 he had subtly modernized that restaurant's cuisine, giving the "Silver Tower" a new spirit, and restoring its luster. Highly esteemed, well-paid, and doing the work he loved, he was set for life, right? Wrong. Dominique and Françoise Bouchet wanted to go home, where life is quieter and simpler, where his parents still tended their farm.

Bouchet restored the old mill—preserving little of its outer vestiges, and leaning toward Spanish modern. Yet, from the elegant dining room, large windows look out on lush river banks, the millpond, and the stream tumbling over the weir.

Within two years, with inventive changes to the earthy regional dishes, Bouchet earned two Michelin stars. Diners came from as far as Bordeaux and La Rochelle to enjoy one of the few fine restaurants in the area, and to oblige them he added an annex—ten large, luxurious rooms, furnished with antiques, each with a balcony over the river, or with private garden and patio. *Now* he is set for life.

FOOD & WINE

Prior to the Tour d'Argent, Bouchet was Chef des Cuisines at Paris' two-star Jamin. Before that, he worked for Joël Robuchon. His résumé, awards, and honors would require another chapter. He is active in the international community—consultant to Japanese institutions; culinary demonstrations in the U.S. and many countries in Europe, Africa, and Asia—yet he has not let this activity affect the quality of his own kitchen.

On our last visit, Bouchet offered three menus with four to seven courses, and an à la carte list that extended the offerings to 59 items! There is literally something here for everyone. We present a recipe for a first course: *Salade de canard aux pêches fraîches* (duck and fresh peach salad). Each dish we tried was a delightful discovery. One of our favorite main courses was a casserole of chicken and sweetbreads, with wild mushrooms *(Cocotte de volaille et ris de veau aux champignons sauvages)*. A pleasant dessert: *Pêches blanches au granité de champagne* (white peaches with champagne ice).

The wine cellar—actually a circular tower by the reception room—is heavy in Bordeaux, some at reasonable prices.

You can't go wrong at the Moulin de Marcouze.

SIGHTS & SUCH

The mill has its own heliport, and Mme Bouchet can arrange a helicopter trip over the Bordeaux vineyards. Better, you can drive to Médoc via the Royan ferry, and return on N137 or A10, seeing Bordeaux on the way. Several of the classified Médoc wineries offer tours and tastings. Also, visit another of the most picturesque villages of France: Saint-Émilion[34]. Although more famous for its wines, the village is worth a detour on its own.

Saintes and Royan deserve a visit, as does La Rochelle. And, as mentioned in Chapter 65, several famous Cognac firms offer tastings. (See Michelin's *Poitou/Vendée/Charentes,* and *Pyrénées/Aquitaine).*

SALAD WITH DUCK AND FRESH PEACHES
Salade de canard aux pêches fraîches

24 leaves of red leaf lettuce
(washed and dried)
3 duck breasts (about 4 oz.
or 120 g. each)
3 fresh peaches

1 carrot cut in julienne
2 stalks celery cut in julienne
salt and pepper
fresh coriander seeds

Vinaigrette:
2 oz. (6 cl.) sherry vinegar
3 oz. (9 cl.) walnut oil

3 oz. (9 cl.) canola oil
salt and pepper

Salt and pepper the duck breasts and cook in a frying pan as a steak. The meat should be rare. Let the meat cool for 30 minutes so that the juices stay in the meat and the flesh firms.

Peel the peaches and cut into thin slices. Place them on a plate and cover with 2 to 3 tablespoons of the vinaigrette. Sprinkle with ground coriander. Mix the carrot and celery juliennes and top with some vinaigrette.

Cut the duck breasts in thin slices.

Place 4 leaves of lettuce on each salad plate. Distribute the juliennes of vegetables on these leaves. Place alternate slices of peach and duck breast on the vegetables, forming a circle. Lightly cover with vinaigrette and a sprinkling of ground coriander.   Serves 6.

★ ★ ★ ★ LE MOULIN DE MARCOUZE, 17240 Mosnac-sur-Seugne.
   Tel: 46 70 46 16. Fax: 46 70 48 14.
PROPRIETORS: Dominique and Françoise Bouchet. CHEF: Dominique Bouchet.
ROOMS: 10, plus 1 suite, all with bath or shower and WC, direct telephone, TV,
   mini-bar, air conditioning, safe.
PRICES: Rooms: 525–700 F ($105–140); suite: 1200 F ($240); ½-pension: 710–760 F
   ($142–152). Breakfast: 70 F ($14). Menus: 150–420 F ($30–84). Credit cards: AE,
   CB, EC, MC, Visa.
AMENITIES: Bar, lounge, garden, terrace, swimming pool. Tennis: 1 km. Golf: 23
   km. Fishing: in Seugne River. Riding: 1 km. Parking, heliport.
MARKET DAYS: Pons: Sat.
DIRECTIONS: From Paris, 470 km. SW on A10 to Saintes, then 31 km. S on N137
   to St.-Genis-de-Saintonge, left 5 km. on D146 to Mosnac, then follow signs.
OPEN: Mar 15–Oct 30; Restaurant closed: Wed lunch & Tue, except Jun 15-Sep 15.

67. LE MOULIN DE CHALONS
"Chalons," Le Gua, Charente Maritime, Poitou-Charentes

Water lapping, birds singing, trees fluttering in the breeze—the romantic countryside of Charente soothes the Moulin de Châlons on the banks of the Seudre River. Sea, meadows, forests and river are its environs. Nearby are a golf course, swimming pool, tennis courts, riding stables, and Royan and its beaches.

Constructed with blond stone, the mill is a large, three-story, building, with millpond in front, and millrace running underneath. The grounds comprise a private, two-acre shady park, with private fishing. An 18th-century tidal mill, it operated by filling the pond from the high ocean tides, supplemented by water from the river.

The hotel and its gastronomic restaurant "L'Ecluse" open their doors into an atmosphere of yesteryear, a proud display of handsome stonework, lustrous wooden beams, antique furniture, and velvet. There is something uniquely elegant in each of the 14 guest rooms, the bar, lounges, and breakfast terrace. This was the dream of owner Claude and chef Colette Dupin.

FOOD & WINE

Dupin has earned a GaultMillau toque, and seems well on the way to a second. Specialties include lobster; a luscious *Soupe de moules au safran* (Mussel soup with safran—the mussels are grown near Royan); and fish such as *Filet de turbot au gingembre et agrumes* (Filet of turbot with ginger and citrus—see recipe).

The wine list is, appropriately, heavy in Bordeaux, and includes a nice Muscadet Clos des Orfeuilles.

SIGHTS & SUCH

In addition to the activities mentioned—swimming, golf, tennis, fishing, riding—there is punting on the pond, sailing and hang-gliding nearby.

A short ferry ride will take you to Haut-Médoc, the Atlantic entrance to what many believe to be the greatest red wine region in the world. Some of the vineyards welcome visitors, even some of the great ones—see Michelin's green guide *Pyrénées/Aquitaine*. After a day's touring, return to the Moulin de Châlons by A10 to Mirambeau, then D730/D17, with visits to Bordeaux and Saint-Émilion en route.

Other nearby sights: Cognac, where you can visit and taste same; La Rochelle, a fascinating city with an old fishing harbor and an important place in French History; the old city of Saintes; and the picturesque Île d'Oléron, which has a toll causeway. For details, see the Michelin green guide *Poitou/Vendée/Charentes*.

TURBOT FILET WITH GINGER AND CITRUS
Filet de turbot au gingembre et agrumes

2½ lb. (1.2 kg.) filet of turbot or other firm white fish	½ cup (12 cl.) cream
	2 tablespoons cold butter
2 grapefruit	½ cup (12 cl.) white wine
2 oranges	½ teaspoon fresh grated ginger

Peel the oranges and grapefruit, making sure to leave no white pulp. Separate the segments of fruit from their membrane, conserving any juice that runs out. Set the fruit aside.

Bring to a boil the juice of the fruit, the white wine and ginger.

Add the cream and reduce for about 5 minutes. Just before serving, slowly stir in the butter cut in small pieces until the sauce is a smooth and slightly thickened consistency.

While the sauce is being prepared, cook the fish filets either by steaming or poaching.

To serve, pour one fourth of the sauce on each warmed plate. Place the fish on the sauce and surround with the segments of orange and grapefruit which have been warmed in the microwave. Decorate with sprigs of chervil or mint.   Serves 4.

★★★ LE MOULIN DE CHALONS, 2, rue du Bassin, "Chalons" 17680 Le Gua. Tel: 46 22 82 72. Fax: 46 22 91 07. (Restaurant L'ÉCLUSE.)

PROPRIETOR/CHEF: Claude Dupin. HOSTESS: Colette Dupin.

ROOMS: 14, all with bath or shower and WC, direct telephone, TV, mini-bar.

PRICES: Rooms: 350–510 F ($70–102); ½-pension: 400–480 F ($80–96). Breakfast: 60 F ($12). Menus: 155–390 F ($31–78). Credit cards: AE, CB, DC, EC, MC, Visa.

AMENITIES: Bar, lounge, terrace, 2.5-acre park, Seudre River, pond, fishing. Parking. Swimming 2 km. Tennis , riding, boating, golf, beach and water sports 10 km.

ASSOCIATIONS: Moulin Étape; Châteaux et Hôtels Indépendants; Chaîne des Rôtisseurs; Académie des Arts de la Table.

MARKET DAYS: Royan, Saintes: Tue to Sun.

DIRECTIONS: From Paris, 470 km. SW on A10 to Saintes, then 24 km. W on N150 to Saujon; 6 km. N on D1 to Le Gua; follow signs to the mill.

OPEN: May 8–Sep 20; Restaurant closed: Wed lunch and Tue (except Jul–Aug).

68. AUBERGE À LA BELLE GASCONNE
Poudenas, Lot-et-Garonne, Aquitaine

This delightful 14th-century mill on the Gélise River is as much a family home as a hotel. We once arrived at the staff's dinner hour, and found them all seated around a table under a rear verandah, just like a family.

The name means "inn of the pretty Gasconne," which describes Marie-Claude Gracias—a bubbly, red-haired dynamo—pretty well. She is also one of the foremost women chefs in France. Like her mother, grandmother, and great-grandmother, she has dedicated her life to feeding the public. She shows what Gascon home cooking should taste like, and if the food doesn't come from her garden, or from her neighbors, she doesn't serve it.

Marie-Claude was born in this tiny village (population 275), far from the tourist flux. Her husband Richard is mayor, and founder of the local wine cooperative. His cellar is rich in southwest wines.

The mill stream flows around and under the mill—you can see the flowing water through a window in the floor of the restaurant—and over a small weir.

The inn contains six rooms and one suite, all well-equipped, and decorated with taste that reflects the personality of Mme Gracia.

FOOD & WINE

Of 20 items on the carte, eight involve duck. The "traditional dishes of our Gascony" *all* involve duck: *Le Magret de canard braisé et sa vinaigrette gasconne à l'echalote* (duck breast with a Gascon shallot vinaigrette); *Le Confit de canard et sa charlotte de pommes à la sauge* (preserved duck with sage-flavored potatoes); and *Le Civet de canard au vin de Lot et Garonne* (duck stew made with wine from this department).

Marie-Claude makes her own duck foie gras, which is available off-sale as well as in the restaurant. She makes a dish called *La Macaronade*, consisting of foie gras and noodles. She produced a cookbook, from which she selected six recipes for us, three of which we present below: *Tourte de blancs de poireaux* (Leek tart); the Gascony duck stew mentioned above; and *"Mon Gâteau au Chocolat"* (Marie-Claude Gracia's own chocolate cake).

Another specialty we enjoyed: *Tourtes aux blancs de poireaux et aux ris de veau* (leek and sweetbread pie). Wines: Colombard, Côtes de Duras, and a large selection of other regionals.

The food is superb, and the service smiling and competent.

SIGHTS & SUCH

The inn offers residents fishing, canoeing, and tennis. Also, cooking demonstrations, and visits to wine growers. Half of the inn, as well as the green park behind, and the swimming pool, lie on an island formed by the stream passing under the mill, and the river. It is most-easily accessed through a door at the end of the restaurant.

Another medieval *"village de charme,"*[34] Poudenas is at the edge of the Landaise forest, in the heart of Armagnac. The old stone houses, of various shades of yellow and brown with round tile roofs, are terraced up the hillside. At the top of the village sits a château where "Henry IV used to tumble a pretty Gasconne or two." The château is private, but can be visited.

Gascony was the home of d'Artagnan, who was a real-life hero on which Dumas based *Les Trois Mousquetaires*. It is also the home of Armagnac, which some connoisseurs prefer to Cognac. Several firms offer tastings of Armagnac, and local wines.

Don't miss the picturesque town of Nérac, 21 kilometers to the northwest. For more information, see Michelin's *Pyrénées/Aquitaine*.

LEEK TART
Tourte de Blancs de Poireaux

Pâte brisé:
    2 cups (275 g.) flour
    1 teaspoon salt
    ¼ lb (120 g.) butter
    1 egg, beaten
    1 tablespoon ice water

Filling:
    1 lb. (500 g.) leeks
    ½ lb (250 g.) mushrooms
    1 cup (20 cl.) crème fraîche
       or thick whipping cream
    1 egg, beaten
    salt and white pepper

Butter and flour a 9-in. (23-cm.) spring-form pan.

Make a pâte brisé or pastry dough: In a food processor, combine flour and salt. Cut butter into small pieces and process into the flour with short pulses. Add water and mix just until it starts to make a ball. Remove from processor, wrap in plastic wrap and let rest in refrigerator for 1 hour.

After dough has rested, divide it into 2 unequal parts: one third and two thirds. Roll out the larger part so that it is about 2 inches bigger than the spring form pan. Line the pan. Roll out remaining dough to fit top of tourte.

For the filling, julienne or thinly slice the leeks using the white and only a little of the green part. Put leeks in a heavy dry frying pan and stir with a wooden spoon until the water of the leeks is gone and the leeks are quite dry and emerald green (about 6 minutes).

Remove the stems of the mushrooms (reserve for another use) and finely mince the caps. Do not wash the mushrooms.

Put the leeks in the pastry-lined pan. Top with the finely minced mushrooms. Add the cream and salt and pepper. Cover with the rest of the pastry and paint the top with beaten egg.

Bake in a hot preheated oven 425°F (220°C) for 45 minutes. Serve while still warm.

Serves 8.

GASCONY DUCK STEW

Le Civet de Canard de la Belle Gasconne

Civet is a stew, usually thickened with blood. Outside of France, this blood may be hard to find. Although it's absence makes it impossible to reproduce the same rich, silky, unctuous sauce, thickening the sauce other ways (such as a beurre manié or purée of the vegetables in the sauce) makes this a very good dish.

2 legs of a duck	1 bouquet garnie
1 bottle red wine	2 cloves garlic
1 clove	4 carrots, cut in rounds
1 onion	salt and pepper

Remove the skin from the duck legs. (You can cut the skin in fine slices and render out the fat over low heat. This is good to add to salads in place of croutons.)

Brown the duck legs in some fat from the duck When it has a nice color, add the wine, bouquet garnie, onion pricked with the clove, garlic, and carrots. Salt and pepper and cook one hour on a low fire. When the legs are tender, set them aside.

Pass the sauce through a strainer. Just before serving, tie the sauce with the blood of the duck. (Or other thickening.)

Serve with boiled red potatoes.

Serves 2.

MARIE-CLAUDE GRACIA'S CHOCOLATE CAKE
Mon Gâteau au Chocolat

10 oz. (300 g.) bittersweet chocolate   5 eggs
6 oz. (180 g.) butter   1/3 cup (40 g.) flour
1¼ cups (160 g.) powdered sugar

Break the chocolate into pieces and put in a bowl. Add butter cut in pieces (reserving 1 tablespoon for later use), and the powdered sugar. Put the bowl in a pan and add hot water to the pan so that it comes two thirds up the bowl. Heat over a low fire to melt the butter and chocolate. Remove from the heat and stir until smooth.

Separate the eggs and add the yolks, one at a time to the chocolate mixture. Add the flour to the chocolate, pouring through a strainer or sifter. Mix well.

Whip the egg whites until firm and fold gently into the chocolate.

Butter a nine-inch (23-cm.) spring form pan. Gently pour the batter in and bake 45 minutes at 375°F (190°C). The cake will still be very soft. Let it cool completely before unmolding it on a plate

This cake can be served plain or sprinkled with powdered sugar.

Serves 8.

★★ AUBERGE À LA BELLE GASCONNE, Poudenas 47170 Mézin.
  Tel: 53 65 71 58. Fax: 53 65 87 39.
PROPRIETORS: Marie-Claude and Richard Gracia. CHEF: Marie-Claude Gracia.
ROOMS: 6, plus 1 suite, all with bath, WC, direct telephone; 3 with TV
PRICES: Rooms: 500–550 F ($100–110); suite: 630 F ($126); ½-pension: 570–715 F
  ($114–143). Breakfast: 50 F ($10). Menus: 175–280 F ($35–56). Credit cards:
  AE, DC, EC, MC, Visa.
AMENITIES: Bar, lounge, garden, terrace, shaded park, Gélise River, swimming
  pool, parking. Fishing, canoeing on premises. Tennis 1 km. Golf 15 km.
  Exercise trail and hiking trails (across bridge).
MARKET DAYS: Condom: Wed, Sat; Mézin: Thu, Sun; Nérac: Sat.
DIRECTIONS: From Bordeaux 139 km. SE on A62 to Agen. From Agen: 47 km
  SW on D656 to Poudenas.
OPEN: Mar 1–Jan 1; Restaurant closed: Sun dinner and Mon (except Jul–Aug, and
  Mon lunch in Sep).

69–70. ADDITIONAL SOUTHWEST FAVORITES

69. AUBERGE DU MOULIN D'ANÉ

Marmande, Lot-et-Garonne, Aquitaine

The shady terrace at the river's edge is perfect for dining. The view is superb from this very rustic inn. And the food should be worth a toque. (Restaurant only.)

★★★ AUBERGE DU MOULIN D'ANÉ, 47200 Marmande. Tel: 53 20 18 25. Fax: 53 89 67 99.
PROPRIETOR-CHEF: Jacques Amiel. HOSTESS: Mme Amiel.
SPECIALTIES: Seafood, sweetbreads, duck.
PRICES: Menus: 98–230 F ($20–46), children 65 F ($13). Credit cards: AE, CB, DC, EC, MC, Visa.
AMENITIES: Bar, lounge, terrace. Parking. Dining inside, or on terrace.
DIRECTIONS: Marmande is on the Garonne River, 90 km. S of Bordeaux. The mill is 7 km. E, by D933 and D267.
OPEN: All year except Feb vacations; restaurant closed Sun dinner, Mon.

---

70. LA RIBOTE

Les Junies, Lot, Midi-Pyrénées

La Ribote dates from the 14th century, and is hidden in a valley on the Masse River. It has a flowered garden, waterfall, rotating water wheel, and, to make it complete, a GaultMillau toque. Try the following recipe.

BRAISED SQUAB WITH SHALLOT MARMALADE AND CRANBERRIES,
FRIED APPLES, AND SCALLOPED POTATOES WITH THYME

Pigeon mijoté en cocotte à l'echalotte confite et aux airelles;
Pomme reinette poêlée; et Gratin de pomme de terre au thym

4 squab	duck fat
4 shallots	4 cooking apples
6 oz. (180 g.) cranberries	6 potatoes
1 glass port	2 cloves garlic, minced
1 cup (25 cl.) beef	butter
or chicken stock	salt, pepper, thyme

Prepare the squab for roasting, tying down legs and wings, and seasoning with salt and pepper. Melt a little duck fat in a baking dish and add the squab. Bake in a hot oven until the squab are half cooked and beginning to brown. Remove and set them aside.

Prepare the gratin of potatoes. Peel the potatoes and cut in thin slices. Mix them with a little duck fat, thyme, garlic, salt and pepper. Place in a gratin dish and bake in a medium 375°F (190°C) oven.

In the meantime, chop the shallots and add them to the squab's baking dish. Deglaze the squab dish with the port and add the stock, cranberries, a little water, salt and pepper. Return the squab to the oven and finish baking.

Cut the apples in eighths, not peeling them, and sauté in butter with a pinch of sugar, salt and pepper.

To serve, place a squab on each warmed plate. Coat with their juice and cranberries. Serve along side the sautéed apples and the gratin of potatoes with thyme. Serves 4.

★★★ LA RIBOTE, "La Mouline" on D660, 46150 Les Junies. Tel: 65 36 25 55.
Fax: 65 36 28 91.
PROPRIETORS: The Manenq family. CHEF: Franck Manenq.
SPECIALTIES:
PRICES: Menus: 95–290 F ($19–58); Menu Gourmand, wine incl.: 225 F ($45);
children 65 F ($13). Credit cards: AE, CB, DC, EC, MC, Visa.
AMENITIES: Bar, lounge, flowered garden, waterfall. Parking.
DIRECTIONS: From Cahors, 15.5 km. NW on D911 to D660, then 6 km. NW on
D660. (Cahors is 565 km. S of Paris on N20.)
OPEN: Feb 13–Jan 4; closed Wed (Sep 15–Jun 30).

Appendix A

LIST OF WATER-MILL INNS

Appendix B

BIBLIOGRAPHY & REFERENCES

Provincial France and its People

1. Ardagh, John: *France Today*, Penguin Books, 1990. Examines the profound changes in French society since World War II: the lives and attitudes of the people.

2. ———: *Rural France*, Century Publishing, London, 1983. The people, places, and character of the Frenchman's France.

3. ———, with Colin Jones: *Cultural Atlas of France*, Facts on File, Inc., New York, 1991. An extraordinary book for those interested in France and the French.

4. Barberousse, Michel: *La Normandie–ses Traditions, sa Cuisine, son Art de Vivre*. Librairie Hachette, Paris, 1974. After more than 20 years, still a useful reference (in French).

5. Bond, Michael: *Monsieur Pamplemousse and . . .* , Fawcett Crest, an Imprint of Ballantine Books. A series of tongue-in-cheek "gastronomic mysteries" centered in France, by the author of *Paddington Bear*.

6. Braudel, Fernand: *The Identity of France, Volume I: History and Environment*, Harper & Row, 1986.

7. ———: *The Identity of France, Volume II: People and Production*, Harper & Row, 1986.

8. Carroll, Raymonde: *Cultural Misunderstandings*, U. of Chicago Press, 1988. A thoughtful analysis of the ways in which members of different cultures can misunderstand each other—even when speaking the same language.

9. Fisher, M.F.K.: *Long Ago in France—the years in Dijon*, Simon & Schuster, 1992.

10. Fried, Eunice: *Burgundy: The Country, The Wines, and The People*, Harper & Row, 1986.

11. de Gramont, Sanche: *The French: Portrait of a People*, G.P. Putnam's Sons, 1969. Explores everything French, from bureaucracy, politics, and philosophy, to food, wine, and sex.

12. Mayle, Peter: *A Year in Provence*, Random House, Inc., New York, 1989. An amusing best-seller, with insight into the southern French.

13. ———: *Toujours Provence*, Random House, Inc., New York, 1991. An amusing best-seller, sequel to the book above.

14. Moulin, Pierre, Pierre le Vec, and Linda Dannenberg: *Pierre Deux's French Country*, Crown Publishers, Inc., New York, 1984. A style and source book.

15. Platt, Polly: *French or Foe?* Culture Crossings, Ltd. 1995. The best—and most amusing—compendium on the differences and similarities between French and American cultures. Failing to understand these differences is what leads to inaccurate and unfair stereotypes.

16. Taylor, Sally Adamson: *Culture Shock!: France*, Graphic Arts Center Publishing, Portland, Oregon, 1990. Gives informative tips on the do's and don'ts in France, and insights into what makes the French such a wonderful people. "Outsiders go wrong by looking at France through their own optics."

17. Zeldin, Theodore: *The French*, Pantheon Books, New York, 1983. A brilliant and witty portrait of today's France .

Touring in Regional France

18. Aubarbier, Jean-Luc, and Michel Binet: *Wonderful Périgord*, Ouest-France, 1988 (in English).

19. Bentley, James: *A Guide to the Dordogne*, Penguin Books, 1985. Complete and informative.

20. Chamberlain, Samuel, with Narcissa Chamberlain: *Bouquet de France: An Epicurean Tour of the French Provinces*. Gourmet, 1969.

21. De Combray, Richard: *European Travel & Life*, "Places We Love" Department, June/July 1990 issue.

22. Elsy, Mary, with Jill Norman: *Travels in Normandy*, Merehurst Press, London, 1988. Itineraries and commentary about places, and foods.

23. ———: *Travels in Burgundy*, Merehurst Press, London, 1989. Itineraries and commentary about places, and foods.

24. ———: *Travels in Brittany*, Merehurst Press, London, 1988. Itineraries and commentary about places, and foods.

25. Fennell, Fiona: *Travels in the Dordogne*, Merehurst Press, London, 1988. Itineraries and commentary about places, and foods.

26. Galy, Roger: *Promenades dans Bordeaux: pittoresque promenades dans Bordeaux et autour du Bassin d'Arcachon*, Raymond Picquot, 1962.

27. GaultMillau: *France 1996*, (issued annually). Reviews and rates restaurants and hotels. Much more detailed than the Michelin red guide, but sometimes overweening. (In French.)

28. ———: *The Best of France*, 1995. Revised every three years. In English, but less complete and up-to-date than the French version.

29. Grizell, Rex: *Southwest France*, Harper & Row, 1989.

30. Michelin: Michelin road maps are the standard: Map 989 (red) covers all of France at a scale of 1:1,000,000; the departmental and regional maps (yellow; 1:200,000) show almost all villages and minor roads. Michelin maps are available throughout France.

31.   ——: *Road Atlas of France,*The Hamlyn Publishing Group, Ltd., distributed in the United States by Crown Publishers, Inc. A bound copy of the yellow maps mentioned above, with every village indexed. Updated periodically.

32.   ——: Red Guide *France*, issued annually. Contains reliable hotel and restaurant ratings and descriptions, in four languages.

33.   ——: Green Tourist Guides. For tourist sights, we recommend this series. Itineraries are proposed, sights are described in detail, and rated: one star for "interesting," two stars for "worth a detour," and three for "worth the journey." Covers France in 21 guides (eight in English).

34.   Mouriès, Nathalie: *Guide des Villages de Charme en France* (Rivages, Paris, 1993). Color photos and brief text, describing 279 of the most charming villages in France.

35.   Relais & Château: *Relais Gourmands*, 1995.

36.   Sanger, Andrew: *Exploring Rural France* (Passport Books, 1990). Sanger proposes itineraries in most areas, and provides a lot of useful data.

37.   Simpson, Norman T.: *Country Inns and Back Roads–Continental Europe.* Harper & Row, 1985.

38.   Wells, Patricia: *Food Lover's Guide to France* (Workman Publishing 1987)—An excellent book, and we keep hoping for an update. Wells reviews restaurants, food shops, kitchen supply stores, open-air markets—anything associated with food or drink, in France. Also, *Food Lover's Guide to Paris*, 1995.

39.   Vergé, Roger: *Entertaining in the French Style*, Stewart, Tabori, & Chang, New York.

40.   Vergé, Roger: *Cuisine of the Sun*, MacMillan.

41.   White, Freda: *Three Rivers of France—Dordogne, Lot, Tarn*, Faber and Faber, Ltd., London, 1972.

French Wines and Vineyards

42.   Access Press: *France Wine Country Access*, 1995. Details about vineyards, their wines, visiting times, and fees (if any).

43.   Clarke, Oz: *Oz Clarke's New Encyclopedia of French Wines*, Simon and Schuster, 1990. "A lively and comprehensive A–Z guide to more than 400 wines, grapes, and regions."

44.   Comité Régional du Tourism de Bourgogne: *La Bourgogne: de Vignes en Caves: Guide de Visites et Dégustations*, 1992. (In French.)

45.   Dussert-Gerber, Patrick: *The Best French Wines*, Editions Vintage, Paris, 1989. A wealth of information about individual vineyards.

The Water Mill

46. Candoré, Annie: *Guide des Moulins en France—Moulins à eau, Moulins à vent, Moulins-auberges, Musées, Artisanat.* Pierre Horay, Paris, 1992.

47. Cazals, Rémy: *Cours d'Eau Moulins et Usines,* Archives de l'Aude, Carcassone, 1985. History of water mills in the Departement de l'Aude.

48. Macaulay, David: *Mill,* Houghton Mifflin, Boston, 1983. An illustrated history of the mill, by the author of *How Things Work.*

49. Orsatelli, Jean: *Les Moulins,* Editions Jean Laffitte, Paris, 1979. Virtually a design manual for mills (in French).

50. Reynolds, John: *Windmills and Watermills,* Praeger Publishers, New York, 1975.

BASIC RECIPES REFERENCED IN TEXT

CHOCOLATE GENOISE

4 large eggs
5/8 cup (125 g.) sugar
1 cup (110 g.) flour

3 Tablespoons (30 g.) cocoa powder
1 Tablespoon (15 g.) melted butter

Preheat oven to 375°F (190°C).

Combine eggs and sugar in a large bowl. Set bowl in a larger bowl of hot (not boiling) water. Beat with mixer at low speed until warm (100°F, 40°C) and pale yellow. Remove from heat and beat at high speed until batter has risen and cooled.

Sift flour and cocoa and dust the flour over the batter, a little at a time, folding in gently along with butter.

Pour batter onto a cookie sheet that has been brushed with melted butter, and floured. Bake about 10 minutes.

SWEET TART PASTRY
Pâte sablée

1 cup (125 g.) flour
¼ teaspoon salt
4 oz. (110 g.) chilled butter
    cut in pieces

3 tablespoons sugar
1 egg yolk
1 teaspoon vanilla
1 tablespoon water

Combine flour, salt and butter in the food processor. Process for 1 minute until butter is blended. Add in sugar, egg yolk, vanilla and water and process just a few seconds until the dough masses. Form a ball, cover with plastic wrap and refrigerate one to two hours.

Flour the work surface and beat cold dough with a rolling pin to soften. Roll to one-eighth inch thickness. Cut dough ½ inch larger than tart pan and fit dough into pan, fluting edges.

PASTRY CREAM
Crème pâtissière

3 egg yolks
¼ cup (60 g.) sugar
pinch of salt
¼ cup (30 g.) flour

1 cup (25 cl.) milk, brought to boil
1½ teaspoons vanilla
1 tablespoon butter

Beat egg yolks, gradually adding the sugar and salt. Continue beating until mixture is thick and creamy. Add the flour and fold it in. Slowly add the hot milk. Transfer the mixture to a saucepan and bring to a boil over moderate heat, stirring constantly. Boil about 2 minutes to cook the flour. Add the vanilla or other flavorings and the butter. Cool. Cover with plastic wrap, pressing onto surface to avoid a skin forming.

CRÈME ANGLAISE

6 egg yolks
2/3 cup (180 g.) sugar
1½ cups (37 cl.) milk

1 tablespoon vanilla or other flavoring
1 tablespoons butter

Beat egg yolks and gradually add the sugar. Continue beating until the mixture is thick and creamy. Gradually stir in the milk and pour the mixture into a saucepan. Cook over low heat, stirring constantly until it coats the back of a wooden spoon. (Be careful not to overcook or bring to a boil, or the egg will scramble.) Add butter and flavoring. Serve warm or cold.

INDEX

Order Form

_____

Send order to: Corinthian Publications, Lou Francis,
P.O. Box 3028, Redondo Beach, CA 90277-3028

Please send the following books:

_____

_____

_____

Name: _____
Address: _____
City: _____ State: _____ Zip:_____
Telephone: (___) _____

Sales tax:
Please add 7.75% for books shipped to California addresses.

Shipping:
Book rate: $2.00 for the first book and 75 cents for each
additional book. (Surface shipping may take three to four
weeks.) Air Mail: $3.00 per book.

Payment: By check.

Order Now